Grove Park Inn
ARTS & CRAFTS FURNITURE

Grove Park Inn
ARTS & CRAFTS FURNITURE

Bruce E. Johnson
DRAWINGS BY KEVIN PIERCE

POPULAR WOODWORKING BOOKS
CINCINNATI, OHIO
www.popularwoodworking.com

Read This Important Safety Notice

To prevent accidents, keep safety in mind while you work. Use the safety guards installed on power equipment; they are for your protection. When working on power equipment, keep fingers away from saw blades, wear safety goggles to prevent injuries from flying wood chips and sawdust, wear headphones to protect your hearing, and consider installing a dust vacuum to reduce the amount of airborne sawdust in your woodshop. Don't wear loose clothing, such as neckties or shirts with loose sleeves, or jewelry, such as rings, necklaces or bracelets, when working on power equipment. Tie back long hair to prevent it from getting caught in your equipment. People who are sensitive to certain chemicals should check the chemical content of any product before using it. The authors and editors who compiled this book have tried to make the contents as accurate and correct as possible. Plans, illustrations, photographs and text have been carefully checked. All instructions, plans and projects should be carefully read, studied and understood before beginning construction. Due to the variability of local conditions, construction materials, skill levels, etc., neither the author nor Popular Woodworking Books assumes any responsibility for any accidents, injuries, damages or other losses incurred resulting from the material presented in this book. Prices listed for supplies and equipment were current at the time of publication and are subject to change. Glass shelving should have all edges polished and must be tempered. Untempered glass shelves may shatter and can cause serious bodily injury. Tempered shelves are very strong and if they break will just crumble, minimizing personal injury.

GROVE PARK INN ARTS & CRAFTS FURNITURE.
Copyright © 2009 by Bruce Johnson. Printed and
bound in China. All rights reserved. No part of this
book may be reproduced in any form or by any elec-
tronic or mechanical means including information
storage and retrieval systems without permission
in writing from the publisher, except by a reviewer,
who may quote brief passages in a review. Published
by Popular Woodworking Books, an imprint of F+W
Media, Inc., 4700 East Galbraith Road, Cincinnati, Ohio,
45236. First edition.

Distributed in Canada by Fraser Direct
100 Armstrong Avenue
Georgetown, Ontario L7G 5S4
Canada

Distributed in the U.K. and Europe by David & Charles
Brunel House
Newton Abbot
Devon TQ12 4PU
England
Tel: (+44) 1626 323200
Fax: (+44) 1626 323319
E-mail: mail@davidandcharles.co.uk

Distributed in Australia by Capricorn Link
P.O. Box 704
Windsor, NSW 2756
Australia

Visit our Web site at www.popularwoodworking.com
for information on more resources for woodworkers.

Other fine Popular Woodworking Books are available
from your local bookstore or direct from the publisher.

13   12   11   10   09   5   4   3   2   1

Library of Congress Cataloging-in-Publication Data

Johnson, Bruce.
  Grove Park Inn arts & crafts furniture / by Bruce John-
son. -- 1st ed.
     p. cm.
  Includes index.
  ISBN 978-1-55870-849-5 (hardcover : alk. paper)
  1. Arts and crafts movement. 2. Furniture--History-
-19th century. 3. Furniture--History--20th century. 4.
Grove Park Inn (Asheville, N.C.)--History. I. Title. II. Title:
Grove Park Inn arts and crafts furniture.

  NK2394.A77J64 2009
  749.09756'88--dc22

                                    2008039236

EXECUTIVE EDITOR: David Thiel
DESIGNER: Brian Roeth
PRODUCTION COORDINATOR: Mark Griffin
PHOTOGRAPHER: Al Parrish
ILLUSTRATOR: Kevin Pierce

Metric Conversion Chart

TO CONVERT	TO	MULTIPLY BY
Inches	Centimeters	2.54
Centimeters	Inches	0.4
Feet	Centimeters	30.5
Centimeters	Feet	0.03
Yards	Meters	0.9
Meters	Yards	1.1

Author's Note

I can recall as if it were only yesterday the first time I ever heard about the Grove Park Inn. It was 1980 and I was living in Iowa City, operating an antiques shop and refinishing business I named Knock On Wood, and I had just purchased a reprint of the 1912 *Roycroft Furniture Shop Catalog*. I nearly wore out the pages consuming the thin volume of photographs of rare examples of Roycroft furniture, Arts & Crafts gems I only dreamed of encountering in Iowa.

There, in the final pages, was a copy of Elbert Hubbard's 1912 essay "The Inn Superbus Maximus," with its glowing description of the six-story granite Arts & Crafts resort hotel then under construction on Sunset Mountain overlooking Asheville, North Carolina. Accompanying Hubbard's essay was a letter written on July 20, 1915 by Fred L. Seely, manager of the Grove Park Inn, to Hubbard's son, Bert, extolling the virtues of the Roycroft furniture and lighting he had purchased for the resort hotel.

Little did I know that just six years later I would be standing in the Great Hall admiring the Roycroft copper chandeliers, massive twin sideboards, corner cabinets and the now famous Roycroft "GPI" chairs. My infatuation with the Grove Park Inn and its collection of furniture inspired me to organize the first Arts & Crafts Conference, held at the Grove Park Inn in February of 1988. Twenty years later what began with a handful of antiques dealers and three hundred collectors had mushroomed into an annual event bringing together thousands of Arts & Crafts collectors from across the U. S., Canada, Australia, Mexico and England.

My own first book about the hotel, *Built for the Ages: A History of the Grove Park Inn*, appeared in 1990; an enlarged edition, containing new information gleaned from my insatiable research, was published in 2005. Both books chronicle the history of the hotel, from the early years of owner Edwin Wiley Grove and its designer and manager, Fred L. Seely, through two world wars and into the twenty-first century.

And while the history of any structure and the men and women who brought it to life can never be totally complete, I am proud of *Built for the Ages*. I knew then, as I know now, that the purpose of that first book was to tell the fascinating story of nearly a hundred years' history of this grand hotel. What I also knew was that the opportunity would soon present itself for a book focused on the Arts & Crafts furniture and hammered copper lighting which the craftsmen at the Roycroft Campus had created in 1913 for the Grove Park Inn. I knew there would be a chance to relate the role of the Roycrofters in the Grove Park Inn commission. Such a book would, I knew, also examine the role both the Grove Park Inn and the Roycrofters had played in the national dissemination of the Arts & Crafts philosophy of Head, Heart and Hand.

That book is now in your hands, and while it — like all books — will invariably fall short of my goal of including every piece of information, bit of trivia and known example, I am equally as proud of it as I am of my earlier books and as I am of the Grove Park Inn — the jewel of Sunset Mountain.

Acknowledgements

I owe a debt of gratitude to those unselfish individuals who have shared their research, experience and expertise with me, whether it be in the past twelve months or the past twenty-five years.

Among those whom I would like to thank are Lee Ainsworth, Margaret Augat, Bruce Austin, Gus Bostrom, Andy Brown, Bob Brunk, David Cathers, Michael and Jill Thomas-Clark, Jerry Cohen, Kevin Cross, Mark Ellis-Bennett, Stephen Gray, Raymond Groll, Charles Hamilton, Robert Hause, Linda Hubbard, Bill Kelley, Dave Kornacki, Michael Lehr, Boice Lydell, Douglas McFarland, Warren Moffit, Ron Morin, Anne O'Donnell, Christine Peters, David Rago, Patricia Reed, Zoe Rhine, David Rudd, Robert Rust, Marjorie Searl, Alburn Sleeper, Mary Anne Smith, Sandra Starks, Jennifer Straus, David Surgan, Doug Swift, Kitty Turgeon, Jill West, Marie Via, Harold

Wright, the entire staff of the Grove Park Inn — and countless others.

Few, fortunate authors have the opportunity to work with an editor who shares their passion, enthusiasm and knowledge of their subject. David Thiel's insight into both the Roycrofters and the Arts & Crafts movement — and his own admiration for the Grove Park Inn — provided me with the guidance, understanding and encouragement I needed to make this book complete. His literary fingerprint remains etched onto every page of this book.

David also brought to this project a team of talented individuals who fell in love with their subject. Photographer Al Parrish and illustrator Kevin Pierce roamed the rooms, hallways, alcoves, nooks and crannies of the Grove Park Inn searching for the perfect shot, the ideal ray of light and the small but critical detail that not only would represent the Arts & Crafts

style and philosophy, but would bring it to life for veteran Arts & Crafts collectors and budding woodworkers alike. Designer Brian Roeth and Editor Jim Stack blended the words, images and illustrations seamlessly to make a beautiful book for all to enjoy.

I also want to extend my thanks to my two sons, Eric and Blake, who grew up with a father who always worked at home, though they often could not quite figure out exactly what he was doing. They both learned to walk down the long hallways of the Grove Park Inn, while their father crawled beside them, peering under dark pieces of furniture with a flashlight. Eventually, they each worked beside me at the annual Grove Park Inn Arts & Crafts Conference, an honor no award could ever match. And today, although their lives take them far beyond the walls of my office, they invariably ask each time we are together, "How's your new book coming?" That's inspiration enough for any author.

Finally, I would like to thank my wife, Dr. Leigh Ann Hamon, DVM, who also has learned to cope with the challenges of a husband who works at home, for she has helped me hone both my self discipline and my organization, making me a better writer in the process. A convert to the Arts & Crafts style, she has embraced and adapted it to her own, personal philosophy, while providing me with a new, fresh perspective on life, love and the Arts & Crafts home.

BRUCE E. JOHNSON

Contents

Introduction

"Our atmosphere at the Grove Park Inn is so wholesome and homelike that we come out pretty square with the world. How could anyone do other than behave himself when he is surrounded with so many beautiful Roycroft things — hand-hammered lighting fixtures and table lamps in every bedroom, the great copper pans in the dining room and lobby, the beautiful Roycroft furniture in the dining room and so many other straight-forward honest things."

FRED L. SEELY

27 JUNE 1921

When on July 12, 1913, the Grove Park Inn officially opened, newspapers across the country hailed the six-story, granite structure, firmly imbedded in the western slope of Sunset Mountain overlooking Asheville, North Carolina, as "the finest resort hotel in the world."

Four hundred of the South's most important men — "a cabinet officer, senators and congressmen, men high in various professions, men whose total wealth would run up into the millions" — gathered that evening to celebrate the completion of the 150-room hotel, which a reporter described for his readers as "a marvel of the builder's art, a triumph of architectural skill." As Secretary of State William Jennings Bryan stated so eloquently that evening, "Today we stand in this wonderful hotel, not built for a few, but for the multitudes that will come and go. I congratulate these men. They have built for the ages." ["Secretary Bryan Is Guest Of Honor At Great Banquet That Dedicates Grove Park Inn," *The Sunday Asheville Citizen*, Asheville, NC, July 13, 1913, pg. 1.]

In March of that same year, Elbert Hubbard, founder of the Roycroft Shops and publisher of *The Philistine* and *The Fra* magazines, had declared that "the Grove Park Inn could never be complete without the assistance of The Roycrofters, [for] the dining room will be entirely furnished with Roycroft furniture — plain, simple, straight-lined pieces, genuinely handmade and with their quality the first and last endeavor." ["The Inn Superbus Maximus," by Elbert Hubbard, *The Fra*, March, 1913, pg. 34..]

In addition to the Roycroft furniture Hubbard had touted, Fred Loring Seely, who designed the hotel for his father-in-law, Edwin Wiley Grove, had also selected Arts & Crafts furniture from the respected White Furniture Company, the Heywood Brothers & Wakefield Company and the Old Hickory Company, as well as hundreds of hammered copper lighting fixtures from the Roycroft Copper Shop. When assembled that July of 1913 inside what historians now recognize as the largest and finest example of Arts & Crafts public architecture, the Grove Park Inn and its collection of Arts & Crafts furnishings represented the zenith of the American Arts & Crafts movement. Nearly a century later the Grove Park Inn stands not a mere shadow of its former glory, but as a mecca for Arts & Crafts enthusiasts, for today it proudly bears the title of "the finest Arts & Crafts resort hotel in the world."

"Do you like things that are simple, genuine and exactly what they purport to be," Elbert Hubbard asked his readers in 1908, "and are made to last a century?" While his question may seem self-serving, no one will deny that one hundred years later the furniture which his Roycroft woodworkers created during the Arts & Crafts era (1895-1939) not only has survived several decades of neglect and abuse, but has risen to become some of the most valuable and most sought-after furniture in the history of American decorative arts.

Gustav Stickley, the dean of the American Arts & Crafts movement, sensed it as well when he predicted in 1912 that Arts & Crafts furniture "will be a permanent part of the home surroundings, and in

fifty or one hundred years will be worth many times its first cost." Though four years later he would be mired in bankruptcy, his prediction rang true in 1988, when an oak sideboard which Gustav Stickley had made for his home at Craftsman Farms was auctioned at Christie's in New York. The winning bidder was Barbra Streisand, who walked away with the sideboard for $363,000. Indicative of the continued strength of the Arts & Crafts market, ten years later that same Stickley sideboard was purchased by a private collector for a record price of $596,500.

And if there is any example of Arts & Crafts furniture prepared to match the Gustav Stickley sideboard in terms of historical importance, design, construction, condition and provenance, it would be the eight-foot tall clock designed and completed by Elbert Hubbard's Roycroft Furniture Shop in 1913 for the Grove Park Inn.

The Grove Park Inn represents the largest and most important commission in the history of the Roycroft Shops. Never before nor after 1913 did the Roycroft Furniture Shop rise to the level of excellence in design and construction which it achieved that

year for the Grove Park Inn. Twenty-five years later, in 1938, the hammers, saws and anvils fell silent, as the Roycroft Shops succumbed to the economic paralysis of the Great Depression. But, in Asheville, evidence of the dedication of the Roycroft craftsmen and craftswomen remained in the form of sturdy oak furnishings and hammered copper chandeliers still in service throughout the Grove Park Inn.

The world famous hotel was built by Edwin Wiley Grove (1850-1927), a pharmaceutical manufacturer and real estate developer from St. Louis, but credit for the Arts & Crafts design and furnishing of the hotel belongs to his son-in-law Frederick Loring Seely (1871-1942). With only minimal experience in construction and no training in either architecture or interior design, Seely undertook the challenge of designing, furnishing and managing the 150-room hotel. A friend of Elbert Hubbard's and a regular customer of the Roycroft Furniture Shop, Fred Seely had embraced the philosophy of the Arts & Crafts movement both in his home and in the planning of the Grove Park Inn.

In the years since Fred Seely's reign at the hotel ended in 1927, the Inn has more than tripled in size,

yet has remained dedicated to the Arts & Crafts ideals of hand-craftsmanship, honest construction, native materials and simple elegance without dependence on what Gustav Stickley described as "badly constructed, over-ornate, meaningless furniture." During the addition of new wings in both 1984 and 1988, the owners and management of the Grove Park Inn purchased scores of Arts & Crafts antiques for the hallways and public areas, including pieces by Gustav Stickley, L. & J.G. Stickley, Charles Limbert, J.M. Young, Stickley Brothers and the Roycrofters.

In addition, the hotel's staff has also recognized the important role currently being played by living Arts & Crafts furniture designers and craftsmen. They have purchased key pieces of furniture to take their place alongside the original Roycroft, Limbert and Stickley antiques in their collection — a collection that, since its conception in 1913, has grown to become the largest assemblage of Arts & Crafts furniture and lighting in the world. Unlike museums, the Grove Park Inn's collection has since 1913 remained available for the public not only to study, but to touch, inspect, sit in and enjoy, just as its original designers had intended.

The result both of their efforts and those of E. W. Grove and Fred Seely is not simply a 512-room monument to the founders of the Arts & Crafts philosophy, but is proof that at the Grove Park Inn, the Arts & Crafts movement never ended.

The Arts & Crafts Movement

"In the beginning, there was no thought of creating a new style, only a recognition of the fact that we should have in our homes something better suited to our needs and more expressive of our character as a people than imitations of traditional styles, and a conviction that the best way to get something better was to go directly back to the principles of plain construction and apply them to the making of simple, strong, comfortable furniture."

GUSTAV STICKLEY

FOUNDER, CRAFTSMAN WORKSHOPS

The Arts & Crafts movement began as a social revolution, but this upheaval did not start on the streets of London, nor did it begin in the workshops of the craftsman Gustav Stickley or at the desk of the prolific Roycrofter, Elbert Hubbard. Instead, it began in the writings and lectures of Englishman John Ruskin (1819-1900), the controversial 19th-century art and social critic whose ominous prediction that the impending Industrial Revolution would dehumanize the English working class inspired generations of reformers on both sides of the Atlantic Ocean. In his book, *The Seven Lamps of Architecture* (1849), John Ruskin called for a return to handcraftsmanship in the belief that no structure or object could be of value if it had not been created by hand with a sense of enjoyment and pride. It would not be until 1887, however, that the term Arts & Crafts would be coined, as the reformers who followed Ruskin established as one of their goals the raising of the status of the artisan to that of the artist, hence the name Arts & Crafts.

John Ruskin shocked the British public by his outright condemnation of classical architectural as being repressive and without moral basis. Similarly, he criticized the revered Old Master artists for their inaccurate portrayals of nature, exposing their practice of manipulating clouds, trees and waves as it suited their needs in their studios rather than painting them outdoors as they actually appeared. He attacked capitalistic industrialism, calling instead for a revival of the medieval guild system of the late Middle Ages, wherein each worker would have the opportunity to learn the skills of handcraftsmanship, would work in healthy, pleasant surroundings, would be given creative freedom of expression, and would share in the profits with his employer. Ruskin advocated a close working relationship between architect and builder, designer and craftsman, utilizing the skills, talents and experience of each individual involved in the process from the beginning to the end. Although the experimental Guild of St. George that he founded in 1871 failed to live up to his high expectations, it established the philosophical foundation and the model on which future craft guilds in England would be based.

Among the college students at Oxford who read, listened to and was influenced by John Ruskin was a young man named William Morris (1834-1896), who, like the famous professor and social critic, had been born into the privileged upper class. But whereas Ruskin remained a cultural theorist for much of his life, Morris became an outspoken activist and one of the founders of the Socialist party in England. He challenged politicians and manufacturers to improve the standard of living of the working class by recognizing and assimilating the principles of the budding Arts & Crafts movement. Morris believed that by simplifying design, by studying the forms of nature and by working with natural materials, the production process could be freed of its growing dependence on machinery and could accomplish Ruskin's goal of drawing the manufacturer, the designer and the worker closer together for the benefit of all.

After graduating from Oxford, William Morris spent time in the offices of the architect G. E. Street (1824-1881), who steadfastly believed that before an architect could properly design any structure he had to first learn the trades for which he was designing, including blacksmithing, cabinetmaking, bricklaying, painting and stained glass. While serving an apprenticeship under Street, Morris met architect Philip Webb (1831-1915), who shared Morris and Ruskin's appreciation for historic buildings and the skills of the men who built them. Working together, Morris and Webb developed a theory that an architect's plan had to take into foremost consideration the purpose the structure was to serve and the site on which it was being constructed, so that the two — structure and site — could live and work in harmony, not unlike the designer and craftsman.

In 1859 Morris and Webb applied their theories in collaboration on the home and gardens Morris presented to his new wife, Jane Burden, as a wedding gift. Located in Upton, Kent and named for the red brick they selected for the exterior, Morris, Burden, Webb and several of their friends designed, decorated and furnished the Red House in a fresh style inspired by nature and now considered the first true Arts & Crafts house. Their collaboration led to the suggestion that the group form an interior design business, which in 1861 they called Morris, Marshall, Faulkner & Company, "Fine Art Workmen in Painting, Carvings, Furniture and the Metals." The heady mixture of talent and artistic egos, however, eventually resulted in the dissolution of the original firm and in 1875 the emergence of Morris & Company, with William Morris as the sole proprietor in his office located in Kelmscott Manor, a country estate in Oxfordshire.

Morris & Company offered clients hand-printed wall coverings and textiles, hand-knotted rugs and tapestries, as well as furniture, all crafted by hand from designs originating from or approved by Morris. Although Morris & Company proved profitable, Morris grew disheartened over the realization that only the wealthy could afford the handcrafted items his craftsmen and craftswomen so carefully created. His dream of discovering a means of producing high-quality, handcrafted and well-designed items inexpensively never materialized and haunted him his remaining days. His final enterprise, the Kelmscott Press, formed in 1890 when Morris was fifty-six, was devoted to the revival of the book as an art form. Founded as a reaction against cheaply produced commercial books, the Kelmscott Press reprinted works of literature ranging from Chaucer to Ruskin, as well as Morris' own writings. Artistic borders, hand-illuminated illustrations

William Morris (1834-1896)

and handcrafted leather bindings fulfilled Morris' dream of producing beautiful works of art, but once again he found that only the wealthy could afford them.

The Arts & Crafts movement continued in England even after the deaths of William Morris in 1896 and John Ruskin in 1900. The books, articles, lectures and business models of these two influential Arts & Crafts reformers inspired architects, builders, designers and craftsmen across the British Isles and Europe. Among the most successful enterprises in England was the Century Guild, a collective of designers and artisans organized in 1882 by architect A. H. Mackmurdo (1851-1942), who studied under and traveled alongside John Ruskin. The Century Guild also produced what many consider the first literary journal dedicated to the ideals of the emerging Arts & Crafts philosophy of design and decoration, *The Hobby Horse* (1884-1892).

Other organizations influenced by Ruskin and Morris included the School of Handicraft and the Guild of Handicraft, both founded in 1888 by architect C. R. Ashbee (1863-1942), as well as the Art Workers' Guild. One of the guild's members T. J. Cobden-Sanderson (1840-1922), a respected book designer, first suggested the phrase "Arts & Crafts" to be used in conjunction with an exhibition they were organizing in 1887 under the auspices of the Arts & Crafts Exhibition Society.

The Arts & Crafts Movement in America
The dissemination of ideas spawned in the writings of John Ruskin and the workshops of William Morris — the revival of handcraftsmanship, the improvement of working conditions, the return to nature for both design inspiration and working materials, a harmony

of structure and site, and the elimination of unnecessary ornamentation — was made possible through a number of different means. While neither Ruskin nor Morris lectured in the United States, many other prominent English reformers did, including Morris' daughter, May, architect C. R. Ashbee and author Walter Crane. Members of several English guilds exhibited their work at international exhibitions held in San Francisco, Chicago, Philadelphia and Buffalo. In addition, regular trips to England and Europe were a prerequisite for American Arts & Crafts designers, artists, architects and business owners. Those who could not afford to travel abroad to study the art, architecture and decorative arts of England and Europe could view them in a growing number of international art journals.

While in England many of the Arts & Crafts reformers played active roles in the politics of the time or dedicated their efforts to a revival of the medieval guild system, most of their American counterparts elected to separate their political leanings from their manifestation of the Arts & Crafts ideals. Individuals such as Gustav Stickley, Elbert Hubbard, Frank Lloyd Wright, Leopold Stickley and Charles Limbert chose to pursue innovative entrepreneurial enterprises that could appeal to a wider audience while avoiding the political and internal differences that often threatened to stifle the Arts & Crafts movement in England.

Proponents of the Arts & Crafts movement in America faced the same challenges that Ruskin, Morris and others did in England in their attempt to produce handcrafted, artistic furniture, pottery, textiles and metalware that was at once affordable for the middle class, yet profitable for the craftsmen and craftswomen. But whereas the English reformers remained steadfast in their determination to form modern interpretations of the medieval craft guilds, American entrepreneurs adapted the prevalent factory system to produce quality Arts & Crafts furnishings while remaining true — at least in spirit — to the Arts & Crafts ideals.

In Binghamton, New York, five brothers rose from relative poverty to become emblematic of the Arts & Crafts movement in America. The Stickley brothers — Gustav, Albert, Charles, John and Leopold — first learned the craft of cabinetmaking in their uncle's chair factory. Gustav, the oldest, became the factory foreman and by 1884 had organized the Stickley Brothers Company, which produced popular reproductions of classical styles of chairs. The five brothers only worked together for a few years, however, before Gustav and Leopold left in 1888 to pursue other opportunities. By 1902 each of the five brothers had settled into their roles in the Arts & Crafts field: Gustav was designing and making early forms of his Arts & Crafts furniture

Gustav Stickley (1858-1942)

in Syracuse; Leopold, who had been working as Gustav's shop foreman, was formulating plans to start the L. & J. G. Stickley Company with brother John George, a noted furniture salesman; Charles had remained in Binghamton to manage the Stickley & Brandt Chair Company; and Albert had moved to Grand Rapids, the furniture capitol of the country, taking with him the original family business name, where he also began producing Arts & Crafts furniture. Throughout their lives and careers, the five brothers would struggle to maintain their family ties while competing with each other for public recognition and financial success.

Unlike their English counterparts who held rigidly to Ruskin's admonitions to eliminate machinery from their workshops and to replace capitalism with guilds and cooperatives, the Stickleys and most other American manufacturers recognized that a compromise would be necessary in order to produce hand-made items at a reasonable cost. While a few owners did make feeble attempts at establishing profit-sharing plans with their employees, the majority believed in the strong leadership of a benevolent sole proprietor who could provide his workers with a healthy and pleasant working environment and who would, through the success of the business, be able to pay them a fair wage.

And while a few small workshops, most notably furniture maker Charles Rohlfs and metalsmith Dirk van Erp, did adhere strictly to the tenet of handcraftsmanship, the majority of American manufacturers concurred with architect Frank Lloyd Wright who, in his landmark 1901 lecture at the Hull House entitled "The Art & Craft of the Machine," called not for the elimination of the machine, but for the proper use of it. Wright believed that machinery could be utilized to reduce the drudgery of certain tasks and to free the workers for more creative application of their time and talents. To furniture manufacturers like Gustav Stickley, Leopold Stickley, Charles Limbert and Elbert Hubbard, that meant building workshops and factories powered by electricity or steam and equipped with planers, sanders, table saws, band saws and mortise and tenon cutting machines. By all indications, productivity increased dramatically and workmen became even more involved with the creative aspects of their trade, from selecting boards for their grain pattern to the assembly, coloring and finishing of each piece.

Even so, the acceptance of the machine into the Arts & Crafts workshop remained a sensitive issue for many of these same furniture manufacturers. While reporters touring the furniture workshops of both Gustav Stickley and Elbert Hubbard noted the existence of power machinery, all such machines are conspicuously absent from the workshop photographs Stickley and Hubbard published in their magazines. Other manufacturers made no attempt to dodge the question, including Leopold Stickley, who declared — almost as a rebuke to his older brother — "the work of L. & J. G. Stickley, built in a scientific manner, does not attempt to follow the traditions of a bygone day. All the resources of modern invention are used as helps in constructing this thoroughly modern product, more suitable, as many notable authorities believe, to the house of today — your house, that is — than is the furniture of past centuries." [*Stickley Craftsman Furniture Catalogs*, Introduction by David Cathers, Dover Publications, New York, 1979, pg. 131.]

In the final analysis, the success or failure of any of the firms that produced Arts & Crafts furniture had less to do with the extent to which they utilized machinery in their factories or workshops than it did with their ability to adjust to changing public tastes and the country's volatile economy. Nowhere was that more apparent than in the furniture factories of the five Stickley brothers.

Gustav Stickley and his designers had gradually moved from his heavy, massive early forms to an experimental line of spindle chairs and settles and finally, in 1912, to a complete line of Arts & Crafts furniture consisting of thinner boards, few exposed tenons and lighter finishes. Unfortunately, Stickley had also begun an overly ambitious and costly expansion of his business, including the purchase of 650 acres of land in New Jersey for an unsuccessful farm school for boys and fifty thousand dollar annual lease on a 12-story office building in Manhattan. Adding to his burgeoning debt, Stickley spent thousands of dollars outfitting the building for his editorial and architectural services, showrooms for his furniture, a library and lecture hall, an interior decorating service and a restaurant.

In 1914, just as his Craftsman Building was nearing completion, war broke out in Europe. Although President Wilson kept American troops on the sidelines until April of 1917, the threat of America's involvement, punctuated by the sinking of the *Lusitania* in 1915, cast a pall over the country's economy. Unable to generate the cash required to maintain the Craftsman Building and Craftsman Farms, Stickley was unable to weather the economic storm and was forced to declare bankruptcy in 1916 with debts totaling a quarter of a million dollars. His spirit broken, he never fully recovered prior to his death in 1942.

Leopold Stickley, who throughout his long career remained focused solely on furniture production, had also begun implementing a line of lighter Arts & Crafts furniture. Without such costly ventures as Gustav, Leopold and John George Stickley were not only able to remain in business, but also purchased much of their brother's assets at bankruptcy auction. In 1922, recognizing the decline in demand, Leopold Stickley phased out production of Arts & Crafts furniture and in its place began offering a quality line of Colonial reproductions that are still being manufactured today. Albert Stickley of Stickley Brothers also survived the swing away from Arts & Crafts; although he died in 1928, his firm remained in business manufacturing English-inspired furniture until the 1940s.

The Arts & Crafts movement in America had at various times during the first half of the twentieth century influenced the design and manufacture of furniture, art pottery, metalware, textiles, wall coverings, art and architecture. But, the devastating effects of two world wars and the collapse of America's economic system caused the Arts & Crafts movement to slip into obscurity, symbolized by the closing of the Roycroft Shops in 1938.

The Arts & Crafts movement began its slow ascent back into public consciousness. Along with it came the recognition that many of the ideals of the Arts & Crafts movement had been manifested in the design, construction and furnishing of the "finest resort hotel in the world" — the Grove Park Inn.

RIGHT Early guests at the Grove Park Inn enjoyed hiking along many of the trails leading up Sunset Mountain, several of which still remain.

A Brief History of
the Grove Park Inn

"After a long mountain walk one evening, at the sunset hour, I sat down here to rest, and while almost entranced by the panorama of these encircling mountains and a restful outlook upon green fields, the dream of an old-time inn came to me — an inn whose exterior, and interior as well, should present a home-like and wholesome simplicity, whose hospitable doors should ever be open wide, inviting the traveler to rest awhile, shut in from the busy world outside".

EDWIN W. GROVE

12 July 1913

Edwin W. Grove

Raised on a small farm in Hardeman County in southwest Tennessee, Edwin Wiley Grove (1850-1927) moved to Memphis as a young man, where he enrolled in pharmacy school. At the age of twenty-four Grove traveled to Paris, TN, where he sought out Dr. Samuel Caldwell, a local physician who had served with Grove's father during the Civil War. Dr. Caldwell hired Edwin Grove to manage his small pharmacy and by 1880 the enterprising and ambitious young pharmacist had purchased the business and renamed it Grove's Pharmacy.

In 1876 Edwin Grove married Mary Louisa Moore (1855-1884), a beautiful young woman he had met in Paris. Their daughter, Evelyn, was born in 1877, but all three of their subsequent children died in infancy. Tragically, in 1884 both twenty-nine year old Mary Louisa Moore and their son, Lawrence, died in the couple's home during childbirth.

After his wife's death, Edwin Grove remained in Paris, where he continued to

Edwin W. Grove, COMPLIMENTS OF THE GROVE PARK INN

operate his pharmacy while experimenting with various formulas for new medicines. At that time malaria threatened nearly every family in the rural South, killing thousands of people each year, the majority of them being pregnant women and children under the age of five. No cure for malaria existed, although scientists had determined that quinine, a bitter powder extracted from the bark of the cinchona tree, could ward it off. As scientists would later learn, the female mosquito carried the malarial parasite from infected to healthy individuals, injecting the parasite through the skin as she sought food. Once in the individual's bloodstream, the parasite would attack the liver, where it could infect the victim's red blood cells. The resulting high fever and chills marked the first stage in the disease. As the infected red blood cells multiplied, they collected within the arteries, often restricting the flow of blood to the brain and causing a fatal coma. It is quite possible that the deaths of Edwin Grove's three children and that of Mary Louisa may have been linked to malaria, explaining, in part, his determination to discover a means of thwarting the disease.

In 1886 Grove introduced his first successful formula, Grove's Tasteless Chill Tonic, a dark syrup containing refined quinine crystals, whose bitter taste Grove disguised with "reduced iron, sugar syrup and lemon flavor," in addition to a small percentage of alcohol. The ability of quinine to prevent the spread

ABOVE   While the original rustic gates have since been removed, the granite gatehouse at the entrance to the hotel still stands.

LEFT   Grove's Tasteless Chill Tonic proved to be an effective deterrent against malaria, making Grove a millionaire by age forty.

of malaria had been known for centuries, but its effectiveness had been diluted by its bitter taste. In India, the British colonials tempered the bitter quinine, commonly referred to as 'the tonic,' by mixing it with gin, hence creating the popular drink 'gin and tonic.' Today, tonic water still derives its acrid taste from the quinine it contains.

Grove had undoubtedly learned in pharmacy school that quinine could only act as a preventative and not a cure for malaria, prompting him to advise his customers to take "two tablespoons, three times a day…for a period of eight weeks or during the entire malarial season." Despite a cost of fifty cents per bottle — half a day's wages for many men — Grove's Tasteless Chill Tonic became a staple in nearly every household in the South, and made Edwin Wiley Grove a millionaire by the time he was forty.

In 1890 Grove moved his business, officially called the Paris Medicine Company, to St. Louis, along with thirteen-year old Evelyn and his second wife, Gertrude. Later that same year their son Edwin Wiley Grove, Jr., was born. St. Louis offered Grove a larger work force for his factory and a well-developed transportation system for distributing Grove's Tasteless Chill Tonic, a number of other pharmaceutical products he had begun to manufacture and his latest invention, Grove's Laxative Bromo Quinine Tablet — an

early version of the first cold tablet. Despite his move to St. Louis and his growing fortune, Edwin Grove never forgot his friends in Paris, many of whom had invested in his fledgling business. Over the ensuing years he provided funds for charities, local churches and the town cemetery, as well as endowing the county's first public high school in 1906.

Fred L. Seely

Once the formula for Grove's Tasteless Chill Tonic had been perfected and his factory had been established in St. Louis, Edwin Grove turned his attention to his latest project, Grove's Laxative Bromo Quinine Tablet. While his Tasteless Chill Tonic had proven even more successful than he had hoped, Grove recognized that sales would always be seasonal and, should the day come when either a cure or a better preventative for malaria would be discovered, might someday end. Noting, too, the public's growing preference for pills over powders and liquid pharmaceuticals, Grove embarked on a new series of experiments intended to produce the first popular cold tablet.

Frederick Loring Seely (1871-1942),
COMPLIMENTS OF BILTMORE INDUSTRIES, INC.

In 1898 his search brought him to the laboratories of Parke, Davis & Company in Detroit, where the firm had begun manufacturing tablets for clients who lacked the specialized equipment and the advanced knowledge necessary to combine the proper ingredients in a tablet which would be durable, yet palatable, attractive, yet effective. It was at Parke, Davis & Company that Edwin Grove met the man who would have the greatest impact on his life — Frederick Loring Seely (1871-1942).

Like his father and eventual father-in-law, Fred Seely

had embarked upon a career in the pharmaceutical industry. Born in New Jersey, Seely first went to work for Johnson & Johnson, and then moved to Detroit to take a position in the new tablet division of Parke, Davis & Company. While working at Parke, Davis & Company, Fred Seely was introduced to Edwin Grove on one of Grove's trips there in the spring of 1898. Seely was assigned to work with Grove on his tablet formula, but rather than, as expected, securing a lucrative contract for Parke, Davis & Company, five months later Seely tendered his resignation and accepted a position working for Edwin Grove and the Paris Medicine Company. His first project for Grove was the refinement of the formula and the development of a machine to produce Grove's Laxative Bromo Quinine Tablets.

Rather than reporting to the Paris Medicine Company factory in St. Louis, however, twenty-six year old Fred Seely was asked by Grove to come to Asheville, North Carolina. Years of running the Paris Medicine Company had taken its toll on Edwin Grove, who suffered from physical exhaustion, insomnia, near-deafness and long bouts of the hiccups. When his doctor suggested that he begin avoiding the hot, muggy and polluted St. Louis summers, Grove began vacationing in Asheville, a quaint city of fifteen thousand inhabitants nestled in the French Broad River valley in the Blue Ridge Mountains of western North Carolina.

At the center of the city, located on a twelve-acre wooded knoll with commanding views in every direction, stood the luxurious Battery Park Hotel, a sprawling Queen Anne style hotel complete with turrets, balconies, porches, individual fireplaces and a water-driven elevator. At the time the city experienced a paradox of visitors: boarding houses and sanitariums were sprouting up to compete for the growing number of tubercular patients being sent to the mountains of North Carolina to recuperate, while upscale inns and hotels, including The Manor Inn and the Battery Park Hotel, were catering to wealthy tourists escaping either the summer heat of Georgia and Florida or the punishing winters of the Midwest and Northeast. Ten years earlier George Vanderbilt and his mother had stayed at the Battery Park Hotel and, after inhaling the view from his private balcony to the towering Pisgah Mountain to the southwest, had decided to purchase what would amount to nearly 125,000 acres of land on which to built his Biltmore Estate, including his 250-room French chateaux.

Like Vanderbilt, Edwin Grove had also fallen in love with Asheville. By 1898 Grove had established a small office and laboratory for his experiments, as well as a summer home for his family: his wife Gertrude, their eight-year old son Edwin and Grove's daughter

Evelyn, who was now twenty-one years old. Fred Seely stayed that summer in the Swannanoa Hotel, but at Grove's insistence took most of his evening meals at their spacious home in north Asheville. Before long he began courting Evelyn Grove and on October 24, 1898, the two were married.

In addition to gaining an intelligent, hard-working son-in-law, Edwin Grove also gained a new manager with greater than normal skills in organization and efficiency. After designing a tablet producing machine larger and faster than anything at Parke, Davis & Company, Seely built and patented a device which could count and package the tablets as they left the stamping machine. Two years later Grove transferred Seely from the Asheville laboratory to the main factory in St. Louis, where he made Seely a corporate officer in the Paris Medicine Company and gave him the authority to completely reorganize and manage the firm's production, sales, advertising and bookkeeping departments.

While his son-in-law took charge of the daily operation of the Paris Medicine Company, fifty-one-year old Edwin Grove embarked on a new career: investment property. Before long he had purchased cattle grazing tracts in Texas and Mexico, timberland in Arkansas, coal fields in West Virginia and residential real estate in parts of Florida, as well as on the outskirts of Atlanta and Asheville. In 1905, however, both men longed for a change. With every department at the Paris Medicine Company running smoothly and efficiently, and with sales breaking records each

ABOVE The original rooms in the Grove Park provided guests with a panoramic view of the Blue Ridge Mountains to the west.

BELOW Downtown Asheville's Battery Park Hotel (1886-1921) served tourists such as George Vanderbilt, William Jennings Bryan and President Theodore Roosevelt before being purchased and demolished by Edwin W. Grove.

The third floor Palm Court provided guests with a quiet, sunny retreat beneath the sixth-floor skylight. The stenciling on the parapet walls was reproduced after meticulously uncovering the original Arts & Crafts design.

Plans for the Grove Park Inn

As Fred Seely concentrated on the daily task of running the *Atlanta Georgian* and on the transition of ownership over to Hearst, Edwin Grove was spending a great deal of time thinking about ways of developing some of the 600 acres of land he had purchased in north Asheville into residential neighborhoods. As someone who loved to walk, Grove enjoyed the many parks and wide boulevards in turn-of-the-century St. Louis. In each of his subsequent residential developments, Grove made it a point to include parks, boulevards and inviting sidewalks. Included in the plans for his first residential development in north Asheville was a small park near the end of Charlotte Street, which, after naming it the E. W. Grove Park, he donated to the city.

Even with the lure of the lush countryside, views of the mountains surrounding the city, the convenience of the extended streetcar line and a city park complete with a fountain and roofed stone benches for people waiting for a streetcar, sales of his residential building lots did not match the pace expected by E. W. Grove. As the aging Battery Park Hotel approached its twenty-fifth anniversary, civic leaders and private investors began to approach Grove with suggestions for a new hotel to be constructed on the western slope of Sunset Mountain. Grove's initial rejection gradually turned to acceptance, once son-in-law Fred Seely endorsed the idea, pointing out that a steady stream of wealthy guests to a resort hotel would spur sales of Grove's surrounding land.

The two men selected a site for the hotel high enough on Sunset Mountain to offer guests panoramic views of the Blue Ridge Mountains to the west, yet low enough to be able to remain open during the winter months — and to be able to offer guests the convenience of walking to the adjacent Asheville Country Club's golf course. Inspired by the Old Faithful Inn and the new Grand Canyon Hotel at Yellowstone National Park, Grove began soliciting plans from architects across the country for a 150-room hotel complete with every modern convenience. Grove's personal preference, as well as his penchant for cutting costs, were revealed in a letter written September 19, 1911: "The hotels and cottages, as I now propose to build them, will be of logs, stone and hewn and rough sawed lumber, using mill stuff only where the details of construction demand it. The stone and timber needed for the various buildings are on the property and accessible." [private collection]

His ultimate motivation was also revealed in the same letter: "If we make Asheville the most desirable place in the whole mountainous section to live in, we can bring people there who have means and who could

year, Edwin Grove indicated that he was rested and ready to return to the helm. Simultaneously, Fred Seely seemed anxious for a new challenge. They agreed that Fred and Evelyn should move to Atlanta, where Fred would manage Grove's real estate developments while determining whether the two men should buy one of the struggling Atlanta newspapers as an investment or start a fresh newspaper.

With no experience in the newspaper business, Seely and Grove founded the *Atlanta Georgian* in 1906. Grove provided the capitol while Seely served as publisher and, later, as editor-in-chief. Although his circulation figures grew annually, Seely found it difficult to lure major Atlanta advertisers away from the two established newspapers. By 1912 the *Atlanta Georgian* was able to show a small profit, but by that time both Grove and Seely had tired of the ordeal. They struck a deal with William Randolph Hearst, who made it the ninth in his growing syndicate of newspapers.

stay in hotels and cottages to their tastes, and many of them would buy and build homes of their own."

With his mind made up and materials at hand, it only remained for Edwin Grove to select an architect and a set of plans for his new hotel. Of the scores of architects who had submitted rough sketches, Grove seemed ready to turn the project over to the Chicago architect Henry Ives Cobb (1859-1931), who had impressed Grove with his experience working with fieldstone construction in Massachusetts. Cobb had achieved national fame when he was among the architects selected to design the buildings for the 1893 World's Fair and had gone on to design several Chicago landmarks, including the Chicago Opera House and the campus of the University of Chicago. Grove remarked in a letter to his Asheville property manager dated March 26, 1912, "Mr. Cobb also states that when you have concluded you have enough stone to complete this building, to go ahead and haul twice as much more. I forgot to state that Mr. Cobb suggested very attractive columns could be made in the big lobby room out of boulders." [*May We All Remember Well,* Vol. 1, edited by Robert S. Brunk, Brunk Auction Services, Publisher, Asheville, NC, 1997, pg. 222-223.]

The very next month, however, Fred Seely, who at age 41 and the father of four children now found himself out of work after the sale of the *Atlanta Georgian* to William Randolph Hearst, presented Grove with a proposal: he would move his family to Asheville in order to serve as Grove's general contractor on the hotel project. Although Seely had little prior experience in construction, having only built a few rental houses and one church during his brief stint in 1905 as a contractor in Atlanta, Grove accepted Seely's offer, offering him as compensation $1500 and nearly twenty acres of land on top of Sunset Mountain for Seely to build a home for his family.

In typical Seely fashion, Fred also offered to relieve Grove of the financial negotiations that Grove had begun with Henry Ives Cobb. The famous Chicago architect had earlier submitted a preliminary set of plans to Grove, which Grove had approved and had forwarded to Seely in Atlanta. When Cobb balked at Seely's proposal to pay the architect in interest-bearing bonds issued by William Randolph Hearst and given to Grove in exchange for the *Atlanta Georgian,* Seely suddenly announced that they would not need his services. Although Fred Seely had no experience as either an architect or draftsman, he informed Cobb, "I was at the time working on a sketch of my own. The sketch proved, strangely, to be entirely satisfactory to Mr. Grove and he came over here a little over a week ago, when the sketch was finished, approved of it, and requested that I go to Asheville with him to locate the building and start the work." [Brunk, pg. 225-226]

How much indebtedness Fred Seely's 'sketch' owed to the plans Cobb had submitted to Grove several weeks earlier remains undetermined, for, whatever reason, the drawings which Henry Ives Cobb had made for the proposed hotel have yet to surface.

A former newspaper publisher, Grove's son-in-law Fred L. Seely drew this sketch of the proposed hotel, which he subsequently built and managed from 1913-1927. COMPLIMENTS OF THE GROVE PARK INN RESORT & SPA

Construction and Furnishing of the Hotel

Although E.W. Grove professed in April of 1912 that he was in no great hurry to start or complete the massive project, Fred Seely thought differently. In May he submitted his own sketch of the hotel for Grove's approval. In June he withdrew Grove's earlier offer to hire Henry Ives Cobb as the architect. That same month he procured the services of two Atlanta men: Oscar Mills to serve as construction foreman and architect G.W. McKibbin to draw the final plans. In June he also arranged for reporters and Asheville dignitaries to be present on the site on July 1, when Grove's wife, Gertrude, turned the first shovel of dirt to officially begin construction. That day Fred Seely announced to the press — much to everyone's surprise — that the Grove Park Inn would be open for business exactly one year later.

Those in attendance at the ground breaking that afternoon could view some of the preparations made in advance of construction. Piles of granite rocks and boulders hauled in by wagon encircled the site, where a steam shovel — the only motorized piece of machinery employed in the project — stood ready to begin cutting a ledge in the side of the mountain for the foundation. That summer more than four hundred men of all ages, races and nationalities built forms, poured concrete and laid rocks — each hauled by wheelbarrow up long ramps. Seely's plans called for a full basement, a main floor with an expansive lobby, restaurant, offices and parlors, and five upper floors containing 150 guest rooms. The central section consisted of six stories; each of the two side wings terminated at the fifth floor. Hollow concrete blocks provided the skeleton for each of the walls, which the stonemasons encased on both sides with granite stones. The finished walls ranged in thickness from four feet at the ground floor to a mere two feet on the sixth floor. Huge granite lintels, some more than six feet long, were carefully selected to cap each door and window opening.

At that era, the threat of fire plagued nearly every wooden hotel, inn and boarding house in America, many of which had inadequate electrical wiring added long after the initial construction. Seely and Grove took great measures to be able to assure their guests that the Grove Park Inn would be fireproof, including topping the Grove Park Inn with a poured concrete roof. The workmen began by building a wooden form over which they placed a total of ninety thousand

TOP LEFT The poured concrete roof on the hotel was one of the first of its type in America.

BOTTOM LEFT Building materials were stored in the Great Hall during construction. BOTH COMPLIMENTS OF THE GROVE PARK INN RESORT & SPA

Fred L. Seely designed the hotel's two original elevators inside the massive granite fireplaces in the Great Hall to muffle the sound of the machinery from his guests. Both elevators are still in operation today.

pounds of steel reinforcing bar, woven like a giant spider's web draped over the hotel. Once pouring commenced, the men worked around the clock, bringing wheelbarrows of wet concrete up a makeshift elevator and dumping them down over the slope of the roof to where men with rakes worked the concrete in and around the reinforcing bar. Electric bulbs were strung from temporary poles on the roof to enable them to work after dark, ensuring that there would be no seams in any of the sections of roof. As Oscar Mills wrote to his family on March 24, 1913, "I had to come back to the hotel tonight. They are pouring the concrete roof on and are working sometimes all night. The wind is blowing up on the roof like fury. I can see all over Asheville, but Good Lord how one peep of dear Old Atlanta would stir the latent blood in my veins." [*Built for the Ages: A History of the Grove Park Inn*, by Bruce Johnson, Grove Park Inn: Asheville, NC, 1991, pg. 16.]

Later the men would seal the concrete with layers of hot asphalt before covering the entire roof with red clay tiles from the Murray Roofing Company in Cloverport, Kentucky. The result was that of an English cottage, built of stone and covered with random-spaced clay tiles. As one writer reported, "There will be no angles anywhere in the roof. There will be only lazy, graceful slopes and the effect will be something unique for this section of the country." [Johnson, pg. 17.]

Six floors below, workmen were covering the floor of the expansive lobby, measuring 80' × 120', with small square tiles. Six stone-encased concrete columns

Photographer John G. Robinson documented the twelve-month construction of the Grove Park Inn, capturing workmen in this photograph dismantling the wooden scaffolding standing on the western terrace. BLACK & WHITE PHOTOS THIS PAGE COMPLIMENTS OF THE GROVE PARK INN RESORT & SPA

rose from the floor more than twenty feet in height to support the poured concrete beams and floor above them. At either end stood massive twin fireplaces, each firebox large enough for a man to stand in and capable of burning twelve-foot logs on hammered andirons. Fred Seely directed his workmen to hide the elevators to the guest rooms on the upper floors inside the thirty-foot wide fireplaces in order to insulate any noise coming from them to the guests relaxing in the Great Hall. Like the six columns and the twin fireplaces, all of the interior walls in the Great Hall were constructed of granite rocks and boulders picked up — not quarried — from the slopes of the surrounding mountains. As Seely later wrote, "The men worked

under instructions that when the Inn was finished not a piece of stone should be visible to the eye [unless] it showed the time-eaten face given to it by the thousands of years of sun and rain that had beaten upon it as it had lain on the mountainside. These great boulders were laid with the lichens and moss on them just as they were found." [Grove Park Inn brochure, attributed to Fred L. Seely, Asheville, NC, ca. 1919, pg. 9.]

Once construction had begun, E. W. Grove returned to St. Louis to oversee operations at the Paris Medicine Company. His son, Edwin W. Grove, Jr., also lived in St. Louis and now worked for his father in the family business. The elder Grove received weekly progress reports from Fred Seely, who conferred almost

LEFT   This staircase once led guests from the front desk to the left up to the third floor Palm Court and surrounding rooms. It has since been moved to a different location.

BELOW   View from the west showing what the town of Ashville saw during construction of the Grove Park Inn.

OPPOSITE TOP   Nearly one hundred years has had little effect on the Grove Park Inn's stone walls.

OPPOSITE BOTTOM   The Great Hall was originally furnished with wicker furniture from the Heywood-Wakefield Company of Boston resting on rugs handwoven in France. The chandeliers were made in the Roycroft Copper Shop. BLACK & WHITLE PHOTOS THESE PAGES, COMPLIMENTS OF THE GROVE PARK INN RESORT & SPA

daily on the site with their foreman, Oscar Mills. Correspondence between Seely and Grove indicates that Grove's overriding concern were the mounting costs of construction, driven beyond his initial expectations by Seely's insistence on the highest quality of materials, from plumbing fixtures to Arts & Crafts furniture. Indicative of Fred Seely's tastes — and his attention to detail — is this description which he wrote for an early Grove Park Inn brochure: "The plumbing material is the finest that the world has ever seen. The soil pipe was hydraulically tested and then galvanized. The hot water pipe, 18,000 pounds in weight, is solid brass. The steam pipes are of Byers' genuine lap-welded wrought iron. The bathtubs and fixtures are all solid porcelain, made to our order by Haines, Jones & Cadbury of Philadelphia, the oldest plumbing manufacturers in the United States. Even the lighting fixtures in the bathrooms are porcelain. The toilet seats are celluloid." [Grove Park Inn brochure, attributed to Fred L. Seely, Asheville, NC, ca. 1919, pg. 2.]

Two Asheville photographers, John G. Robinson and Herbert Pelton, documented the construction of the Grove Park Inn from groundbreaking to its official opening little more than twelve months later. As their photographs reveal, during the summer and fall of 1912 a skeleton of scaffolding blurred the view from downtown Asheville of the rising granite walls. That spring, however, as the red clay tile was being laid on the roof, the workmen removed the scaffolding, giving the people of Asheville their first full view of the hotel on Sunset Mountain that would help define their city. It was, as has often been observed, literally built *of* the mountain, not *on* the mountain.

E. W. Grove was content to let his son-in-law select all of the furnishings for the Grove Park Inn, from the flatware in the dining room to the chandeliers hanging from the ceiling of the Great Hall. No detail escaped the discerning eye of Fred Seely, who, as a seasoned traveler, knew what the wealthy and elite clientele he hoped to lure to the Grove Park Inn would expect during their stay at the resort. For their entertainment he provided an indoor swimming pool, two billiard tables, a three-lane bowling alley, evening movies, live musical performances each afternoon, guest speakers, guided tours, a stable of horses, hiking trails, tennis courts, access to the adjacent golf course of the Asheville Country Club and scores of Old Hickory rocking chairs stretching along more than 500 feet of open terraces overlooking Asheville, the French Broad River Valley and the distant Blue Ridge Mountains.

To soften the sounds reverberating off the granite walls and tile floors in the Great Hall, also referred to as the "Great Lobby" or the "Big Room," Fred Seely ordered rugs and tapestries from the looms of Charles Henry Sallandrouze of Aubusson, France. The chairs, tables and rockers in the room were made of wicker and upholstered in red tufted leather by the Heywood Brothers and Wakefield Company of Boston. The Asheville Supply and Foundry Company provided "four great andirons weighing 500 pounds apiece, and an average of twenty-four days' blacksmith work was done on each of them." [Grove Park Inn brochure, attributed to Fred L. Seely, Asheville, NC, ca. 1919, pg. 8.]

TOP LEFT Each of the original guest rooms was furnished with Arts & Crafts furniture designed by the Roycrofters but constructed by the White Furniture Company of Mebane, N.C. The walls were first decorated with natural burlap trimmed in stained oak. COMPLIMENTS OF THE GROVE PARK INN RESORT & SPA

BOTTOM LEFT The pattern on the original dining room china came from that used by Fred L. Seely's grandmother. The souvenir plate on the left was sold through the hotel's News Stand for nearly three decades and remains highly collectible.

ABOVE The terrace on the west side of the hotel was left uncovered until the 1960s. During all but the winter months it now serves as one of the hotel's most popular restaurants.

RIGHT Rustic rockers from the Old Hickory Chair Company lined the nearly five hundred feet of terraces that originally ran alongside three sides of the hotel. COMPLIMENTS OF THE GROVE PARK INN RESORT & SPA

The guest rooms that Fred Seely designed included Arts & Crafts furniture by the Roycrofters and the White Furniture Company (see separate entries), with beds meeting Seely's specifications that they each be six feet, four inches long. The box springs and mattresses were provided by the Sealy Company; the bedspreads, pillowcases and even the curtains in the room were all of pure brown linen. In the dining room Fred Seely ordered nickel-silver flatware in a hammered Arts & Crafts style from the Wallace Silversmiths of Wallingford, CT. The dinnerware produced by the Syracuse China Company for the Grove Park Inn was definitely not influenced by the Arts & Crafts movement. Instead, the Victorian floral and fruit border was inspired by a teapot that had been in the Seely family for over one hundred years. A designer at the Syracuse China Company by the name of J. T. Wigley drew the final version, satisfying Seely's desire for "some simple embossed design in old blue or mulberry." [Syracuse China News, E. J. MacMillan, Syracuse China Corporation, Syracuse, NY, 1931, pg. 25.]

But the company that would have the greatest impact on the furnishing of the Grove Park Inn and its recognition both in 1913 and today as the finest Arts & Crafts resort hotel in the country was the Roycroft Shops of Elbert Hubbard. Although some of the original Roycroft lighting fixtures and furniture has left the Inn, what has survived and what has returned now comprises the country's largest collection of Arts & Crafts furniture and lighting. The role of the Roycrofters in the history of the Grove Park Inn is without equal. Working together, the Roycroft Shops and the Grove Park Inn, their owners Elbert Hubbard and E. W. Grove, their managers Elbert Hubbard, Jr. and Fred Seely, and one talented designer and craftsman by the name of Victor Toothaker combined to create an Arts & Crafts legacy that not only has survived, but has prospered.

Elbert Hubbard and the Roycroft Shops

"We make this simple, substantial straight-lined furniture with our Head, Hand and Heart. We believe that which serves best distracts least. Things in evidence must be unassuming and dignified. You cannot afford to harass your nerves with gaudy and noisy surroundings."

ELBERT HUBBARD

ca. 1912

Born on June 19, 1856 in Bloomington, Illinois, Elbert Hubbard left school at the age of fifteen to begin doing what he always did best — selling. The flashy, handsome young man began his career peddling soap from the back of a wagon to farm wives on the Illinois prairie. The year he turned eighteen his older sister, Frances, married John D. Larkin (1845-1926), a twenty-nine year old soap manufacturer from Chicago. Larkin's earlier business partnership had just soured, prompting him to begin looking for a new location and an equally as energetic business associate. He and Elbert Hubbard joined forces and in 1875 selected Buffalo, New York, as the headquarters for the Larkin Soap Company.

At the beginning of the firm's history Larkin and Hubbard sold soap by the traditional method — through middlemen, independent retail shops and wholesalers. In 1881, drawing upon his own experience in Illinois, Hubbard suggested that the firm send out its own door-to-door salesmen to sell Larkin's laundry detergent, which Hubbard had named "Sweet Home Soap," and their toilet soap, "Crème Oatmeal." Soon thereafter Hubbard hit upon an idea that would prompt business historians to label him a marketing genius. He suggested that the company begin including small gifts, such as a postcard or handkerchief, with each soap order a customer placed directly with the company. Soon they replaced the gifts with premiums redeemable for a growing assortment of household items, including bath towels, pottery, glassware, leather goods and even furniture.

Hubbard set as his goal the complete elimination not only of all middlemen and wholesalers, but also of the Larkin door-to-door salesmen, replacing them with a mail order network stretching across the country. He even coined his first motto: "From Factory to Family — Save All Costs Which Add No Value." Hubbard's parade of marketing ideas convinced the American public that the Larkin Soap Company was looking out for their good. Among his most popular ideas was the Combination Box, a six-dollar assortment of Larkin soaps and creams sent to the family on a thirty-day trial, along with a coupon worth six dollars in the Larkin catalog. In 1893 the Larkin Soap Company mailed out 1.5 million copies of their catalog containing hundreds of gifts redeemable with Larkin coupons. That year the company shipped more than 80,000 Morris chairs and nearly 125,000 oak dining chairs, all which had been purchased using coupons included in Elbert Hubbard's Combination Box.

Several years earlier, in 1884, Hubbard, his wife of three years, Bertha Crawford Hubbard, and their first

Elbert Hubbard in 1904. COMPLIMENTS OF THE ROYCROFT CAMPUS CORPORATION

son had moved to East Aurora, a small town sixteen miles southeast of Buffalo. His years in the city had left him longing for the country and his self-described "weakness for horses." [*Art & Glory: The Story of Elbert Hubbard*, by Freeman Champney, Kent State University Press, Kent, Ohio, 1968, pg. 36.] In East Aurora, where he purchased a large house on an acre of land, Hubbard enjoyed not only riding horses, but also buying and selling them as well.

It was in East Aurora that by 1889 Elbert Hubbard had also met Alice Moore, a local schoolteacher and a friend of Bertha Hubbard. For a short time Alice Hubbard boarded with the Hubbards; all three were members of the Chautauqua Literary and Scientific Circle. Years later, after their secret and stormy relationship had surfaced, Hubbard declared that it was Alice who had "caused me, at thirty-three years of age, to be born again." [Champney, pg. 37.] But as a married man and the father of three sons, Elbert Hubbard was not yet prepared to publicly declare his love for Alice.

Despite the success which he and John Larkin had achieved, Elbert Hubbard longed to be remembered for more than just his role as an advertising and marketing executive. Although he lacked a formal education, Hubbard had quietly been writing a novel entitled *The Man: A Story of Today*, which in 1891, the J. S. Ogilvie Company of New York published under his pseudonym of Aspasia Hobbs. Alice Moore, historians believe, both encouraged and helped Hubbard to write his first novel.

Although neither critics nor the public found any merit in *The Man*, which Hubbard seldom, if ever, acknowledged, he remained determined to pursue a literary career. In 1892 the Larkin Soap Company incorporated, prompting John Larkin to reward Hubbard handsomely with a considerable number of shares of company stock. Later that year Hubbard shocked Larkin, his family and his friends by announcing that at age thirty-six he would be retiring from the soap business to pursue his goal of becoming a novelist. His stock settlement has been estimated to have been in the neighborhood of $65,000 — the equivalent today of approximately $1,500,000.

Freed from his responsibilities at the Larkin Soap Company, Hubbard churned out three more mediocre novels, attempted unsuccessfully to become a 37-year old student at Harvard University and maintained separate households with two women: Publicly with Bertha and their three sons in East Aurora, and secretly with Alice, who was then living in Boston. Adding to the turmoil in his life, in 1894 Alice gave birth to their daughter, Miriam; less than two years later Bertha bore her fourth child by Hubbard, a daughter they named Bertha. In 1894 Elbert Hubbard attempted to escape the pressures of his dual households by sailing to England, where he visited the home and printing operation of William Morris, the father of the Arts & Crafts movement.

After two months touring the British Isles, Hubbard returned to East Aurora determined to establish

Fra Elbertus
and the little De Luxe.

ALICE AND ELBERT HUBBARD

LEFT Early postcards captured Elbert Hubbard with his daughter on the steps of the Roycroft Inn.
COMPLIMENTS OF THE ROYCROFT CAMPUS CORPORATION

RIGHT In the Print Shop with wife, partner and fellow writer Alice Moore Hubbard.
COMPLIMENTS OF THE ROYCROFT CAMPUS CORPORATION

CALIFORNIA NUMBER

THE FRA

(NOT FOR MUMMIES)
A JOURNAL OF AFFIRMATION

Vol. III   JUNE, 1909   No. 3

PUBLISHED·MONTHLY·BY·ELBERT·HUBBARD
EAST·AURORA·ERIE·COUNTY·NEW·YORK
2 5 CENTS·A·COPY·2·DOLLARS·A·YEAR

Elbert Hubbard was the most prolific writer of the Arts & Crafts era, filling numerous books and magazines, including *The Fra* and *The Philistine*, with his views on everything from social customs and religion to politics and architecture.

chapel right alongside of my house. There was a basement and one room upstairs. I wanted it to be comfortable and pretty, so we furnished our little shop cozily. We had four girls and three boys working for us then. The shop was never locked and the boys and girls used to come around evenings. It was really more pleasant than at home." [*The Roycroft Shop: A History*, by Elbert Hubbard, The Roycroft Print Shop, East Aurora, NY, 1908, pg. 3.]

Hubbard's partnership with Henry Tabor proved to be short-lived. By November of 1895 Elbert Hubbard was the sole owner of the Roycroft Printing Shop, along with the orb-and-cross shopmark, both of which historians now agree had been first conceived not by Elbert Hubbard, but by little known Henry Tabor. [Via and Searl, pg. 24.] That same fall Hubbard had struggled with two other partners as well: His wife Bertha asked to design the cover of *The Song of Songs*, while his mistress, Alice Moore, secretively assisted with the text from her apartment in Boston. His dual relationships with the two women in his life lurched along unsteadily for eight more years, until it became impossible for him to hide the existence of his nine-year old daughter and Alice, whose demands for his time and recognition for her creative role at the Roycroft Shops increased with each of his visits. Faced with public humiliation, Bertha Hubbard filed for divorce from her husband in 1903 and moved to Buffalo. A few months later Hubbard married Alice Moore and brought her and Miriam to live in East Aurora. It was a shocking turn of events, one that brought national scorn and ridicule down upon Hubbard and cost him the friendship of John Larkin and his sister, Frances Hubbard Larkin.

The rapid success of *The Philistine* prompted Hubbard to continue publishing his avant-garde periodical. Looking back on those early days, Hubbard recalled, "the country had grown tired of soft platitude, silly truism and undisputed things said in such a solemn way. So when *The Philistine* stepped into the ring and voiced in no uncertain tones what its editor thought, thinking men and women stopped and listened. Editors of magazines refused my manuscript because they said it was too plain, too blunt, sometime indelicate — it would give offense, subscribers would cancel, et cetera. To get my thoughts published I had to publish them myself; and people bought them for the very reason for which the editors said they would cancel. The readers wanted brevity and plain statement." [Hubbard, pg. 7.]

Hubbard proved capable of wearing several hats, serving at various times as publisher, editor, writer, marketing director and, quite naturally, salesman.

his own printing enterprise based on the ideals and philosophy of the newly emerging Arts & Crafts movement. Having no experience in the printing business, he entered into a partnership with Harry Tabor, an established East Aurora printer, with whom he published the first editions of a magazine called *The Philistine: A Periodical of Protest* and the first Roycroft book, *The Song of Songs* (1896). Years later Hubbard recalled that pivotal first year:

"I decided to run *The Philistine* magazine for a year — to keep faith with the misguided and hopeful parties who had subscribed — and then quit. To fill in the time, we printed a book: We printed it like a William Morris book — printed it just as well as we could. It was cold in the old barn where we first set up *The Philistine*, so I built a little building like an old English

Between issues he continued to print, illuminate and bind books by hand in the Arts & Crafts tradition espoused by William Morris. As his work load increased, Hubbard hired local young men and women to work for him, often in a variety of tasks ranging from bundling magazines as they rolled off the press to binding books, illuminating pages or unloading wagonloads of granite boulders brought in by area farmers for Hubbard's many building projects on the expanding Roycroft campus.

Hubbard's flamboyant style and his natural gift for public speaking provided a source of income far in excess of what the Roycroft Printing Shop could generate during its early years. He discovered eager audiences on the lecture tour, where he espoused his personal philosophy on life, big business, small towns, relationships, literature, politics, religion, medicine or whatever topic interested him at the moment, including — or especially — his own Roycroft Shops. Many of his lecture tours he arranged himself, others were in association with the Chautauqua circuit and one year he actually traveled with a vaudeville act. The townspeople of East Aurora often joked, "whenever Hubbard needed money for a Roycroft project, he went on the road lecturing." [Via and Searl, pg. 8.]

And Hubbard would have agreed, for as he noted in 1908, "my lectures have been of double importance, in that they have given an income and at the same time advertised the Roycroft Wares. The success of the Roycroft Shop has not been brought about by any one scheme or plan. The business is really a combination of several ideas, any one of which would make a paying enterprise in itself. So it stands thus: First, the printing and publishing of two magazines. Second, the printing of books. Third, the publication of books. Fourth, the artistic binding of books. Fifth, authorship. Sixth, the lecture lyceum. Seventh, blacksmithing, carpenter work, terra cotta and weaving. These industries have sprung up under the Roycroft care as a necessity. Men and women, many of them seventy years young or so, in the village, came to us and wanted work, and we simply gave them the opportunity to do the things they could do best. We have found a market for all our wares, so no line of work has ever been a bill of expense." [Hubbard, pg. 8.]

It should be noted, however, that Hubbard's statement was made in 1908, a year when an economic recession caused him to temporarily close the Roycroft Furniture Shop and two years before the Roycroft Copper Shop [see separate entry] began to bloom under the steady hand of Karl Kipp. The "terra cotta and weaving" which Hubbard referenced are now considered to have been experimental endeavors that were soon dropped, for few examples of either Roycroft pottery or textiles have since been identified.

On his travels Hubbard spoke with pride of the working and living conditions he provided for the men and women who worked for him at Roycroft, a number which quickly grew from seven the first year to 50 in 1898, 310 in 1908, and more than 500 at its zenith in

THE ROYCROFT SHOPS, EAST AURORA, ERIE COUNTY, NEW YORK.

ABOVE The Roycroft Campus stretched along Grove Street in East Aurora, N.Y. While the well-sweep in the foreground is gone, the majority of the original buildings shown here still exist. COMPLIMENTS OF THE ROYCROFT CAMPUS CORPORATION

COMPOSING-ROOM
The hand-press here shown is the first printing-press owned by Elbert Hubbard

1913 during the Grove Park Inn commission. "At the Roycroft Shop," he explained, "we are reaching out for an all-round development through work and right living. And we have found it a good, expedient and wise business policy. Sweat-shop methods can never succeed in producing beautiful things. And so the management of the Roycroft Shop surrounds the workers with beauty, allows many liberties, encourages cheerfulness and tries to promote kind thoughts, simply because it has found that these things are transmuted into good, and come out again at the fingertips of the workers in

beautiful results. So we have pictures, statuary, ferns, palms, birds and a piano in every room. We have the best sanitary appliances that money can buy; we have bathrooms, shower-baths, library, rest-rooms. Every week we have concerts, dances and lectures." [Hubbard, pg. 9.]

Hubbard shared the belief with William Morris that "the involvement of ordinary unskilled people in the production of the work itself — the process of making — was as important as the finished product." [Via and Searl, pg. 15.] He preferred to take the untrained workers and teach them a skill, whether it be metalsmithing, leatherworking, bookbinding, printing production, illuminating or furniture making. "We do not encourage people from a distance who want work to come on," he explained, "they are apt to expect too much. They look for Utopia, when work is work, here as elsewhere." [Hubbard, pg. 3.]

But they came. Word of the activities and opportunities at the Roycroft Shops brought hundreds of people to East Aurora, some seeking work, others wanting simply to spend a few days amid the Arts & Crafts environment Elbert Hubbard had created. Always alert to the next opportunity, Hubbard opened the Roycroft Inn in 1903. The following year, after his cabinetmakers had provided all of the Arts & Crafts furniture for the Roycroft Inn's guest rooms, library and dining rooms, as well as for the new Print Shop (1899-1901) and Copper Shop (1902), he set them to work building a three-story workshop in preparation for an expanded line of Arts & Crafts furniture he intended to sell to the general public from the Roycroft Furniture Shop (see separate entry).

While Hubbard began various enterprises, including metalsmithing, leather craft, furniture making and, for a brief time, art pottery, he remained a man of literature. No evidence exists which indicates any significant involvement or interest of his, beyond the success of the venture in supporting and promoting the Roycroft Shops, in any of the Roycroft branches other than printing and publishing. To his credit, Elbert Hubbard never made serious claim to have designed or crafted an oak bookcase or sideboard, a copper bookend or candlestick, a leather purse or table mat. He could write as prolifically as any man or woman in America and loved nothing better than to see his ideas and opinions in print. While at the Larkin Soap Company, Hubbard ran the advertising and marketing departments while John Larkin served as the financial and business manager. During the early years at Roycroft, at a time when the Roycroft Printing Shop was the only established branch, Hubbard could manage the financial, the creative and the promotional aspects of the business. It was no accident, however, that the rapid expansion of the Roycroft Shops to include the Roycroft Inn and three workshops specializing in metalsmithing, leatherworking and furniture making, as well as a staff which grew to include approximately five hundred people, coincided with the arrival of Alice Moore Hubbard. Her role, as she and only she could define it, was not to merely be the wife of Elbert Hubbard, but to be the business manager of the Roycroft Shops. Credit for the founding of the Roycroft Shops, for the proposal of a colony of artists and artisans sharing a belief in the ideals and principles of the Arts & Crafts movement clearly belongs to Elbert Hubbard,

Though since reduced to two stories by a fire, the original Furniture Shop, seen here ca. 1904, still stands on the Roycroft Campus, where it houses a pottery, an art gallery and an antiques shop. ALL PHOTOS THIS PAGE ARE FROM THE ROYCROFT CAMPUS CORPORATION

The first Roycroft Blacksmith Shop was a low, wooden shanty that was torn down after completion of the Copper Shop, seen here under construction around 1901.

Completed in 1902, the Roycroft Copper Shop grew in size as Roycroft hammered copper items grew in popularity. The craftsmen shown here worked under the discerning eye of master designer Karl Kipp.

The Copper Shop has survived and serves today as a gift shop and the offices of the Roycroft Campus Corporation.

ABOVE A canopy of maple trees once lined Grove Street, where twin glass globes marked the front entrance to the Roycroft Inn.

LEFT The Salon Room inside the Roycroft Inn served as a lecture hall for Elbert Hubbard and other speakers who entertained Roycroft workers and guests. COMPLIMENTS OF THE ROYCROFT CAMPUS CORPORATION

but as Elbert Hubbard recognized and declared in 1907, Alice Hubbard provided the financial backbone for the company: "In manufacturing she studies cost, knowing far better than most business men that deterioration of property and overhead charges must be carefully considered, if the Referee in Bankruptcy would be kept at a safe distance. She is a methodizer of time and effort…. She is an economist and a financier, making a dollar go farther without squeezing it than any man or woman I ever saw. Her ability to manage people and serve the public is shown in the fact that the Roycroft Inn, of which she is the sole manager, made a profit the past year of a little over some thousand dollars." [*White Hyacinths*, by Elbert Hubbard, The Roycroft shops, East Aurora, NY, 1907, pg. 30, 47.]

While Alice Moore Hubbard has often been criticized for having driven from Roycroft such talented and creative individuals as printer and designer Cy Rosen and metalsmiths Karl Kipp and Walter Jennings, she is recognized today as being an early and vigorous leader in the women's rights movement, a popular speaker whose audiences eventually rivaled in size those of her husband's, a gifted writer and skillful editor and an individual unafraid to tackle the most controversial issues of her day, regardless of the risk. As one Roycroft historian has observed, "Alice and Elbert were a balanced pair. Where Elbert was impetuous, Alice was reserved; where he was too generous, she was too frugal. He took the part of father-patron, while she watched the books." [Via and Searl, pg. 54.]

Under Alice and the patronage of Elbert, the Roycroft Shops prospered from 1904 through 1915. The finest of the books printed, illuminated and bound by the Roycroft Printing Shop were unsurpassed in America; the metalware designed and executed by Karl Kipp, Walter Jennings and Victor Toothaker reflected a sophistication rarely found in other metalshops; and the Furniture Shop, while it never sought to equal the production levels of any of the Stickley furniture makers, produced a line of Arts & Crafts furniture which is treasured by Arts & Crafts collectors today.

Unfortunately, as every Roycroft collector knows, Alice and Elbert Hubbard did not live to enjoy the legacy they created together. They stood, helpless, on the bow of the Lusitania and watched that clear Friday morning, the 7th of May in 1915, along with hundreds of other passengers destined for Ireland, as a single German torpedo cut a foamy white swath across the icy Atlanta Ocean. Experts theorize the ship might have survived the torpedo's initial damage, but a second, still unexplained explosion signaled her doom, sending the Lusitania to the ocean's floor in just eighteen minutes.

The sudden heavy list of the ship made lowering the lifeboats on the starboard side impossible. A survivor recalled that Elbert and Alice Hubbard had made their way to lifeboat #14 on the port side and were safely in it when the Lusitania suddenly lurched, fouling the ropes and causing the crew to lose control as they were attempting to lower the boat. The lifeboat and her occupants dropped several feet into the ocean where it struck another lifeboat, shattering her hull on impact. Lifeboat #14 began taking water and within minutes it, too, had sunk, leaving its passengers, including Alice and Elbert Hubbard, struggling to stay afloat in the near-freezing water. They, along with nearly 1,200 other men, women and children, drowned that clear Friday morning, just eight miles from their destination.

THE ROYCROFT SHOPMARK

Contrary to popular belief, Elbert Hubbard did not coin the word Roycroft. After divesting himself of his interest in the Larkin Soap Company in 1893, Hubbard moved his wife and three sons to East Aurora, a small town approximately twenty miles southeast of Buffalo. Frustrated over his failure to gain recognition either as a Harvard academic or as a successful novelist, Hubbard joined forces with Henry Taber, an East Aurora printer and publisher who in 1895 established the Roycroft Printing Shop. The two men then formed a short-lived partnership, which ended in a quarrel resulting in Hubbard buying Taber out in November of that same year. What remained for Elbert Hubbard was to supply the story behind the Roycroft mark, which he often revised as he told it:

"I got this trademark out of a book printed at Venice in the year 1472. Since then I have found the device was used by the makers of manuscript books as far back as the year 1300, and where the merry monks got it I do not know." [*Roycroft Hand Made Furniture*, 1912, House of Hubbard reprint, East Aurora, NY, 1973, pg. 58.] Additional research reveals that the mark may have been designed by Cassiodorus, a monk in the Middle Ages known for the books which he hand-illuminated and carefully bound. On each of his books "he placed his mark which was the cross and circle representing Unity and Infinity. When Hubbard adopted this mark he divided the circle into three parts signifying Faith, Hope and Love and added the "R" to stand for the Roycrofters. 'Roycroft' is coined from "roi craft" or Royal Craftsman and may as such be interpreted as the 'King's Craft.' " [ibid., pg. 58.] It has also been noted that two famous English printers were the brothers Samuel

and Thomas Roycroft, knowledge of whom may have inspired either Henry Taber or Elbert Hubbard.

In what became typical Hubbard fashion, the Roycroft mark was boldly positioned on the center of the front cover of his first book, *The Song of Songs*, designed in late 1895 and released in January of 1896. Thereafter it appeared on nearly every Roycroft product, from their books, magazines and ephemera to copper bookends, oak furniture and pecan patties. Although he had used the mark continually since 1895 on his printed material, as well as pieces made in the fledgling Roycroft Furniture Shop, Hubbard did not file formal trademark papers until 1906. Soon thereafter he

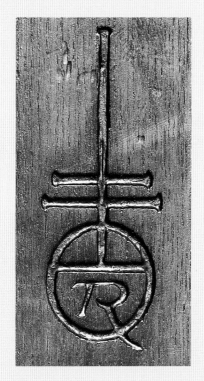

became embroiled in a bitter trademark battle with the National Biscuit Company, also known as Nabisco. "More than that," Hubbard lampooned in 1907, "a pudgy, peascodical, pestiferous, pettifogger, who called himself the Attorney for the Bum Biscuit Aggregation, wrote me a letter demanding that I cease using their trademark, on serious penalty. I wrote back, 'Uneeda punch in the mazzard, and so do your clients.' " [ibid., pg. 58.] Whether the National Biscuit Company felt intimidated by Hubbard's threat or simply decided he and his small band of craftsmen were of no consequence to them may never be known, but nothing ever came of the matter and each continued using their trademarks.

Fred L. Seely and the Roycroft Connection

"If you should ever want a piece of beautiful furniture for your office, try Roycroft hand-made furniture, and get more than your money's worth. I have a house full of it, and wish I had more."

FRED SEELY

On August 12, 1902 Elbert Hubbard wrote to Fred Seely, who then was living in St. Louis and working for his father-in-law, Edwin W. Grove, at the offices of the Paris Medicine Company, "We are in receipt of a letter from [a mutual friend] requesting us to place your name on the Roster of Philistine, all dues paid by him for 99 years. This we have done, so *The Philistine* and *Little Journeys* will go forward every little while." [private collection]

And with that began a relationship with the Roycrofters that would last until Fred Seely's death in 1942.

A few months later, in 1903, Fred Seely wrote to Elbert Hubbard requesting that *The Philistine* be sent to his new address in Princeton, N.J. At the end of his letter Seely added this brief note: "Please send catalog of Furniture, etc." It appears that once settled into his new home in Princeton, Seely began inquiring about Roycroft furniture. In one of their letters, dated September 30, 1904 and signed only "The Roycrofters," someone wrote to Seely, "Of course, the sketches are only crude, but the furniture itself is not." [private collection]

In October of that same year Fred Seely ordered one of the Roycroft Magazine Pedestals, model #080, noting that it "looks so real Roycroftie that I cannot exactly be satisfied without it." In this same letter Seely also ordered custom bookcases for his encyclopedias and dictionary, each made, as he requested, with sloping sides like those on the Magazine Pedestal. [private collection]

The following month Seely also ordered a "combination Serving Buffet and China Closet, Serving Table and Dining Table, as per sketch enclosed, all for $165." Seely did make one special request, however, adding, "Please be sure to put the Roycroft mark on the table in two places as marked, and, if an appropriate place can be found on the Serving Buffet, carve the full word 'Roycroft,' which also do to the Serving Table as well." The acknowledgement from the Roycroft Furniture Shop dated November 28, 1904, ends with the following: "The writer is personally looking after it, and will see to it that every piece is up to its highest and best. With all kind wishes, ever, Elbert Hubbard II." [private collection]

In 1904 Elbert "Bert" Hubbard, Jr., (1882-1970), his father's oldest son, had been placed in charge of the Furniture Shop. He and Fred Seely, just eleven years his senior, formed a friendship which would last until Seely's death nearly forty years later. Despite never living close to one another, the two men eventually shared several similarities: Each worked in the shadow of a nationally-known figure, each managed a large hotel, and each owned and operated an Arts & Crafts enterprise.

The two men met for the first time in February of 1905, when Bert Hubbard and brother Sanford took the train from East Aurora down to Princeton on their way to conduct business in New York City. The two Roycrofters presented Seely with tickets to hear their father speak in New York on March 12.

Seely continued to order furniture from the Roycrofters based on sketches Bert mailed him. Seely, in addition to making notations and suggestions on the sketches before returning them, paid special attention to the location of the Roycroft mark. On March 3, 1905 he wrote, "each chair shall have the word "Roycroft" engraved upon it, so we will have the "S" [for Seely] upon the back as already understood, and "Roycroft" in front of the seat, as shown on some of your cuts." [private collection]

Seely visited the Roycroft campus in April of 1905, delivering a talk to the Roycrofters on his around-the-world trip taken in 1900. A few weeks later he wrote, partially in jest, to a friend, "Mr. Hubbard is a new species of Crank, who writes books and does a few other things and people, and is the first writer and philosopher who has ever been guilty of writing philosophy from experience, or supporting himself while he did it. You know all philosophy is manufactured in garrets, the Philosopher's shirt protruding through holes in the bosom of his pants, and his board bill a few years behind. Means of inspiration, you know.

"Hubbard not so. He is away off on some of his notions, but the fact is he tries to tell the truth, and

Elbert Hubbard, Dr. Cook, and Elbert Hubbard, Jr. in 1911. FREDERICK A. COOK SOCIETY COLLECTION, OHIO STATE UNIVERSITY

keeps his board bill paid, and better yet has instituted an enterprise that pays the board bills of several hundred plain attractive people, The Roycrofters, and educates them and broadens them. It makes me like him, and value the results of his handiwork." [private collection]

In 1907, two years after becoming publisher of the *Atlanta Georgian,* Seely wrote to Elbert Hubbard, chiding Hubbard for omitting any mention of the Georgian in a recent talk on newspapers. On January 23, 1908 Hubbard apologized, adding, "I expect, however, to be down your way the first week in March and will meet you face to face; after which I will write some things about the Georgian that will be worth while. I know of your good work and success and congratulate you upon it, so here is a handclasp over the miles." [private collection] The two men met in Atlanta on March 2, 1908, when Seely introduced Elbert Hubbard to the audience gathered in The Grand, Atlanta's finest opera house. His talk was entitled "The Professions," about which he said, "the doctor is supposed to have charge of the body; the priest of the soul, and the lawyer of one's property. The doctor charges anywhere from five to five hundred dollars, the lawyer takes everything you have, and the preacher is content with what he can get." ("Elbert Hubbard Talks of The Professions," *Atlanta Constitution,* March 3, 1909.)

Despite a few problems which Fred Seely had experienced with his Roycroft furniture in 1905, the following year he placed another large order for several mahogany pieces for his new home in Atlanta, including two custom bookcases, two dining chairs, two "special" chairs, a piano bench, rocking chairs #039 and #051-B, a round lamp table #074, arm chair #034 and side chair #030. This final chair is especially interesting in that it is a forerunner of the model of chair Seely selected seven years later for the Grove Park Inn's dining room.

Correspondence between Fred Seely and Bert Hubbard slowed from 1907 through 1911, as both men turned their attentions toward their new business responsibilities and their growing families. In 1908, however, Seely did ask the Roycroft Furniture Shop to make him a special chair for the organ in his Atlanta home and the following year ordered three more dining room chairs, all of which Herbert Buffum, the shop foreman, turned out in short order.

In a letter which is curious more for what he omitted than for what he included, on the day following the July 1, 1912 groundbreaking for the Grove Park Inn in Asheville, Fred Seely wrote to Bert Hubbard: "Will you kindly send me all the sketches or prints you have of furniture? I want to get another crop of stuff from you, and would like to have everything you can give me before me: especially dining room, office and library stuff." [private collection]

Twin massive sideboards, attributed to designer Victor Toothaker and produced by the Roycroft Furniture Shop, have resided at the Grove Park Inn since 1913. Their original finish and hardware remain intact.

By this date Seely had moved to Asheville to supervise the construction of the 150-room hotel. At the outset, while his new Asheville home was also being built, all of the Seelys' furnishings, including their substantial collection of mahogany Roycroft furniture, had been placed in storage. Fred and Evelyn Seely, along with their four children, had moved into his father-in-law's spacious home, located less than a mile from the construction site for the hotel. Given the fact that Seely had no reason to be inquiring about additional Roycroft furniture for his own home, it stands to reason that he was already considering Roycroft furniture for the new hotel. For whatever reason, however, Seely chose not to share with Bert Hubbard either the news of the previous day's groundbreaking or his ideas as to how he might furnish the new hotel.

Fortunately for the Roycrofters, that same summer they had revived the Roycroft Furniture Shop, had increased their staff of woodworkers and, just a few days before Seely's letter arrived, had issued a new catalog entitled *Roycroft Hand-Made Furniture*, produced under the direction of Herbert Buffum and Bert Hubbard. Seely, however, seemed unimpressed by some of the new designs and, in a letter dated July 12,

1912, let Bert know it in no uncertain terms: "There never was anything quite as pretty as the stuff you used to make, and I would very much rather have the sketches of the old furniture with the ends sticking through [and] with the pegs in them than to have these Grand Rapids pictures you have sent me." [private collection] In defense of the Roycrofters, Bert Hubbard sent his friend and longtime client copies of the three previous Roycroft furniture catalogs, pointing out that "a great many of the old pieces are shown in the new catalogue and that there are no changes whatever in their style or design. Of course, we have made some new pieces and I do not expect or ask that you like them all." [private collection]

That September of 1912, as the granite walls of the Grove Park Inn were taking shape, Seely and Hubbard began discussions of the furniture commission for the Grove Park Inn, culminating with Bert Hubbard's arrival in Asheville on October 30, 1912. The following day the *Asheville Citizen* and the *Asheville Gazette-News* both ran press releases prepared by Fred Seely. They read, in part:

"Through Elbert Hubbard, Jr., who spent yesterday here, the management of the Grove Park Inn yesterday closed a deal with the Roycrofters for 700 pieces of furniture which will be used in furnishing a portion of the hotel when it is completed.

"The order is one of the largest which has ever been given in this city and the furniture is very expensive. The plant of the Roycrofters at East Aurora, N.Y., has furnished some of the most magnificent hotels in the world and the company has an international reputation.

"The furniture will be shipped on a date which will allow it to reach Asheville in time for installing it before July 1, when the Inn will be opened. The order requires that all of the furniture be made according to the specifications of the buyer and no pains or expense will be spared to furnish the inn in the most elaborate, although unique style.

"Mr. Hubbard, who has visited all parts of the nation and who has figured with owners of the most famous hotels in the country, was greatly pleased with Asheville and the new inn. He spent the greater part of yesterday in conference with W. F. Randolph [E.W. Grove's representative in Asheville] and F. L. Seely, and, after completing the business transaction, was shown over the city."

It should be noted that the newspaper article did contain some inaccuracies and a few exaggerations. The Roycroft furniture "plant" was in truth a modest, three-story wooden structure more apt to be called a 'workshop' than either a 'plant' or even a 'factory.' And while the Roycrofters could claim an "international

The Roycrofters produced a wide variety of items during their forty-three year history. Many were sold at the Grove Park Inn, all of which are coveted by Arts & Crafts collectors today.

reputation," it would more likely have been attributed to their magazines, their hand-bound books or their hand-hammered metalware than to their modest output of furniture. As for other commissions, no research has yet been published that has linked the Roycroft Furniture Shop with any "magnificent hotels" — other than the 1904 sixty-room Roycroft Inn — before or after the Grove Park Inn project. Finally, the Mr. Hubbard, "who has visited all parts of the nation and who has figured with owners of the most famous hotels in the country," was the senior Elbert Hubbard, who spent a great deal of his time delivering speeches across the country. Prior to his father's untimely death in 1915, young Bert Hubbard rarely traveled outside the state of New York, for he was typically left in charge of the Roycrofters during the extended trips often taken by Alice and Elbert Hubbard.

Despite the minor inaccuracies contained in the newspaper article, Bert Hubbard had to be smiling — a little nervously, perhaps — as he boarded the Southern Railway train back to East Aurora. In his briefcase he carried a signed contract with an order that dwarfed anything either the Roycroft Copper Shop or the Roycroft Furniture Shop had ever attempted. Herbert Buffum and his small team of woodworkers would have to design, produce and finish more Roycroft furniture in the next eight months than they had in the past eight years. Fortunately for all of them, the Roycrofters had reopened the three-story furniture building just a few months earlier in preparation for orders they expected after the release of their new catalog that July.

The total number of pieces of Arts & Crafts oak furniture which Fred Seely and E.W. Grove had

This twenty-two inch version of the American Beauty vase was designed expressly for the Grove Park Inn by the Roycroft Copper Shop, where it was sold for almost ten years.

determined they would need for the 150-room hotel approached 2,000, a number which Elbert and Bert Hubbard knew they could not even dream of completing by July 1. The order fell into two categories: The furniture for the private guest rooms and the furniture for the public areas. The Hubbards elected to undertake the order for the public areas, even though it would consist of fewer pieces of furniture, hoping that the additional exposure and national publicity would generate future orders for the Furniture Shop. Elbert Hubbard wasted no time in announcing the awarding of the contract to the Roycroft Furniture Shop, proclaiming that "the Grove Park Inn could never be complete without the assistance of The Roycrofters, [for] the dining room will be entirely furnished with Roycroft furniture — plain, simple, straight-lined pieces, genuinely handmade and with their quality the first and last endeavor." ["The Inn Superbus Maximus", by Elbert Hubbard, *The Fra*, March 1912, pg. 34.]

Undoubtedly, as soon as Bert Hubbard arrived back in East Aurora, a meeting would have been held in the Roycroft offices, where Elbert and Alice Hubbard, along with Herbert Buffum and Victor Toothaker, the new Copper Shop foreman, [see separate entry for Victor Toothaker and the Roycroft Copper Shop.] would have listened intently as Bert Hubbard went over the order for the Grove Park Inn commission:

For the Dining Room: 400 oak chairs (model #030 ½), six large copper chandeliers, 32 copper wall sconces, two eight-foot long custom oak sideboards, four large custom oak corner servers, approximately 30 oak folding tray stands and the same number of 24-inch diameter hammered copper serving trays.

For the Great Hall: Approximately twelve standing oak and copper smoker's stands (model C-606), at least three large hammered copper spittoons, a custom oak newspaper rack, six massive copper chandeliers, and two oak three-panel folding screens with leather inserts.

For the Guest Rooms: Approximately 300 copper table lamps (models C-901 and C-903), 150 copper ceiling lights and three suites of oak bedroom furniture, each to include two beds, two nightstands, a tall chest of drawers, a vanity and chair, a writing desk and chair, a wastebasket and a rocking chair. One bedroom suite had to be designed, crafted and shipped immediately to the White Furniture Company to serve as a model. (see separate entry.)

For the Ladies' Parlor, the Writing Room and the Recreation Room: An assortment of oak chairs, rocking chairs, smoking stands, waste baskets, library tables and settles, plus the necessary copper lighting and American Beauty vases for the center tables (see separate section).

Fred Seely's and Staff Offices: An assortment of oak office furniture, including desks, library tables, chairs, a magazine pedestal (model #080) and the necessary lighting.

As Herbert Buffum and Victor Toothaker left the office of Alice and Elbert Hubbard, heading back across the Roycroft Campus to their modest workshops and awaiting men, they must have wondered — and worried — if they could fill the Grove Park Inn's enormous order by the deadline just eight months away. Had they seen Fred Seely's press release and his fictitious reference to their having "furnished some of the most magnificent hotels in the world" or to their "international reputation," the two foremen might have enjoyed a laugh together, for they knew the little they had done in the past few years could not have possibly prepared them for what was sure to be the most challenging eight months of their lives.

THE ROYCROFT MOTTOS

"Get Your Happiness Out of Your Work
Or You Will Never Know What Happiness Is."

Nearly everyone familiar with Elbert Hubbard is aware of his propensity for inspirational quotations or, as they were called in his day, mottos. These tidbits of wisdom — often tempered (or twisted) with Hubbard's irreverent humor — were originally intended to motivate and educate the workers at Roycroft.

What very few Roycroft collectors realize is that Fred Seely may have been the first to suggest to Elbert Hubbard that he market his mottos to a wider audience. When Seely asked Elbert Hubbard about the mottos, on December 28, 1904 Hubbard replied, "we have never printed them except for our own use."

As Fred Seely implored Hubbard early in 1905, "What better missionary work can be done than to sell these little things to businessmen who may spread the gospel of friendship without other motive than the good-feeling within his heart? I have nearly every one you have ever sent and they are pasted up in front of me so I can see them often. The ones I haven't were sent to fellows to whom I wanted to say what they said for me, but which one could not well write as cold-blooded advise." [private collection]

On February 27, 1905 Seely was still so enthused about his idea that he wrote to Hubbard once again: "You can do so much good by placing this form of missionary work in reach of Roycrofters and others, and I once more beg you to consider printing the little mottos in quite large assortments, and sell them, say, in packets of one hundred." [private collection]

Later that year Lyle Hawthorne, manager of the Print Shop, wrote to Seely, "Burt has just shown me your letter in regard to the little mottos, and I believe something can be done along that line. In any event, as soon as [Elbert Hubbard] returns from the little trip he is taking, we will endeavor to get action on the thing. We have sent out a lot of them and have had a great many calls for them. I want to thank you for your suggestion and will let you know if there is anything doing."

Not long afterwards the Roycrofters began printing the mottos of Elbert Hubbard in large quantities, offering them for sale to business owners, readers of *The Philistine* and *The Fra* and to visitors to the Roycroft Campus. They remained a popular Roycroft item right up to the day the presses fell silent in 1938.

A Selection of Roycroft Mottos

"Blessed is the man who has found his work."

"A bad compromise is better than a good lawsuit."

"Don't make excuses! Make good!"

"Don't pray cream on Sunday and live skim milk the rest of the week."

"Do your work as well as you can and be kind."

"Fences are only for those who cannot fly."

"Folks who never do any more than they get paid for, never get paid for any more than they do."

"Lazy men are just as useless as dead ones and take up more room."

"Society is very tolerant; it forgives everything but Truth."

"The leader of the orchestra is always a man who has played second fiddle."

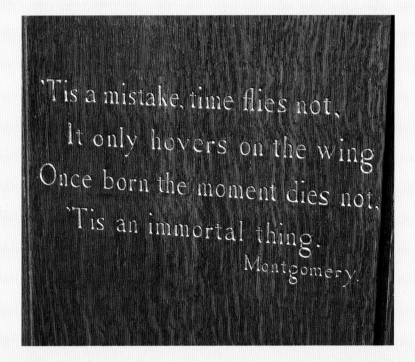

'Tis a mistake, time flies not,
It only hovers on the wing
Once born the moment dies not,
'Tis an immortal thing.
　　　　　　　　Montgomery.

FRED SEELY AND THE GROVE PARK INN MOTTOS

Soon after the Grove Park Inn opened in July of 1913, Fred Seely assumed the roles of president and general manager of the hotel. Recalling the Roycroft mottos that had motivated him years before, he selected several of his own favorite inspirational sayings to have lettered on the rocks in the Great Hall. A few years later, when he constructed buildings for his craftsmen and craftswomen at Biltmore Industries, he repeated the process. While some of the Grove Park Inn mottos have since been covered or removed in subsequent remodelings, a number of them have survived. Show on these two pages are some of the mottos which Fred Seely had selected — for both his staff and his guests to muse — and are stilled viewed daily in the public spaces of the Grove Park Inn.

"Unless what we do is useful, our glory is vain."

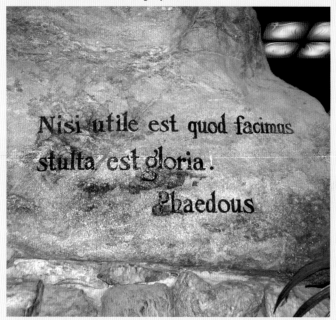

Nisi utile est quod facimus stulta est gloria.

Phaedous

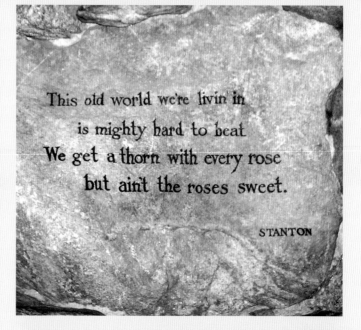

This old world we're livin in
is mighty hard to beat
We get a thorn with every rose
but ain't the roses sweet.

STANTON

Be not simply good
— be good
for something

Thoreau

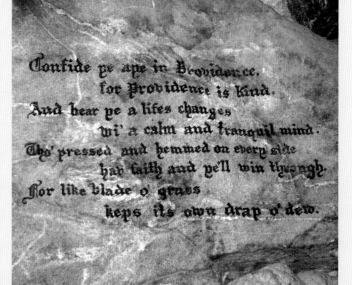

Confide ye aye in Providence,
for Providence is kind.
And bear ye a lifes changes
wi' a calm and tranquil mind.
Tho' pressed and hemmed on every side
hae faith and ye'll win through.
For like blade o' grass
keps its own drap o' dew.

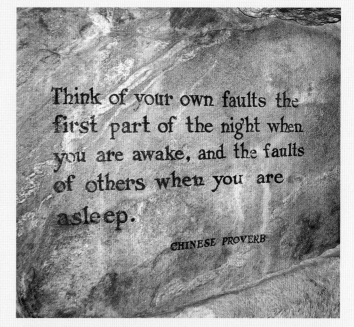

If a man can write a better book, preach a better sermon or make a better rat trap than his neighbor; though he build his house in the woods, the world will make a beaten track to his door.

Think of your own faults the first part of the night when you are awake, and the faults of others when you are asleep.

CHINESE PROVERB

The gem cannot be polished without friction, nor man perfected without trials.

DUTCH PROVERB

Every book is a quotation: every house is a quotation out of all forests and mines and stone quarries and every man is a quotation from all his ancestors.

EMERSON

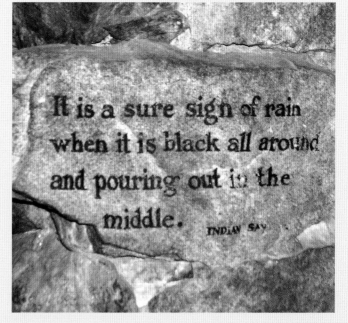

The sun will shine after every storm

EMERSON

It is a sure sign of rain when it is black all around and pouring out in the middle.

INDIAN SAY

The Roycroft Furniture Shop

"The construction of our Furniture is very simple, indeed, and it ought not to be any trouble for you to pick out the way we make it by simply studying the illustrations. All the joints are mortised and tenoned and where extra strength is necessary, we pin the tenon with wooden pins."

ELBERT "BERT" HUBBARD II
AUGUST 20, 1918

According to Roycroft folklore, proliferated by Elbert Hubbard in his many speeches and writings, as his publishing business grew after its founding in 1895, "the place got too small when we began to bind books, so we built the wing on one side; then a wing on the other. To keep the three carpenters busy who had been building the wings, I set them to making furniture for the place. They made it as good as they could — folks came along and bought it." [*Furniture of the American Arts & Crafts Movement*, David Cathers, Turn of the Century Editions, Philmont, NY, 1996, pg. 95.]

Establishing a precise date for the founding of the Roycroft Furniture Shop has been challenging, but the building expansion Hubbard referred to took place in late 1897, leaving open the possibility that furniture production may have begun in 1898. That conclusion is supported by furniture ads that began appearing in

1899 in *The Philistine*, Hubbard's own magazine. Their work caught the attention of the *Furniture Journal*, a trade publication within the furniture industry, which in 1900 noted that Elbert Hubbard "cannot begin to meet the demands for his quaint furniture, and has not yet been able to sell anything to the trade, so many private parties having a prior claim to his production, but he hopes before long to make a few pieces that he can place with leading decorators around the country." [Cathers, pg. 97.].

We do know that in July of 1900 Elbert Hubbard, while on a speaking tour in Grand Rapids, Michigan, toured a furniture exhibition and, upon seeing the booth of Gustav Stickley, purchased several pieces of his new line of Arts & Crafts furniture. The furniture was shipped back to the Roycroft offices, where much of it remained in use for several years. [*Gustav Stickley*, by David Cathers, Phaidon Press: London, 2003, pg. 34]

The first photograph believed to document the Roycroft Furniture Shop was taken around 1900 and shows seven Roycroft woodworkers seated on a bench in an unidentified building. It may be, as was typical Roycroft fashion, that the fledgling business first started in a makeshift structure, then as it proved profitable or, at the least, promising, Elbert Hubbard would have his carpenters construct a permanent building. The official Roycroft Furniture Shop was not completed until 1904, but Hubbard kept his crew of carpenters and woodworkers busy in the years prior to their move to new quarters. In addition to the new wings added to the original Print Shop between 1897 and 1900, the men built and furnished the three-story Roycroft Chapel in 1899, a sprawling Print Shop in

In his characteristic style, Elbert Hubbard often referred to the Furniture Shop as the "woodpile gymnasium." Completed in 1904, it housed an assortment of modern woodworking machinery, powered by a generator in the basement. COMPLIMENTS OF THE ROYCROFT CAMPUS CORPORATION

Formerly known as the Emerson Hall lounge, seen here around 1910 filled with examples of Roycroft furniture, this room today serves as the lobby of the Roycroft Inn. COMPLIMENTS OF THE ROYCROFT CAMPUS CORPORATION

1901, the Copper Shop in 1902 and, their most ambitious project at that time, the Roycroft Inn in 1903.

Built on the site formerly occupied by the first Print Shop, the remodeling and expansion of the Roycroft Inn began in earnest in 1902. While it does not appear that Elbert Hubbard hired the services of a trained and proven Arts & Crafts furniture designer, his band of carpenters and woodworkers quickly assimilated the tenets of the Arts & Crafts philosophy as espoused by their employer, learning and applying in short order the skills needed to design and construct a wide variety of Arts & Crafts furniture. A photograph taken around 1903 in what is now the lobby of the Roycroft Inn reveals a treasure trove of new Roycroft furniture: two Morris chairs, a tall bookcase, a tall magazine pedestal, several library tables, an 'Ali Baba' bench, a low chest with keyed tenons, a tabouret and a large number of chairs. In addition, in 1903 the woodworkers also designed and constructed numerous beds, chests of drawers, vanities and assorted furniture for each of the sixty guest rooms, as well as furniture for two dining rooms and a library within the Roycroft Inn.

As no doubt promised by Elbert Hubbard, as soon as the men completed the construction and furnishing of the Roycroft Inn, they turned their attention across the street to the site of their new, state-of-the-art furniture shop. What emerged in 1904 was a three-story wooden structure with a mansard-style roof punctuated by four dormers on each sixty-foot side. A central staircase and large freight elevator provided access to the upper two floors. All four exterior walls featured numerous large windows, providing the men with an important Arts & Crafts tenet — pleasant working conditions.

The men brought the rough-sawn lumber in through the loading dock on the first floor, where band saws, table saws, planers, shapers, sanders and joiners,

plus an overhead dust removal system — all powered by a generator in the basement — were utilized by the men to prepare the material. No attempt was made by Hubbard to hide the fact that his craftsmen used modern machinery. His 1906 *Catalog of Roycroft Furniture and Other Things* contained a photograph of the first floor of the new workshop, labeling it the "Machine Floor in Furniture Shop." In addition, he extended an invitation to his readers: "If possible," he wrote, "come and visit us and see how we make Things." [*Roycroft Hand Made Furniture Catalog*, 1906, introduction by Nancy Hubbard Brady, reprinted by the House of Hubbard, East Aurora, NY, 1973, pg. 57.]

The majority of the Roycroft furniture assembly took place on the second floor. A ca. 1906 photograph of the second floor reveals a number of large, sturdy workbenches, each cluttered with boards and hand tools, including mallets, chisels, hand planes, vises and clamps. Neither workmen nor any power machinery are visible in the photograph, but two partially completed chairs remain next to a workbench. The third floor of the Roycroft Furniture Shop appears to have been designated for staining, finishing and temporary storage of completed pieces, as well as for the leatherworkers and upholsterers.

Just two years after the opening of the Furniture Shop building, Hubbard described the Roycrofters' approach to furniture building: "Roycroft Furniture is all made in a Cabinet Shop; we do not have a furniture factory. There is a difference in furniture so made. In a factory each piece of furniture is inspected after it is finished. In our cabinet shop each stick of wood is inspected before it is put into the piece being made." [*Head, Heart and Hand: Elbert Hubbard and The Roycrofters* by Marie Via and Marjorie Searl, University of Rochester Press, Rochester, NY, 1994, pg. 58]

Furniture Design and Construction

Photographs of the interior of the earliest Roycroft buildings reveal that Elbert Hubbard's first carpenters may well have been assigned the task of building simple, yet massive work tables for the men and women who were collating pages and binding Roycroft publications. Within a matter of months, however, Hubbard's woodworkers were turning out more sophisticated Morris chairs, round oak dining tables, library tables, flat-topped desks and chairs for the rapidly expanding Roycroft departments and offices. While historians often lament the lack of a guiding hand in the form of a single, trained designer at the Roycroft Furniture Shop, the craftsmen employed by Elbert Hubbard — who, quite accurately, seldom claimed to be a furniture designer — remained true to the Arts & Crafts style. As Hubbard wrote in the preface to their 1906 *Catalog of Roycroft Furniture And Other Things*, "We would ask you not to class our products as 'Mission,' or so-called 'Mission Furniture.' Ours is purely Roycroft — made by us according to our own ideas. We have eliminated all unnecessary elaboration, but have kept in view the principles of artistic quality, sound mechanical construction and good workmanship." [*Catalog of Roycroft Furniture And Other Things*, 1906, reprinted by Turn of the Century Editions, New York, NY, 1981, pg. 1]

Hubbard's earliest instructions to his woodworkers may well have been influenced by the Arts & Crafts furniture he saw on his well-documented journey to England in 1894. A 1902 advertisement for his Morris chair proclaimed it to be "a close replica of the original chair made by the hands of William Morris." [Via and Searl, pg. 56.] In addition, Hubbard is known to have subscribed to a wide variety of both American and European publications featuring photographs of Arts & Crafts furniture and interiors, including *International Studio* and Gustav Stickley's *The Craftsman*. In a rare break with his practice of only advertising in his own publications, in April of 1905 Elbert Hubbard purchased a full-page ad in *The Craftsman* to tout his own line of Roycroft Arts & Crafts furniture.

Before examining the furniture produced by the Roycroft Furniture Shop between 1898 and 1925, it is wise to note that what a furniture historian might call 'inconsistent,' a furniture craftsman might well call 'innovative' or 'experimental.' Before being too critical of the Roycrofters' lack of a consistent set of design principles, one must also step back and take a look at the furniture produced under a number of different designers at the Craftsman Workshops of Gustav Stickley in nearby Syracuse, New York. Between the years 1901 and 1916 Stickley oversaw the manufacture of wide variety of furniture, from early, dark, massive designs from his own pen and that of Henry Wilkinson to the dramatic arches and the lighter, inlaid furniture of Harvey Ellis, the spindle furniture attributed to Lamont Warner and Peter Hansen, and the scaled-down, weaker furniture of Stickley's final years. In comparison, while the Roycroft Furniture Shop never achieved the popular success or the production levels of the Craftsman Workshops, their adherence to the principles of the Arts & Crafts movement was no less as dedicated.

Like the majority of Arts & Crafts furniture designers, workshops and factories, the Roycrofters worked most often in oak, including the more expensive and more attractive quartersawn oak with its highly-figured grain pattern. In addition, the Roycroft Furniture Shop advertised the availability of any of its furniture designs in mahogany or ash. Examples made in hard maple, walnut or other woods have been attributed either to one of the rooms in the Roycroft Inn or a custom order from a preferred Roycroft client.

One of the design elements favored by the Roycroft Furniture Shop was the swelled or bulbous foot, often referred to as the Mackmurdo foot, a reference to the English architect and Arts & Crafts furniture designer Arthur Mackmurdo (1851-1942), a student of John Ruskin, friend of William Morris and co-founder of the Century Guild. The leaded glass occasionally found in the Roycroft china cabinets and bookcases also reflects an English or Gothic influence. But as David Cathers points out, "Some of the best Roycroft furniture seems free of recognizable influences and succeeds because of its massive simplicity and exciting proportions." [*Furniture of the American Arts & Crafts Movement*, Cathers, pg. 95.]

Oak pegs that pinned key joints together also provided a decorative feature in Arts & Crafts furniture produced by the Roycrofters and other firms.

The Roycroft craftsmen often employed keyed tenons, but unlike some lower-tier American furniture manufacturers who simply nailed false keyed tenons onto their furniture, the Roycroft keyed tenons actually provided support and stability, as well as a decorative feature. In addition, critical joints were generally pinned with wooden pegs sanded flush with the surface of the wood, but the Roycrofters did not over-employ this device as a decorative element. Unlike Gustav Stickley's designers, the Roycrofters showed little inclination to incorporate dramatic arches into the seat rails of chairs or the toeboards of bookcases and china cabinets. Neither were they inclined to produce chairs and settles with either extremely wide slats or extremely narrow square spindles. Instead, they consistently relied on narrow (2"-3") boards when slats were called for either across the back or under the arms of settles and chairs.

Since the Roycroft Copper Shop [see separate section] did not begin to play a significant role in Roycroft production until after 1904, the local blacksmiths whom Elbert Hubbard had hired in 1897 to forge door hardware, lighting fixtures, chandeliers and fireplace andirons — both for his buildings and eventually for sale to the public — were called upon to produce iron or copper door hinges, key escutcheons and drawer pulls on the earliest Roycroft furniture. The results were inconsistent at times, both in terms of their design and construction. Once the Copper Shop came under the influence and eventual supervision of Karl Kipp, the hardware produced for Roycroft furniture improved significantly. The hardware typically found on Roycroft furniture will often include drawer pulls with over-sized backplates and 'butterfly' door hinges, i.e. hinges affixed to the exposed surface of the door and framework, thus forming a shape reminiscent of the wings of a butterfly. On a more petite style of furniture these large pulls and exposed hinges might prove overpowering, but they tend to compliment the massive Roycroft sideboards, desks, china cabinets and servers.

Several of these larger pieces were occasionally photographed for the Roycroft catalogs perched on small castors. While the addition of castors may have seemed practical, especially given the weight of these pieces, they tend to detract from the design and proportions of the piece. Designers of large examples of Arts & Crafts furniture, including Frank Lloyd Wright, Gustav Stickley, George Washington Maher and the Roycrofters, sought to make their furniture appear as if it were firmly rooted to the ground, hence the use of such design elements as reverse tapered legs, additional trim around the base and the bulbous Mackmurdo foot. The final addition of small casters beneath these

This Roycroft dressing table and vanity chair feature the bulbous or swelled foot often termed the 'Mackmurdo foot' in deference to the English architect and furniture designer. PHOTO COURTESY CRAFTSMAN AUCTIONS, WWW.CRAFTSMAN-AUCTIONS.COM

Exposed tenons were occasionally strengthened with the addition of a wedge or 'key.' The medulary rays on the quartersawn oak leg of this table provide an additional decorative feature.

This hand-tooled and embossed leather covered chair with vertical seat-rail slats and tapered legs has the carved orb-and-cross mark on the front rail. This piece was from the estate of Elbert Hubbard and is one of the two chairs shown in the historical photo below. PHOTO COURTESY CRAFTSMAN AUCTIONS, WWW.CRAFTSMAN-AUCTIONS.COM

The tooled leather chairs awaited guest lecturers in the Roycroft Salon Room, where Hubbard entertained and educated the hundreds of men and women who worked in his shops. COMPLIMENTS OF THE ROYCROFT CAMPUS CORPORATION.

larger pieces tends to modify this desired effect. Fortunately, the wooden castors can easily be removed without harming the furniture, but should be labeled and stored with the piece to maintain the integrity of the furniture.

Included in the text for the 1912 *Roycroft Hand Made Furniture Catalog* can be found this description of Roycroft furniture, possibly penned by Elbert Hubbard: "There is a distinctiveness about Roycroft Furniture that places it in a class by itself. The simplicity of design and the intent are strictly Mission — made to use and to last. The monks of the California Missions made their own furniture because they had to. Having the right idea of the simple life, and the belief that beauty and durability were best displayed in the plain, straight-lined effect, they originated the now so-called Mission design.

"Roycroft Furniture resembles that made by the old monks, in its simple beauty, its strength and its excellent workmanship. We use no nails — but are generous in the use of pegs, pins, mortises and tenons. Our furniture is made of the solid wood — no veneer. We use the best grade of quarter-sawed oak and African or Santo Domingo mahogany.

"We do not confine ourselves to the designs shown herein, but will, if you wish, make special pieces to your order, embodying your own ideas." [*Roycroft Hand Made Furniture*, 1912 catalog, reprinted by House of Hubbard, East Aurora, NY, 1973, pg. 1.]

Furniture Designers and Craftsmen

During the initial part of the recent revival of interest in the furniture of the American Arts & Crafts movement, most collectors were content simply to credit all of the designs coming out of the Craftsman Workshops to Gustav Stickley and those coming from the Roycroft Furniture Shop to Elbert Hubbard, just as people had for decades assumed that it was William Morris and only William Morris who made the first reclining arm chair.

We now know that Philip Webb, a friend and associate of William Morris, in all likelihood designed the chair that we so readily call the Morris chair. We also recognize that Gustav Stickley relied on such talented furniture designers as Henry Wilkinson, Harvey Ellis, Lamont Warner and Peter Hansen. Since no one argues that Elbert Hubbard was ever a serious furniture designer or craftsman, the question arises: who designed Roycroft furniture?

The answer has proved somewhat elusive, but the picture is slowly coming into focus. Although Elbert Hubbard once proclaimed that "every piece is signed by the man who made it," [*Roycroft Hand Made Furniture Catalog*, pg. 57.] he was referring to the Roycroft mark, not that of any individual designer or woodworker. Clues to these uncredited craftsmen do randomly appear, however, and inferences can be drawn. In 1900, for instance, when writing the text for *A Catalog of Some Specimens of Art & Handicraft Done by Roycroft Workers*, Hubbard mentions that the Morris chair then being offered had been made by Albert Danner (ca.1843-1913).

This German-born craftsman was mentioned again by Elbert Hubbard, this time in 1902, who noted that the tall magazine pedestal (model #080) — deemed among the finest of all Roycroft furniture — had been "hand made by Uncle Albert [Danner] Roycroft — seventy years young." [Via and Searl, pg. 73.] After serving as a cabinetmaker's apprentice in Germany, Albert Danner had emigrated to the United States, fought and was wounded in the Civil War and finally settled in East Aurora, where he worked as a cabinetmaker. Word of the skilled woodworker undoubtedly reached Elbert Hubbard when he was first recruiting carpenters and woodworkers for the Roycroft enterprise. An 1899 newspaper article based on an interview with Elbert Hubbard may well have been describing Albert Danner as "the East Aurora carpenter and cabinet maker [who] spent his life, until lately, tinkering. The Roycrofters went to him and ordered a table made after the William Morris fashion, circular and some eight feet in diameter, with six or eight great plain legs, and all polished oak. The carpenter doubted, but took the order and filled it. When he heard that a visitor to the shop paid $75 for the table after it was made, he grumbled no more. Now, when he can be spared from the buildings, he makes tables, chairs, and a plain oak pedestal for statuary." [*Furniture of the American Arts & Crafts Movement*, Cathers, pg. 95.]

According to his family, Albert Danner's special skill lay in woodcarving, born out by an early Roycroft photograph showing the elderly man standing next to a Roycroft chair with his mallet and chisel in hand. Danner has been credited with the acanthus leaf carving on the early forms of the model #080 tall magazine pedestal and may well be the individual who carved the motto on the famous front door to the Roycroft Inn, as well as the word "Roycroft," the orb-and-cross shopmark and special names requested by clients on early Roycroft furniture. Albert Danner may not have remained at Roycroft for very long, however, or, as he approached retirement, may have limited his contribution to his woodcarving skills, for his obituary written in the East Aurora Advertiser on February 20, 1913 makes no mention of his time spent at Roycroft.

Two other significant woodworkers both mentioned in print by Ebert Hubbard and identified in

This large oak sideboard features hammered copper strap hinges on the lower doors and leaded glass in the upper cabinets. Quite possibly a custom commission, it is typical of Roycroft furniture: what it lacks in sophistication it more than makes up for in boldness. PHOTO COURTESY CRAFTSMAN AUCTIONS, WWW. CRAFTSMAN-AUCTIONS.COM

Roycroft payroll records include James Cadzow and Herbert Buffum, both of whom had come to Roycroft in time to work alongside the venerable Albert Danner. All three — Albert Danner, Herbert Buffum and James Cadzow — are credited in 1900 with having made some of the furniture shown in *A Catalog of Specimens of Art and Handicraft Done by Roycroft Workers* (1900). Both Cadzow and Buffum subsequently served as managers of the Roycroft Furniture Shop and made major contributions to its development.

In 1902, Elbert Hubbard remarked, "In our woodworking department and the erection of new buildings, I have deferred to James Cadzow, a small and modest man weighing two hundred and forty pounds, who can lift six hundred pounds from the floor. He was born right in the woods, and now has but one desire — to make furniture that will do us proud." [Via and Searl, pg. 59.]

Then, in 1904, as the new three-story workshop was being completed, Elbert Hubbard named his twenty-two-year old son, Elbert "Bert" Hubbard II, as manager of the Roycroft Furniture Shop. The appointment was a reflection more of the senior Hubbard's desire to rotate his son through the various departments

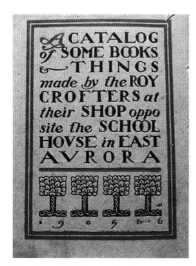

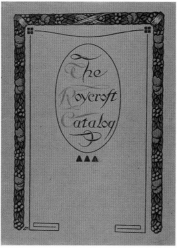

The Roycroft Catalog of Books and Things, 1906.

The Roycroft Catalog, 1909

than it was an indication of Bert's abilities or experience as either a furniture designer or craftsman. In December of 1905, Bert Hubbard was again transferred, this time from manager of the Furniture Shop to head cashier for another Roycroft department — the Elbert Hubbard Bank. As he explained to Fred Seely, his friend and Roycroft client, in a letter dated December 30, 1905, "I had a lot of interest in that Furniture Shop and to drop it all is no small matter with me, but circumstances rounded out to make the change necessary. Our banker left and father thought it better I take the job for various reasons. Now if your interest in Roycroft furniture keeps up, pump it into [James] Cadzow, as I know the stuff needs some things." [private collection.]

Roycroft scholars have long noted that the 1906 *Catalog of Roycroft Furniture and Other Things* contains a substantially larger number of examples of new Roycroft designs than any of their previous material. In a letter dated January 4, 1905, Bert Hubbard wrote to Fred Seely, "I am sorry to say that we cannot send you any ideas on sectional bookcases at present, but we are working along this line and will have sketches out in a few days. It is something we have never taken up before, but think there is a good prospect of selling lots of them." [private collection]

He then continued, "We are also getting out some very special new designs of bedroom, dining room and library furniture. They will be entirely new and we are going to make a special [price] on them. I will see that you get the circulars and illustrations as soon as we have them out. They will undoubtedly interest you. I will be pleased to hear from you about any other pieces of Roycroft furniture that you might want." [private collection]

Since Bert Hubbard neither took personal credit for these "very special new designs" nor did he assign

it to anyone other than "we," determining exactly who was the chief furniture designer for the expanded 1906 line — most of which remained in production virtually unchanged for the entire history of the Roycroft Furniture Shop — has proven to be a challenge. Correspondence from the unpublished papers of Fred Seely, however, has shed additional light into the Roycroft Furniture Shop. During the months just prior to the release of the newly expanded 1906 catalog, it was James Cadzow who wrote to Fred Seely on behalf of the Roycroft Furniture Shop when issues arose regarding his furniture.

Then, in letter dated January 27, 1906, James Cadzow reported to Fred Seely:

"Our new Furniture Catalog is now on the press and it shows a great many pieces — in fact, a complete line up to date. A good many of these pieces we have no prints or pen sketches of and think that possibly you will be able to make a better selection from this than through our sending you sketches at random.

"We are quite satisfied that we have overcome almost entirely the trouble which we had with furniture at the time we made your last order; we have not had a single instance in the last six months where one of our pieces of furniture have gone 'batty.' " [private collection]

Years later, Bert Hubbard made two key recollections in unpublished letters written to his friend Fred Seely. On August 20, 1918, looking back to his time in the Roycroft Furniture Shop, Bert Hubbard recalled, "It may seem like a funny thing, but you know we never had any blue prints for any of our Furniture. The boys make wooden patterns for our stock pieces, and the other things are just sort of made up from a few Working Drawings which the 'Boss' Furniture maker makes." [private collection]

A few years earlier, in a letter written July 17, 1912, Bert Hubbard had recalled that, indeed, "our original furniture maker" was James Cadzow. [private collection] The granddaughter of Elbert Hubbard also stated "Cadzow taught a dozen or more Roycrofters to make furniture by hand...." [*Roycroft Hand Made Furniture Catalog*, pg. i] Some of the furniture makers who may have learned the craft under Albert Danner or James Cadzow were Merritt Jackson, Tom Standeven, Gus Ensinger, William Roth and Herbert Buffum. In addition, individuals who rotated briefly through the Roycroft Furniture Shop and who may have made contributions to Roycroft furniture designs include Hubbard's sons Bert and Sandy, leather designer Frederick Kranz, papermaker and stained glass artist Dard Hunter and, during the time of the Grove Park Inn commission, metalsmith, illustrator and designer

Victor Toothaker [see separate section]. The statements, letters and recollections of three generations of Hubbards — Elbert, son Bert and granddaughter Nancy — confirm that it was James Cadzow who served as the chief designer and foreman for the Roycroft Furniture Shop during the pivotal years of 1902 through 1906.

By the end of 1906, however, orders for Roycroft furniture had fallen off dramatically, prompting Bert Hubbard to lament in a letter dated November 20, 1906, "our friend, Mr. Cadzow, has left here and is now seeking his fortune in Washington, where he is engaged in Railroad work. This is due to the fact that the furniture shop has been practically closed up and there was no work for James." [private collection] Coming on the heels of their release earlier in 1906 of their expanded furniture catalog, the lukewarm response to Roycroft furniture must have proved disappointing to Bert Hubbard.

The following week Bert explained in a letter dated November 28, 1906, "Just at the present there is no possibility of being able to make any furniture for anybody until after the first of the year. The real facts of the matter are that we are going to discontinue the furniture business on a large scale, but it will be necessary for us to keep three or four men to do the work we have to have done for ourselves, and I think that it will be possible to work in a few orders for extra special Roycrofters who desire a little Roycroft furniture from time to time." [private collection]

On February 19, 1907, Bert went on to state in a letter to Fred Seely, "We are not going to quit the [furniture] business entirely, but will keep [Herbert] Buffum and his family at work as long as they want to stay. They are busy now with just about six months' work making various furniture and cases for ourselves." [private collection]

While little is known about Herbert Buffum, he is believed to have come to work for the Roycrofters around 1900 and in 1916 was listed in that year's catalog as superintendent of the Roycroft Furniture Shop. One of the young men in the ca. 1900 photograph of seven Roycroft woodworkers [Via and Searl, pg. 59] bears a striking resemblance to a photograph taken of Herbert Buffum approximately fifteen years later [*Furniture of the American Arts & Crafts Movement*, Cathers, pg. 97.].

The Furniture Shop limped through an economic recession in 1908, although a fresh catalog was issued that same year, largely composed of items which had previously been published in the 1906 *Roycroft* catalog. Elbert Hubbard announced in 1908, "Just for the Very Elect Few we will still make a little Roycroft furniture. We have but six men, Deacon [Herbert] Buffum and

his five sons…making furniture — by hand." [Via and Searl, pg. 60.]

In early 1912, however, Elbert, his wife Alice and his oldest son Bert Hubbard decided to revive the Roycroft Furniture Shop. Even before word had reached East Aurora that Fred Seely and E. W. Grove were planning to build a hotel in Asheville, Bert Hubbard wrote to his friend Seely, "We are making furniture just as before, and I believe better than we ever were before. The same cabinets makers [Herbert Buffum and his sons] are with us and they have learned a lot of things in the last few years. Especially do I think we have improved on our finish. Look over the [new 1912] catalog and let us hear from you. And you may depend that we will get you out some of the best stuff you ever saw." [private collection]

Roycroft Furniture Finishes

Like all Arts & Crafts furniture manufacturers, Elbert Hubbard and the Roycrofters purposely kept their finish formulas shrouded in mystery. In the opening page of their 1912 *Roycroft Hand Made Furniture Catalog* they only reveal that "the oak is finished in our own weathered finish, a combination of stain, filler, and wax polish, that produces a satisfying and permanent effect. The mahogany is finished in exactly the same way, except that the soft, red tones of the natural wood are preserved and brought out."

In an interview conducted in 1979 with Gerald Youngers, who had worked in the Roycroft Furniture Shop during the time of the Grove Park Inn commission, author David Cathers determined that "the essence of the formula was a barrel of soupy water left standing, apparently for years on end, full of rusting nails, scraps of metal and wood stain. This bizarre mixture was brushed on the furniture. After it had completely dried and achieved a uniform color over the entire surface of the piece, the furniture was sanded to smooth the grain raised by the watery stain. Wood filler was next applied to the open-pored oak, and then the furniture was waxed. The Roycroft finish gave a beautiful color to the wood but does not seem to have been as durable as Gustav Stickley's finishes." [*Furniture of the American Arts & Crafts Movement*, Cathers, pg. 101.]

Bert Hubbard, in a letter to Fred Seely dated August 4, 1905, provides additional insight into the early Roycroft furniture finishes: "… the way some of our Furniture has been acting lately has just about put me off my feet, but you know we are unable to control the blooming weather. None of our Furniture has any varnish on it and doubtless the atmosphere would not be taken into the wood so much were the stuff varnished.

A closer view of the original Roycroft finish (with minimal wear) from the chair shown on page 52. PHOTO COURTESY CRAFTSMAN AUCTIONS, WWW.CRAFTSMAN-AUCTIONS.COM

If we used varnish we would not be able to produce the particular weathered oak finish that we make and I think the color and texture of the finish are about the best I have ever seen.

"We are adopting a plan of shellacing all of the tabletops and for that matter any pieces where three or four boards are joined together; I think that this will prevent to a great degree the swelling process that has been going on of late. You see the wood only swells sideways and the dampness is all taken in on the end grain, swelling the ends of the boards first and opening the joints in the middle.

"Perhaps we have been drying our lumber a little too much and we are going to try just a little less time in the kiln and see what this does.

"It might be a very good scheme for you to have the ends of the tabletops sand-papered and varnished or shellacked now so that future trouble may be prevented. I would not suggest varnish on any of the pieces (except on the ends of the tops) as this would spoil the color and general effect of our finish, which is strictly Roycroft." [private collection]

The Roycroft Furniture Shopmark: Carved or Routed?

Perhaps the most familiar of all of the shopmarks associated with the makers of Arts & Crafts furniture, art pottery, metalware and books is that of the Roycroft Shops. The orb-and-cross that Elbert Hubbard adapted as his trademark in 1895 remained in use until his son was forced to declare bankruptcy in 1938. During those forty-three years the Roycroft mark was prominently emblazoned on hundreds of thousands of books, motto cards, magazines, catalogs, pecan patties, pottery, dinnerware, leatherwork, lighting, stationary, metalware and, of course, furniture — all of which was distributed through retail outlets across the country, from Alameda, California to Zanesville, Ohio.

While locating a shopmark on many examples of Arts & Crafts furniture can be frustrating, that never is the case with Roycroft furniture. From the very beginning, when Elbert Hubbard was hiring local carpenters and cabinetmakers to make furniture for his rapidly expanding printing and publishing business, each piece which left the Roycroft Furniture Shop was emblazoned with either a deeply-carved orb-and-cross or, less frequently, the entire word 'Roycroft' in block or flowing script. Hubbard insisted that no one should ever wonder which firm made a piece of Roycroft furniture, directing his craftsmen to carve each shopmark into a prominent location, such as the front seat rail in a chair, centered on the backsplash of a bookcase or incised in the middle of the lid on a fall-front desk. Their diligence in following Hubbard's instructions inspired the modern Arts & Crafts furniture collector's motto: "Unsigned Roycroft isn't."

The decision when to employ the entire word 'Roycroft' or just the orb-and-cross may have been influenced either by the size and significance of the piece or the time allotted to the task. Carving the word Roycroft in flowing scrip demanded considerably more skill and time with a mallet and chisel than did the standard orb-and-cross. A close inspection of many of the 400 dining room chairs which the Roycrofters made for the Grove Park Inn during the winter of 1912-1913 reveals a consistency in the shopmarks which has led more than one woodworker to ask: were the Roycroft shopmarks carved by hand with a chisel and mallet or incised using an electric router?

Among the many paradoxes which plagued the proponents of the American Arts & Crafts movement involved the use of the machine in the Arts & Crafts workshop. At one extreme we find the San Francisco coppersmith Dirk van Erp (1860-1933), who reportedly would not even allow an electric drill to be brought into his workshop [*The Arts & Crafts Studio of Dirk*

Though Hubbard can be accused of over-promotion, this double-insignia can likely be attributed to an overzealous installer at the Grove Park. One orb was carved into the drawer front by the Roycrofters, and then the drawer pull was installed after delivery. The screws are modern replacements.

Van Erp, by Dorothy Lamoureau, San Francisco Craft & Folk Art Museum, San Francisco, 1989, pg. 30-31.]. On the other side of the question we find architect and furniture designer Frank Lloyd Wright (1867-1959), who, throughout his long career, campaigned for a more liberal interpretation of the Arts & Crafts philosophy espoused by John Ruskin and William Morris. Wright called for man to embrace the machine, to use it to relieve craftsmen of the drudgery of certain tasks, to free them to use their time, their talents and their energy toward the more creative tasks that would bring out the beauty of the wood.

Elbert Hubbard, who is believed to have known Frank Lloyd Wright, appears to have accepted the famous architect's more liberal interpretation, as did Gustav Stickley, Leopold and John George Stickley, Albert Stickley and Charles Limbert. While the introductions to each of Hubbard's furniture catalogs harkens back to the principles of Ruskin and Morris — "Roycroft Furniture resembles that made by the old monks, in its simply beauty, its strength and its excellent workmanship. We use no nails, but are generous in the use of pegs, pins, mortises and tenons," [*Roycroft Hand Made Furniture catalog*, 1912, pg. 1] — Hubbard often carefully avoided the issue of machinery in the Roycroft Furniture Shop. It is now known, however, that like other manufacturers of quality Arts & Crafts furniture, Elbert Hubbard did purchase woodworking machinery, including table saws, planers, joiners and mortise-and-tenon cutters, all run on electricity generated in his own Power House.

The care the men in the Roycroft Furniture Shop took in the construction of each piece of furniture carried over into the incising of the Roycroft orb-and-cross into the wood. Unlike the metalworkers who only needed a single drop of the hammer to drive the Roycroft die into the soft copper, the woodworkers had to carefully remove the hardwood — typically oak or mahogany — to a depth of an eighth of an inch. While for years it has always been assumed that each Roycroft orb-and-cross had been chiseled into the wood by hand, the sheer size of the Grove Park Inn commission, including the 400 oak "GPI" chairs with 400 shopmarks and 1200 letters needing to be carved, has prompted the question: Did they actually carve each shopmark and set of letters by hand — or did they employ an electric router to help speed the process?

With more than thirty original pieces of Roycroft furniture still at the Grove Park Inn and available for close inspection, it seemed time, as trivial as the quest might seem to a non-woodworker, attempted to answer the question. After close examination of the Roycroft furniture at the Grove Park Inn, especially the "GPI" chairs, with a flashlight, magnifying glass and calipers, here are the observations I have made and the conclusions I have come to:

1. The Roycroft shopmarks and the GPI letters cut into the dining room chairs are so consistent in height, width, depth and spacing that it appears each one was first outlined with a form or a template. Whether that template was cut from metal or paper or was transferred to the wood as a tracing remains undetermined, but it seems highly unlikely that either the shopmark or the letters were cut freehand without the aid of an outline.

2. As any woodcarver will attest, maintaining a consistent depth in a carving is extremely difficult. In the case of the Roycroft "GPI" chairs, each shopmark and every letter maintained a constant depth — without any evidence of the blade of a chisel in the bottom of any of the grooves, even when inspected with a high-power magnifying glass.

3. At the termination of many of the "GPI" letters carved in the head rail of the chairs, the magnifying glass revealed an obvious round cut in the bottom of the channel, very much like that left by the rotating cutting bit in a router. In each instance the end

of the letter had subsequently been squared with a narrow chisel, but in several cases the craftsman did not achieve the identical depth with the chisel as he had with the router bit, leaving a microscopic ledge of wood above and around the end of the channel created by the router.

4. The only evidence of any chisel work in the lettering appears at the termination of each of the "GPI" letters and then only in what seems to be an attempt to 'square-up' or 'clean-up' the round channel left by the router bit.

5. While the depth of the letters does not vary, on occasion the width of each letter will, leading me to conclude that if, indeed, a router was used to remove the wood, it was hand-held by the craftsman, as opposed to being mounted in and controlled by a piece of machinery.

6. In the case of the Roycroft orb-and-cross on the "GPI" chairs, many of the same characteristics are present: A constant depth, evidence of 'rounding' in the bottom of the channel at the end of each cut and a minimal evidence of chisel work except at the end of each cut. What to a woodcarver seems remarkable — and what first prompted the question — is that in none of the Roycroft shopmarks which were inspected is there any 'break-out,' including in the small island of wood inside the letter "R." Given the brittle nature of oak and the pressure exerted by the hammer and chisel around this particular section of wood as the craftsman cuts out the letter "R," it seems remarkable that not a single incident of breakout was observed.

7. In conclusion, then, it seems very likely that each orb-and-cross on the 400 "GPI" chairs was first outlined with a template, cut by hand using a power router, then cleaned up with a narrow chisel.

LEFT The Roycrofters were never modest about where to place their famous shopmark. This version appears on one of the corner servers at the Grove Park Inn.

BELOW An orb-and-cross is at the top of a rare Roycroft tall case clock, one of two found at the Grove Park Inn.

ABOVE The lack of any break-out in the brittle oak and the near-perfect consistency from example to example appear to contradict the theory that each shopmark was hand-carved with a mallet and chisel.

LEFT Like many Arts & Crafts firms, the Roycrofters shunned ornamentation in favor of the decorative effect of hammered copper hardware, the flake of quartersawn oak and their own shopmark.

Victor Toothaker and
the Roycroft Copper Shop

"Too, from The Roycroft Copper Shop will come the lighting fixtures. These are also being made after special designs, with the loving marks of the hammer still on them. Nothing crude or impractical, but along the line of the most modern methods of illuminating, indirect lighting. Not an electric bulb will be seen. Both our furniture and copper shops are putting forth the very best in them to help make this the most artistic and best equipped hostelry in America."

ELBERT HUBBARD

MARCH 1913

Unlike the Roycroft Furniture Shop, which struggled throughout its history to find and maintain a consistent style and regular clientele, the Roycroft Copper Shop blossomed under a series of talented designers and craftsmen.

As each of the early buildings on the Roycroft Campus were being constructed under the watchful eye of Elbert Hubbard, the need arose for andirons for

Craftsmen in the first Blacksmith Shop (ca. 1899) on the Roycroft Campus produced wrought iron chandeliers and andirons reflecting more of the waning Victorian style than the emerging Arts & Crafts. COMPLIMENTS OF THE ROYCROFT CAMPUS CORPORATION.

each of the many fireplaces, along with strong hardware for the heavy oak doors and both gas and electric lighting fixtures. Two early Roycroft craftsmen — Jerome Connor and Peter Robarge — took it upon themselves to fill these needs.

Jerome Connor (1874-1973) had immigrated to the United States from Ireland and at various times had worked as a carpenter, stonemason, foundry man, draughtsman, woodcarver and prizefighter. Upon the urging of a friend, he traveled to East Aurora where he went to work for Elbert Hubbard in 1898. Though he dreamed of becoming a sculptor, Connor first worked as a designer and craftsman in the Roycroft Blacksmith Shop, where Hubbard also provided him with a studio where he could sculpt. He also designed books in the Print Shop and was instrumental in the construction of several early buildings. In East Aurora, Connor met his future wife, Ann Donohoe, a bookbinder also working for Hubbard, and the two were married in a ceremony held on the Roycroft Campus.

Peter Robarge had been serving the needs of the local farmers and townspeople of East Aurora from his blacksmith shop on Cazenovia Street. Of Peter Robarge, Hubbard later wrote, "Due to the need to furnish the expanding Roycroft Campus, I hired the local smithy and set him up as an attraction for the growing number of visitors." [*The Roycroft Campus*, Robert Rust and Kitty Turgeon, Arcadia Publishing,

Charleston, SC, 1999, pg. 31.] Together, along with Hubbard's carpenters, Conner and Robarge constructed a wooden blacksmith shop on the Roycroft Campus in 1899. Little more than a long, low, wooden shed, it was located on Grove Street, where it served as a temporary home for the Roycroft Blacksmith Shop for three years.

Conner and Robarge set to work producing the andirons and lighting fixtures Elbert Hubbard needed for the earliest Roycroft buildings, including the Print Shop, the Chapel and the dining room. Their first work appears to have been influenced more by the waning Victorian style than the emerging Arts & Crafts movement. A photograph taken in either 1899 or 1900 shows two unidentified men in the Blacksmith Shop, working on a wrought iron chandelier and a pair of andirons featuring ornate curlicues, hearts, interlocking rings, twisted metals supports and spiral arms. Early photographs of the first Roycroft buildings reveal a number of ornate, gaslight chandeliers hanging from the exposed timbers in medieval fashion, a favorite of Hubbard after his trip to England. Subsequent andirons shed their Victorian influences in favor of the emerging Arts & Crafts style. Among those were a line of seahorse andirons designed by the artist W.W. Denslow and cast by Jerrome Connor. These were first used in the fireplace in the Print Shop and later sold to the general public. Today they rank among the most collectable of the Roycroft Blacksmith Shop items.

Almost immediately Hubbard recognized the interest visitors to his East Aurora campus were showing in the ironwork of Connor and Robarge. In his 1900 publication, *A Catalog of Some Specimens of Art & Handicraft Done by Roycroft Workers*, he included for sale both four-light chandeliers and andirons produced in the Blacksmith Shop. Jerome Conner also provided artwork and sculpture for the catalog as well.

The following year Peter Robarge and Jerome Connor set to work designing a permanent home for the Blacksmith Shop. Completed in 1902, it looked much like an English cottage. Constructed of glacial fieldstone provide by local farmers and topped with a tile roof, the Blacksmith Shop provided Robarge with a permanent shop where he and his staff produced andirons and lighting fixtures for subsequent buildings and for sale to the public. For whatever reason, rarely was any of their work marked with the familiar orb-and-cross. Examples which surface today, however, can be identified through vintage photographs and Roycroft catalogs.

In July of 1902, however, just as the new Blacksmith Shop was nearing completion, Jerome Connor was lured away from Roycroft by Gustav Stickley, who was in need of a foreman for his new metalsmithing department

Roycroft Blacksmiths.

TOP Two unidentified blacksmiths at work in the wooden shanty on the Roycroft Campus.

ABOVE After 1902, the metalsmiths worked in the Roycroft Copper Shop, where fancy wrought iron chandeliers and andirons gave way to hammered copper desk sets, vases, bowls and furniture hardware. BOTH PHOTOS COMPLIMENTS OF THE ROYCROFT CAMPUS CORPORATION

This early view of the Copper Shop reveals a workbench of hammered copper drawer pulls and strap hinges designed for cabinet doors. COMPLIMENTS OF THE ROYCROFT CAMPUS CORPORATION

at his Craftsman Workshops in Syracuse. As was the case at Roycroft, Gustav Stickley also provided Conner with the opportunity to sell his artwork while organizing Stickley's metalsmith shop. Two years later, the Connors left Syracuse to pursue a full-time career as a sculptor, eventually returning to his native Ireland.

The permanent Blacksmith Shop was completed in 1902 and, as demonstrated in the 1906 publication of *A Catalog of Roycroft Furniture and Other Things*, continued to concentrate on the production of wrought-iron chandeliers, fireplace sets and andirons, including the ornate designs first introduced in 1899. In stark contrast to the 1903 Furniture Shop, photographs of the Blacksmith Shop published in 1906 reveal a dirt floor and basic, almost crude, equipment. A close examination of a table laden with Roycroft furniture hardware — copper strap hinges, butterfly hinges and drawer pulls — provides a glimpse into the near future. By 1906 hammered copper had taken its place alongside wrought iron in the Roycroft Blacksmith Shop. In addition, two hammered copper items which were not destined for Roycroft furniture — a letter opener and a shallow tray — first appeared for sale in the 1906 catalog, each with a crude, early version of the Roycroft orb-and-cross stamped into the copper.

The earliest examples of Roycroft copper work reflect the fact that they were produced by blacksmiths who were slowly making the transition from forged iron to hammered copper. Most of these first pieces, including strap hinges for desks and over-sized drawer pulls, reveal only a minimal of hammering and no chemical patination. The raw copper was either left to tarnish on its own or was lightly coated with wax or lacquer to retard oxidation.

The 1906 Roycroft catalog signaled a turning point in the development of the metal arts at Roycroft. Two years earlier a talented designer by the name of

Dard Hunter (1883-1966) had arrived in East Aurora seeking work as a Roycrofter. Hunter had come from Ohio, where his father had been a newspaperman. Trained as a printer and a graphic artist, Hunter became infatuated with the work of William Morris and soon learned of Hubbard's parallel interest in the Arts & Crafts movement and in the production of hand-illuminated and hand-bound books. Like many talented individuals who arrived at the Roycroft Campus, Hunter was provided with free room and board, a small weekly wage and the opportunity to try his hand at many of the different departments. While he eventually rose to become art director, Hunter also spent time in both the Roycroft Furniture Shop and the Roycroft Blacksmith Shop — soon to be known as the Roycroft Copper Shop. There he experimented with both iron and copper and shared with the blacksmiths his knowledge of more sophisticated Arts & Crafts-inspired designs. His work there, while limited, influenced Elbert Hubbard's decision to seek a true designer to lead the Roycroft Copper Shop.

That individual turned out to be Karl Kipp (1881-1954), whose career at Roycroft began in 1908 in the bindery, but who by 1909 was directing the Roycroft Copper Shop. That year Kipp and Dard Hunter worked together designing hammered copper lighting fixtures and stained glass windows influenced by European designers from Austria and Vienna. Unfortunately, their collaboration was short-lived, as Hunter departed East Aurora in 1910, but his impact was far-reaching. As historians Marie Via and Marjorie Searl have noted, "His youth, his interest in modern decorative arts, his travels abroad, and his versatility in media as diverse as clay, glass, wood, and printmaking helped propel the Roycroft Copper Shop beyond nineteenth century provincialism." [*Head, Heart and Hand: Elbert Hubbard and the Roycrofters*, University of Rochester Press, Rochester, NY, 1994, 2007, pg. 80-81.]

Inspired by Dard Hunter's designs, Karl Kipp set out to revolutionize the Roycroft metal arts. Drawing upon the design elements of the Viennese Sezession and the Glasgow School, Kipp produced a series of hammered copper items featuring square cutouts and German silver overlay which proved to be immediate successes. Hubbard responded by enlarging the staff at the Copper Shop, including transferring two talent designers and craftsmen — Walter Jennings and Ernest Fuchs — from the bindery to assist Karl Kipp. In addition, Kipp and Hubbard hired several recent graduates of a growing number of regional manual arts schools, helping to explain how the transition from a dirt floor blacksmith shop to a world renown metal arts facility could have been achieved in such a brief period of time.

The familiar dark patina found on Roycroft metalware was achieved by dipping the copper items in tubs of chemical solutions rather than waiting for the copper to oxidize naturally. COMPLIMENTS OF THE ROYCROFT CAMPUS CORPORATION

In 1912, however, just as Elbert Hubbard's friend Fred Seely was designing the Grove Park Inn, a shake-up occurred in the Roycroft Copper Shop. The previous year Karl Kipp had established his own metal arts studio in East Aurora, called the Tookay Shop (a play on words, "two K" — a reference to his double initials) with its own shopmark, back-to-back letter K's. Kipp's venture was apparently done with at least tacit approval from Elbert and Alice Hubbard, for a letter opener with Kipp's new shopmark appears in an ad for the Roycroft Copper Shop in Hubbard's magazine, *The Fra*, in November of 1911. The Tookay Shop was located on Church Street, while his showroom was at 636 Main Street, just a few blocks from the Roycroft campus. The official opening of the Tookay Shop occurred on May 21, 1912, and may have coincided with Kipp's resignation from the Roycroft Copper Shop.

While the precise reason for Karl Kipp's departure may never be known, it has been reported that Kipp and Alice Hubbard, the second wife of Elbert Hubbard and business manager of the Roycroft Shops, had argued over Kipp's wages. With Elbert unwilling to back him, Kipp may well have decided to strike out on his own, offering metalware of his design to the tourists who came to East Aurora to see the Roycroft campus. Adding salt to the wound, perhaps, Kipp

persuaded Walter Jennings, the most talented designer and craftsman working under him at the Roycroft Copper Shop and the obvious choice to become shop foreman, to leave Hubbard's employment and join him at The TooKay Shop.

Another indication of a possible rift between Kipp and the Hubbards is the fact that Karl Kipp began advertising his metalware in *The Craftsman*, a magazine published by Gustav Stickley, a rival of Hubbard's. Kipp's metalware was also displayed in Stickley's Craftsman Building in New York City from 1912 until 1914. Kipp and Jennings did eventually return to work in the Roycroft Copper Shop, but not until the untimely death of Elbert

Karl Kipp and Dard Hunter designs produced in the Roycroft Copper Shop often featured square cutouts or applied nickel-silver overlay. COURTESY OF CRAFTSMAN AUCTIONS

A pair of delicate Karl Kipp candlesticks reflect the influence of European designers on the American coppersmith. COURTESY OF THE CRAFTSMAN AUCTIONS

and Alice Hubbard aboard the Lusitania on May 7, 1915. Although he remained as the head of the Roycroft Copper Shop until the Great Depression, Kipp continued to operate the Tookay Shop as well. [*Tookay Catalog*, ca.1914, edited by Boice Lydell, Roycroft Arts Museum, East Aurora, NY, 1992.]

Victor Toothaker and the Grove Park Inn Commission

As news of the departure of both Karl Kipp and Walter Jennings swept across the Roycroft Campus in 1912, many employees wondered if the Roycroft Copper Shop could meet the anticipated demand for the extensive line of hammered copper items Kipp had just designed for the newly released catalog. Fortunately for Alice and Elbert Hubbard, they had already found the one man who could fill the void left by the departure of their two most experienced designers and craftsmen — thirty-year old Victor Toothaker.

Born in Pueblo, Colorado, Wade Victor Toothaker (1882-1932) learned the trade of blacksmithing from his father before moving to San Francisco, where he quickly established a reputation as a metalsmith capable of working in iron, brass and copper. His work caught the attention of Paul Elder (1872-1948), a noted author, publisher and bookseller and the proprietor of a popular San Francisco bookstore specializing in Arts & Crafts merchandise. Elder's Book and Art Shop at 238 Post Street had risen to become one of the most popular spots in the San Francisco literary and art scene, for in addition to viewing the most recent publications, customers could also buy art pottery by Dedham, Pewabic and Newcomb, as well as Arts & Crafts jewelry, art, leatherwork and metalware, including

candlesticks by Chicago metalsmith Robert Jarvie and Arts & Crafts metalware by Victor Toothaker.

According to Arts & Crafts historian David Cathers, Victor Toothaker may have met Paul Elder as early as 1904, the same year that Gustav Stickley embarked on a journey to California. Stickley's itinerary included a tour of San Francisco, where he may well have paid a visit to Paul Elder, a regular advertiser in Stickley's magazine, The Craftsman. In Elder's shop Stickley may have seen the metalware designed and produced by Victor Toothaker. Given their later connection, Elder could possibly have introduced the young metalsmith to the influential magazine publisher and furniture manufacturer.

On April 18, 1906 the devastating San Francisco earthquake destroyed Paul Elder's store at 238 Post Street. Undeterred, Elder immediately announced plans to build a new shop designed by noted architect Bernard Maybeck. While Maybeck was drawing plans for the new San Francisco bookshop, Elder traveled to New York City and simultaneously began working on a store at 43 East 19th Street. Both the New York store and the San Francisco store opened in August of 1906 and were followed a few months later by Elder's 1906 catalog that included a full page on Victor Toothaker and his metalwork.

Paul Elder's catalog, *An Arts & Crafts Book Shop in Greater San Francisco*, appeared in December of 1906 and included lighting fixtures designed and produced in the Arts & Crafts style by the twenty-four year old Victor Toothaker. [*Gustav Stickley*, by David Cathers, Phaidon Press: London, 2003, pg. 214.] As Elder wrote in his 1906 catalog, "the work of Victor Toothaker, here for the first time exhibited, is typical of this movement, and shows in pleasing variety the possibilities that lie in these humbler metals [copper, brass and iron]. Executed with the technical skill of the finished artisan coupled with the feeling of the artist, each piece will be found to be substantial and individual." [*An Arts & Crafts Book Shop in Greater San Francisco*, by Paul Elder, San Francisco, 1906, unnumbered.] Elder's 1906 catalog lists an impressive assortment of metalware by Toothaker, including desk sets, sconces, candlesticks, andirons, fireplace hoods and electric table lamps. Unfortunately, Victor Toothaker may not have signed his work, for no documented pieces produced for either Paul Elder's San Francisco or his New York bookshops has yet been identified.

In 1906 Victor Toothaker is believed to have left San Francisco, in all likelihood after the April earthquake. He may have been encouraged by either Paul Elder, who had temporarily moved to New York during the summer of 1906, or by Gustav Stickley, who had lost the services of his metalshop foreman that same summer. What has been confirmed is that by early 1907 Victor Toothaker was working for Gustav Stickley in his Syracuse factory and offices. His primary responsibility was managing the growing number of craftsmen in Stickley's metal shop who were making an extensive line of andirons, light fixtures, candlesticks, fireplace accessories, chandeliers, umbrella stands and wall plaques, in addition to strap hinges and drawer pulls for Craftsman furniture.

Although it is not known if Victor Toothaker attended any art classes or studied architecture, his ability to both design and draw impressed Gustav Stickley. Described as being "equally at ease…at forge, at anvil, at bench, at desk," Victor Toothaker soon found himself dividing his time between the metal shop and Stickley's offices, both adjacent to the furniture factory located in Eastwood, a suburb of Syracuse. [Cathers, pg. 150.] In the metal shop Toothaker served as both foreman and designer of a new line of electric ceiling lights, earning $25 a week, the highest of anyone in the shop. [Cathers, pg. 153.] His artistic ability also prompted Stickley to clear a drafting table for him in the offices of *The Craftsman* magazine, where Toothaker designed covers for the magazine and drew architectural renderings of Craftsman homes. Indicative of Stickley's respect and admiration for Toothaker, the publisher permitted him to sign his architectural illustrations for *The Craftsman*, on which he simply wrote "Victor." [Cathers, pg. 153.]

On October 22, 1908 a small notice appeared in the *New York Times* indicating that papers of incorporation had been filed for the Hand Wrought Metal Shops of New York City. Legal documents named three directors for the new business: Lela M. Rosenthal and Adolph J. Rosenthal, both of New York City, and W. Victor Toothaker, whose address was listed as 271 West 11th Street, a five-story brownstone apartment building. While nothing else is yet known of the Hand Wrought Metal Shops, it is interesting to note that the date of the incorporation and Toothaker's move to New York City coincides with the same month Gustav Stickley moved his editorial and architectural offices to 41 West 34th Street in Manhattan.

One could surmise that in 1908 Gustav Stickley asked Victor Toothaker to turn his metalsmithing duties in the Craftsman Workshops over to someone else and to move to New York City. Stickley may well have felt the need for Victor Toothaker in his editorial and architectural offices, for Stickley had just undertaken a number of new projects, including the layout of architectural drawings for Stickley's first book, *Craftsman Homes* (1909), the formation of the Craftsman

This hammered copper drawer pull with a fixed bail was designed by Roycrofter Victor Toothaker for the Grove Park Inn guest room furniture.

Home Building Company, a prototype of a new farm magazine entitled *The Yeoman*, and preparation for his compound of buildings across the river in New Jersey called Craftsman Farms. It may have been Toothaker's intent to maintain his interest and utilize his skills in metalsmithing while living in New York City by forming a new business with the Rosenthals. Since so little is known about the Hand Wrought Metal Shops, his plans may never have achieved the level of success which he had hoped.

Three years later Victor Toothaker terminated his employment with Gustav Stickley. While the reason remains undocumented, he is known to have moved to East Aurora in 1911. He also had begun courting Anne Knights, whose sister, Belle, worked as Elbert Hubbard's personal secretary. Victor and Anne were married and he became a Roycrofter in 1911. Toothaker is known to have occupied at least three different positions during the years (1911-1915) he worked for Elbert Hubbard: He is shown in a white shirt and tie seated at a desk in a 1912 photograph taken inside the Elbert Hubbard Bank, his name appears as illustrator of a 1914 color rendering of a Roycroft interior for that year's catalog and, most important, after the departure of Karl Kipp and Walter Jennings in May of 1912 he assumed the key role as chief designer, craftsman and foreman of the Roycroft Copper Shop.

Toothaker's tenure as foreman of the Roycroft Copper Shop coincided with the largest commission the small workshop would ever undertake: Designing and producing hundreds of ceiling lights and table lamps for the Grove Park Inn. While the first newspaper reports focused on the 700 pieces of Arts & Crafts furniture contracted from the Roycroft Furniture Shop, no mention was initially made of the more daunting task Bert Hubbard brought to Victor

Toothaker in November of 1912. In the following eight months Toothaker and his metalsmiths would have to produce approximately 300 table lamps, 300 suspended ceiling lights, each with matching ceiling plates, 32 interior sconces, nine outdoor lanterns, six chandeliers for the dining room and twelve massive chandeliers for the Great Hall. And if that were not enough, Fred Seely had also requested special Roycroft hammered copper drawer pulls for each of the chests of drawers, nightstands, vanities and writing desks in all 150 guest rooms — a staggering total of nearly 2,900 handles.

As Elbert Hubbard would write a few weeks later, "The Grove Park Inn could never be complete in its fulfillment of purpose without the assistance of The Roycrofters. No one knew this better than [Fred] Seely. And so it is that the dining room will be entirely furnished with Roycroft furniture — plain, simple, straight-lined pieces, genuinely handmade and with their quality the first and last endeavor. Too, from The Roycrofters' Copper Shop will come the lighting fixtures. These are also being made after special designs, with the loving marks of the hammer still on them. Nothing crude or impractical, but along the line of the most modern methods of illuminating, indirect lighting. Not an electric bulb will be seen. Both our furniture and copper shops are putting forth the very best in them to help make this the most artistic and best equipped hostelry in America." ["The Inn Superbus Maximus", by Elbert Hubbard, *The Fra*, March 1913, pg. 34.]

Hubbard's article was accompanied by two illustrations by Victor Toothaker, one a view of the west façade of the Grove Park Inn as it would appear when completed in July of 1913, the other an interior rendering showing a massive sideboard, round dining table and server. Each illustration bears the initials "V. T." [Ibid., pg. 34.]

The Table Lamps

Fred Seely's order for nearly 700 lighting fixtures included 300 table lamps required for the 150 guest rooms. The table lamps were of two strikingly different designs. When they appeared in the 1917 Roycroft catalog they had been assigned individual numbers: model C-901 (18" high) had a circular base and tapering, cylindrical shaft, while model C-903 (14" high) had a square base and rectangular post. Both lamps originally came with hammered copper shades lined on the inside with reflective aluminum.

Each of these two table lamps had also appeared in the 1914 catalog, *The Book of the Roycrofters*, which was published under the direction of Copper Shop foreman Victor Toothaker and features a color illustration of

a Roycroft room interior bearing his signature on the final page. In the 1914 catalog neither lamp has been assigned a number and are listed under the heading "Rare Roycroft Lamps of Hand-Wrought Copper." [*The Book of the Roycrofters*, edited by Elbert Hubbard, East Aurora, NY, 1914, pg 18.] While no designer has been previously credited with these two lamp designs, it is plausible that Victor Toothaker designed them in 1913 for the Grove Park Inn, and then included them in the Roycroft catalog the following year.

Prior to Victor Toothaker's arrival at the Copper Shop in 1912, Karl Kipp had been the chief designer. When Kipp published his own catalog of Tookay Shop metalware in 1912, he included numerous items that he had first designed while working for Elbert Hubbard from 1909 until May of 1912. While his Tookay Shop catalog of 1912 does include one table lamp, it bears no resemblance to either C-901 or C-903 and features, as does his later lamps, a stained glass shade rather than one of hammered copper. [*Karl Kipp and His Work at the Tookay Shop*, 1912 catalog, edited by Boice Lydell, The Roycroft Arts Museum, East Aurora, NY, 1992.] Had Karl Kipp designed either C-901 or C-903 prior to 1912, it would seem likely he would have offered a similar model in his Tookay Shop catalog of 1912. It would seem just as unlikely that these two lamps would have been introduced in the 1914 Roycroft catalog as "Rare Roycroft Lamps" had they been designed and placed into production prior to Victor Toothaker's arrival in 1912. It would seem, then, that both of these table lamps were designed by Victor Toothaker.

Both styles of Roycroft table lamps included two features which eventually fell out of favor with Fred Seely. The solid copper shades, while attractive, only directed light directly down and around the base of each lamp, making it difficult for guests at the Grove Park Inn to read in bed at night. Every known example of model C-901 or model C-903 that either remains in the Grove Park Inn's collection or has surfaced elsewhere has had its original copper shade removed. The story behind the alteration was only recently revealed in letters written in 1920 between Seely and Bert Hubbard. On the 16th of March Seely asked, "Some time ago you remember we returned a lot of copper shades to you when we replaced them with glass. I wonder if the boys have used them up?" A week later Bert Hubbard replied, "I am sorry to say those copper shades which were returned by you a long time ago have all been used up and we have none of them on hand now. I am sorry about this, but that's just the situation." [private collection.]

Fred Seely also complained to Bert Hubbard about the original yokes securing the shades to the top of

Shown here with a replacement parchment shade, the Roycroft table lamps made for the Grove Park Inn originally featured solid copper shades.

the lamps. He noted, quite correctly, that the design of the yokes allowed the shades to tilt unevenly. As Hubbard explained in a subsequent letter, these yokes were manufactured by another firm and purchased by the Roycrofters, for they proved too expensive to make by hand in the Roycroft Copper Shop. On December 4, 1924, Seely instructed his assistant, Ruth Hatch, "to please send him a lamp that needs fixing and refinishing to show him how they are. Send him one with shade holder loose and not straight and send glass shade with it. Tell him none of them sit on straight." On January 15, 1925 Bert Hubbard replied, "We put a copper cap on top of the glass shade on the lamp we returned, and this will make it possible to tighten the screw on top so that the shade won't wobble around, nor is it apt to chip off, as they apparently are doing. The shade holder may wobble a little but that is due to the fact that it hooks up with the socket and it can't be helped." [private collection]

Roycroft Drawer Pulls

While his veteran craftsmen were working on the table lamps for the Grove Park Inn, Victor Toothaker set his less experienced men, many of them undoubtedly newly hired, to the less demanding task of producing the nearly 3000 drawer pulls needed for the chests of drawers, nightstands, writing tables and vanities to be placed in each of the 150 guest rooms. These pulls differed from any illustrated in the Roycrofters 1912 furniture catalog, all of which featured some variation of the traditional swinging bail that, when not in use, hung flat against the drawer front. While no documentation exists to explain the departure from the traditional bail, it is not difficult to imagine Fred Seely specifying that he preferred rigid bails protruding at a right angle from the backplates.

The process began with approximately 3,000 copper rectangles measuring $1\frac{1}{2}$ inches high by $3\frac{5}{8}$ inches long. The surface of each backplate was lightly hammered and the edges softened with carefully aimed blows from the planishing hammer. The workmen also drilled four holes for the screws and two holes for the bails, then used a steel die to stamp the Roycroft orb-and-cross into the center of each backplate. At another workbench, the Roycrofters formed an equal number of rigid bails, each cut, hammered and formed from five-inch lengths of quarter-inch copper rod. The bails were then riveted to the face of each backplate before the completed pull was sent to the finishing room for patination and coating.

Fewer than sixty of the nearly three thousand drawer pulls were walked over to the Roycroft Furniture Shop, however, for the Roycrofters are estimated to have only made three sets of bedroom furniture for the Grove Park Inn (See Roycroft Furniture Shop entry.). The vast majority of the Roycroft pulls were shipped directly to the White Furniture Company in Mebane, North Carolina, where the bedroom furniture, modeled after Roycroft prototypes, was being constructed (See White Furniture Company entry.).

The fixed bail drawer pulls which Victor Toothaker designed for the furniture for the Grove Park Inn have been discovered on other examples of Roycroft furniture that had not been commissioned for the hotel. In all likelihood, once the fixed bails had been designed and produced in 1913, the Roycroft Copper Shop made them available to other clients or may have substituted them for one of the standard Roycroft drawer pulls. While the fixed-bail pulls are typically associated with the furniture of the Grove Park Inn, they cannot be exclusively attributed to this important commission.

Ceiling Lights and Chandeliers

While his craftsmen worked on drawer pulls and table lamps for the guest rooms, Victor Toothaker began designing the custom wall sconces, outdoor lanterns and ceiling lights needed throughout the six-story Grove Park Inn. Drawing upon his early training as a blacksmith, his experience designing light fixtures for Gustav Stickley and guided, no doubt, by Fred Seely's instructions, Toothaker developed a vocabulary of design elements that became his personal trademark, clearly distinguishing him and his work from that of his predecessor, Karl Kipp.

The ceiling lights Victor Toothaker designed for the Grove Park Inn feature parallel, hammered bands of copper-plated iron, separated by sheets of hammered copper attached to the bands with large, exposed rivets. These visible rivets — a Toothaker trademark also found on smaller hammered copper items he designed for the Roycrofters — serve a valuable function while at the same time providing a pleasing decorative element, not unlike the exposed tenons or pegs in a piece of Arts & Crafts furniture. Rather than attaching the chains leading to the ceiling plate directly to these iron bands, Toothaker added another unique, yet still functional design element: hammered copper yokes attached to the outside of the fixtures with additional exposed, hammered rivets. Even the chains leading from these yokes to the domed ceiling plate display yet another distinctive Toothaker trademark: alternating short and long iron links.

Victor Toothaker designed three variations of ceiling lights still in use throughout the Grove Park Inn. Twelve massive, square chandeliers illuminate the Great Hall, each suspended from its four corners by chains leading to square copper plates imbedded in the concrete ceiling. The daughter of one of the early Roycroft metalsmiths recalled seeing the four-foot square chandeliers being assembled on the lawn in front of the Copper Shop, presumably because they were too large to fit through the doorway. [Via and Searl, pg. 95.] Toothaker's original design for these chandeliers included a domed copper bottom, intended to hide the electric bulbs. The interior of the copper dome may have been coated with aluminum, as were the insides of copper shades on the Roycroft table lamps, to reflect a maximum amount of light up toward the ceiling, from which it would softly cascade down over the room. During an ill-fated remodeling shortly after Fred Seely's departure from the hotel in 1927, new owners had the copper bottoms cut out and replaced with frosted glass to provide more direct light for the guests.

The second style of ceiling light, one which Victor Toothaker designed for the 150 guest rooms, as well as for some of the smaller public rooms, suffered an equally ignoble fate. These fourteen-inch diameter lights, each with characteristic Toothaker parallel bands of iron, exposed yokes, three distinctive lengths of chains and raised, hammered rivets, also had hammered-copper, domed bottoms. But they, too, were later taken down and had the copper domes removed and replaced with a flat piece of glass. The only intact surviving example is a ceiling light in an alcove off

When first installed in the Great Hall in 1913, the chandeliers designed by Victor Toothaker had solid copper domed bottoms. COMPLIMENTS OF THE ROYCROFT CAMPUS CORPORATION

Around 1930 the copper bottoms were replaced with etched glass to provide additional light.

Victor Toothaker designed two types of ceiling lights for the hallways and guest rooms. The one shown here had a solid copper bottom.

This ceiling light had a moulded-glass globe. Each featured Toothaker's trademark exposed rivets.

the Great Hall. An undetermined number of Roycroft copper-bottomed ceiling lights were removed during a series of remodeling projects spanning several decades. Many were discarded, some were placed into storage and others made their way into private collections. In only few cases did the original ceiling plates and chains stay with the copper bowl.

Examples of Toothaker's third variation of ceiling light fixture have fared better than the first two. For the hallways outside the guest rooms and in some of the larger public areas, Toothaker designed a second version of his fourteen-inch diameter suspended ceiling light, one which also included parallel bands of iron, exposed rivets and visible yokes for the three chains, but this model featured a moulded, opalescent glass shade in place of the copper bottom. Intended to provide more light than the solid copper version, the original glass shades are distinguished by their six triangular panels, each separated from the other by a tapering, raised buttress. Two inches from the center point of each shade, tucked into one of the triangular panels, is the Roycroft orb-and-cross, etched into the molded glass. Since the Roycrofters had neither the facility nor the capability of producing this style of glass shade, it is safe to presume they were sub-contracted to an established glass manufacturer, possibly Corning Glass Works in Corning, New York. Over the years, as some of the original buttress shades were broken, the Grove Park Inn replaced them with a smooth, cylindrical shade of unknown manufacture.

A fourth variation of ceiling light, the six chandeliers originally suspended from the ceiling of the hotel's first dining room, may represent the only link between designer Karl Kipp and the Grove Park Inn commission. Over the years a few Roycroft historians have speculated that Karl Kipp may have assisted the Roycroft Copper Shop with the Grove Park Inn project. Of all of the lighting fixtures designed and produced for the Grove Park Inn, only the six chandeliers in the dining room appear to support this theory.

Five of the original dining room chandeliers remain in the Grove Park Inn's collection and now hang in the Blue Ridge Dining Room, which replaced the original Plantation Dining Room in 1988. The chandeliers feature Toothaker's parallel bands of iron punctuated by large decorative and functional rivets, but in a dramatic departure from any of Toothaker's known designs, twenty square cutouts, each filled with a sheet of mica, are positioned between the parallel bands. The square cutout is a well-documented design element associated with the Viennese Secessionists style often subscribed to by Karl Kipp; numerous examples of similar square cutouts appear in work known to have been designed by him. [Via and Searl, pg. 79-82.] In another departure from Victor Toothaker's trademark style and technique, the domed bowl of the dining room chandeliers was formed by overlapping and riveting the ends of a long sheet of copper. Nowhere else in the Grove Park Inn commission is this technique employed.

Strictly from a design standpoint, the dining room chandeliers, which, as an added noted of interest, bear the Roycroft shopmark, raise at least three possible explanations as to their source:

First, they may have been designed by Karl Kipp, who, while adding his own distinctive touch with the square cutouts, made it a point to include Victor Toothaker's parallel bands of iron and the exposed rivets in order to maintain continuity throughout the hotel's lighting. The Kipp-designed chandeliers may have been made in his shop or the men in the Roycroft Copper Shop may have made them using his designs.

Second, they may have been designed by Victor Toothaker, who could have paid homage to his friend and mentor by incorporating the square cutouts favored by Karl Kipp into the dining room chandeliers.

Third, they may have been designed by a third and unknown Roycrofter, possibly Walter Jennings or

ABOVE The five Roycroft chandeliers in the Grove Park Inn's dining room bear evidence of two Roycroft designers: Karl Kipp's square cutouts and Victor Toothaker's raised rivets. Originally copper, the chandeliers were later silver-plated.

OPPOSITE TOP This reproduction lantern crafted for the exterior of the Vanderbilt Wing (1988) was inspired by an original Arts & Crafts lighting fixture.

OPPOSITE BOTTOM Larger outdoor lanterns for the more recent additions to the hotel are close replicas of several original Roycroft lanterns which have been in use at the Grove Park Inn since 1913.

Ernest A. Fuchs, both of whom were familiar with the work of both Karl Kipp and that of Victor Toothaker.

As a final note, when they were originally installed in 1913, the six chandeliers bore the standard Roycroft dark patina over the hammered copper. At some still

TOP Victor Toothaker designed several cylindrical outdoor lanterns for the hotel, several of which have survived.

ABOVE Toothaker's raised rivets are evident in the copper wall sconces he designed for the walls of the original dining room in 1913. Nearly all have survived and have since been moved to the hotel's later restaurants.

undetermined point in time the chandeliers were removed and plated with silver, a coating they retain to this day in the Blue Ridge Dining Room. Letters between Fred Seely and the Wallace Silver Company of Wallingford, Connecticut indicate that around 1920 Seely had the firm silver-plate the 24" Roycroft copper serving trays from the dining room. This leaves open the possibility that the Roycroft chandeliers may also have been silver plated at a later date by the Wallace silversmiths.

The Roycroft Outdoor Lanterns and Wall Sconces

The outdoor terraces around the hotel required approximately nine hanging copper lanterns, presumably also designed by Victor Toothaker. The lanterns do not appear to have been a Roycroft catalog item either before or after the Grove Park Inn commission. Each of the tall cylindrical lanterns was formed with a funnel-shaped roof to which a thick metal strap was attached at the top. Each strap was then formed on site around one of the long, narrow rocks that the stonemasons had carefully selected and intentionally laid so that the point of the rock protruded several inches from the wall. Each of the nearly two-foot tall copper lanterns featured six frosted glass panels separated by copper mullions rising out of a flared base. Like the other lighting fixtures at the hotel, the outdoor lanterns display the large exposed rivets characteristic of Victor Toothaker's work.

The original Plantation Dining Room could accommodate 400 diners, but the six copper chandeliers with their solid copper trays could not provide enough light for the diners to read their menus. To solve this problem, Fred Seely ordered from the Roycroft Copper Shop approximately 32 large wall sconces to encircle the dining room. These hammered copper sconces featured a rectangular backplate as well as a rectangular light box, which hung from an iron bracket flaring out from the backplate, and appear to have been designed by Victor Toothaker. Originally the bulbs inside the wall sconces were hidden from view by mica panels, but the mica has since been replaced with white glass.

Nearly all of the estimated 32 Roycroft wall sconces made for the hotel in 1913 have survived and since 1988 have been utilized on the walls of the current restaurants. Unfortunately, the copper sconces were stripped of their original dark patina decades ago. During the construction and furnishing of the Sammons Wing (1984) and the Vanderbilt Wing (1988) the Grove Park Inn commissioned a number of reproduction copper wall sconces nearly identical to the Roycroft sconces. Upon close comparison, however, the hammering on the recent sconces varies in style from those produced in 1913 in the Roycroft Copper Shop. The original sconces also display the Roycroft shopmark stamped into the face of the backplate. The reproduction sconces bear no visible manufacturer's mark.

Installation

Given the scope of the Grove Park Inn commission, the size of the massive chandeliers and the importance of this project, which promised to provide the Roycrofters with a great deal of national publicity, it was agreed that one of the metalsmiths would accompany the final shipment of lights to Asheville to supervise their installation. As the discovery of an unpublished letter written from Bert Hubbard to Fred Seely on April 18, 1924 confirms, the task had fallen to Victor Toothaker:

"Surely you haven't forgotten … the fellow we sent down several years ago and who made your Inn fixtures for you. He is in business for himself here in East Aurora and is not connected with us at all. It will be all right with me if you want to send the [light] fixtures to him and have him make them over again, or, in fact, I will do anything you want me to do about it. His name is Victor Toothaker, East Aurora, N.Y." [private collection]

In June of 1913 Victor Toothaker had boarded a train bound for Asheville, where, in all likelihood, he may well have been the first guest who slept in the Grove Park Inn. There he spent several days supervising the installation of the twelve giant chandeliers in the Great Hall, more than 200 ceiling lights in the guest rooms and public hallways, the nine hanging outdoor lanterns and the six chandeliers in the Grove Park Inn's dining room. He also would have stood alongside Fred Seely as the workmen carefully uncrated the eight-foot tall clock, the twin eight-foot sideboards and the four corner servers, as well as the nearly 700 pieces of furniture handcrafted by the Roycroft Furniture Shop for the Grove Park Inn. In retrospect, it had to have been the crowning achievement in his career as a craftsman and designer.

Victor Toothaker remained as foreman and designer with the Roycroft Copper Shop until 1915, during which time he is credited with having designed and produced a number of items, most of which have been attributed to him by their employment of decorative and functional rivets, often in conjunction with parallel bands of hammered copper. His most significant contribution outside his lighting fixtures may have been his design of the special Grove Park Inn American Beauty Vase.

The American Beauty Vase

One of the most distinctive and most desirable Arts & Crafts antiques associated with both the Roycroft Copper Shop and the Grove Park Inn is the 22-inch hammered copper American Beauty vase.

Over the course of its history, the Roycroft Copper Shop had made versions of the American Beauty vase in seven-inch, twelve-inch and nineteen-inch heights, but Fred Seely requested that Victor Toothaker design and make for the Grove Park Inn a twenty-two inch version with the inscription (photo below) on the bottom

The tall, slender vase featured Toothaker's trademark raised rivets set in a band encircling the bowl of the vase. [Via and Searl, pg. 83.] Some, but not all, of the vases also featured the familiar Roycroft shopmark stamped beneath the inscription. Since so few have surfaced, it was once assumed that the stately copper vases were only made for use at the Grove Park Inn, where they would have held flowers picked from the hotel's garden located on the slope below the Sunset Terrace. A series of letters between Fred Seely and Elbert "Bert" Hubbard II written between 1919 and 1924, however, reveal that the vases were intended to be sold to guests at the News Stand located in the Great Hall (see separate entry.)

"Along about the first of the year," Fred Seely wrote on August 15, 1919, "we will need a new crop of 'G.P.I.' American Beauty vases. Have the boys any idea as to any change in the design that would improve it in any way? I don't mean that it can be improved, but have they thought of anything? [private collection]

Twelve days later Bert Hubbard replied, "About the G.P.I. American Beauty Vases — we haven't been figuring on any

The twenty-two inch version of the copper American Beauty vase featured this unique inscription stamped into the underside of each vase sold at the Grove Park Inn's News Stand. Again, the raised rivets credit this design to Victor Toothaker, Roycroft Copper Shop foreman from 1912-1915.

change in these, and Kippie [shop foreman Karl Kipp] and I think frankly they cannot be improved upon very much. It is a pretty substantial and well-proportioned vase. The last lot we made for you was made in 1917." [private collection]

With a retail price at the Grove Park Inn of $20, the same cost as a Gustav Stickley library table, it does not appear the American Beauty vases were a popular item at the News Stand. Correspondence between Seely and Hubbard indicates that only five were sold in 1919 and the News Stand had none in stock in 1920. The Roycroft Copper Shop shipped the Grove Park Inn twenty-five of the vases in March of 1922 and, in what may have been the final order of American Beauty vases, an additional twenty-four vases arrived in September of 1924.

Examples of the twenty-two inch American Beauty vase without the special Grove Park Inn inscription do occasionally surface. In their 1914 catalog, entitled *The Book of the Roycrofters*, Elbert Hubbard included a twenty-two inch version identical in design to the Grove Park Inn vase, but for a price of only $10, half of what Fred Seely was charging at the Grove Park Inn.

Estimating how many of the special Grove Park Inn American Beauty vases were produced by the Roycroft Copper Shop, as well as figuring how many succumbed to the national scrap drives during World War II, has proven nearly impossible, but Roycroft collectors do consider them extremely rare. As a warning, collectors need to be advised that many of the surviving examples were later drilled through the base for an electric cord, enabling the owner to convert the vase into a table lamp. Such alterations were made after the vases were produced at the Roycroft Copper Shop and should not be considered as original condition.

Victor Toothaker: Furniture Designer

Although the two foremen had only known each other for a few months, Herbert Buffum of the Roycroft Furniture Shop and Victor Toothaker undoubtedly worked together to complete the Grove Park Inn commission by the approaching deadline. The elder Buffum had been a Roycrofter for more than twelve years and had watched the Copper Shop evolve from a crude blacksmith shanty to a sophisticated metal arts facility. Victor Toothaker, while trained as a metalsmith, had worked for nearly five years alongside the furniture designers and woodworkers at the Craftsman Workshops of Gustav Stickley, where, according to Stickley historian David Cathers, Toothaker "devoted his time in the office to designing Craftsman metalwork and, evidence suggests, to designing some standard Stickley

furniture as well." (*Gustav Stickley*, Cathers, pg. 214.) Early Roycroft historian Charles Hamilton considered Victor Toothaker "the principle designer… whose furniture sketches in pen and ink (sometimes in a watercolor of a room setting) appeared in Roycroft and other catalogs, along with his signature." [*Roycroft Collectibles*, Charles F. Hamilton, A.S. Barnes & Company, San Diego and New York, 1980, pg. 92.]

While historians have determined that Victor Toothaker had the capability and the experience to design Arts & Crafts furniture, the extent of Victor Toothaker's role in the design of the Roycroft furniture made for the Grove Park Inn remains undocumented. Clues do exist, however, which may shed light on the question.

For the dining room of the Grove Park Inn, Fred Seely requested two massive sideboards, each measuring eight feet long and nearly six feet high. While the Roycrofters had offered similar sideboards in their 1912 catalog, none were identical to the matched pair the Roycrofters would be designing for the Grove Park Inn. In the March 1913 issue of *The Fra*, Elbert Hubbard published his essay "The Inn Superbus Maximus" describing the role of the Roycrofters at the Grove Park Inn. Accompanying his essay are two line drawings, each signed with the initials "V.T." One is a rendering of what the Inn would look like when completed. It had been modeled after a sketch Fred Seely had drawn in June of 1912 and had distributed widely, including on the hotel's first letterhead stationary printed even before the Inn opened.

The other is a room illustration of a Roycroft server, dining table and sideboard. The sideboard is identical in every detail to the actual sideboards at the Grove Park Inn — with one exception. In Victor Toothaker's illustration, the Roycroft mark is centered above the mirror. In the completed sideboard, the Roycroft mark appears on the left front post. Had Victor Toothaker simply been sketching a sideboard which Herbert Buffum or another Roycrofter had previously designed or constructed, the Roycroft shopmark would have appeared in his drawing where it did on the actual sideboard. Since it does not, one can surmise that Victor Toothaker designed and illustrated the custom Roycroft sideboards for the Grove Park Inn, first placing the Roycroft shopmark in its customary, prominent position. Given Fred Seely's sensitivity regarding the

RIGHT The arched toeboard on the famous 1913 eight-foot Roycroft clock was uncharacteristic of Roycroft furniture, but may reflect Victor Toothaker's earlier five-year tenure at Gustav Stickley's Craftsman Workshops, where arches were commonplace.

location of each Roycroft shopmark, it would follow that before approving Victor Toothaker's drawing of the sideboard Seely would have requested that the Roycroft shopmark be moved from the top of the mirror to a less conspicuous location on the left front post.

The Roycroft Clocks

Tall-case clocks by any of the major Arts & Crafts furniture manufacturers, including Gustav Stickley and L. & J.G. Stickley, are extremely rare. The Roycroft Furniture Shop never offered a tall-case clock in any of their catalogs, but is known to have made them on custom order. They are believed to have only made five, two of which are at the Grove Park Inn. The first example was made for the Roycroft Inn around 1903; it appears in the background in an early photograph, but later was removed. It reportedly still exists in a private collection, but its present location remains undisclosed. The second clock made by the Roycrofters is the eight-foot version crafted in 1913 for the Grove Park Inn. A third Roycroft clock was made around 1914 for a children's hospital in the Midwest, where it currently resides. The fourth stands in the library of the Palmer College of Chiropractic in Davenport, Iowa. Commissioned by founder B.J. Palmer around 1915, it may have been inspired by the Grove Park Inn clock, for Palmer was a friend of both Elbert Hubbard's and Fred Seely's and was an early guest at the hotel. (Via and Searl, pg. 61.] The fifth Roycroft clock is the six-foot version on display at the Grove Park Inn (see separate entry.).

Fred Seely's request for an eight-foot tall clock for the Great Hall at the Grove Park Inn was not included in his original order placed on October 30, 1912. On April 15, 1913 he wrote to E. W. Grove's secretary at the Paris Medicine Company in St. Louis, "Will you ask Mr. Grove if the big clock in your office can be spared and, if so, will you have it boxed up and sent to the Roycroft Shop, East Aurora, N.Y. I want them to put a frame on it and use it in the big room here at the Inn." [private collection] The clock works had been made by the E. Howard Clock Company, to whom Seely wrote on May 22, 1924, "our real father clock of all which holds sway in the Lobby of the Inn is a 24-inch, number 70, that I ordered from you something like 27 years ago and after it having been used about 15 years in its original case I sent it to the Roycroft Shop and had them make a very large floor clock of it." [private collection]

Given the pressure Herbert Buffum must have been under just weeks before his deadline and the distinct possibility that neither he nor any of his craftsmen had any experience designing tall case clocks, Victor Toothaker may have offered to undertake the project. Given the uniqueness and importance of the clock, Toothaker, as the Copper Shop foreman, would have already assumed responsibility for the design and creation of the hammered copper face and strap hinges for the clock. He may have found it more convenient to design the case at the same time than to coordinate his designs with that of one of the craftsmen in the Furniture Shop.

The tapered form of the clock, combined with the thick, overhanging top and the presence of keyed tenons on the sides, may well have been influenced by the well-known Roycroft Magazine Pedestal #080, which had been a Roycroft staple the shop's entire history. What makes this particular piece of Roycroft furniture stand apart from other Roycroft furniture is the inclusion of a furniture element rarely found in Roycroft furniture — the sweeping arch. While adding a dramatic arch to the bottom of the Roycroft clock would be considered uncharacteristic of Herbert Buffum or any other Roycroft furniture maker, it was a design element often associated with the Arts & Crafts furniture designed and constructed in Gustav Stickley's Craftsmen Workshops, where Victor Toothaker had worked for five years just prior to coming to East Aurora.

But one design element present in this clock which does not appear in either the furniture of Gustav Stickley or that coming from the Roycroft Furniture Shop may well enable us to identify Victor Toothaker as the designer. As a coppersmith, Victor Toothaker adopted the exposed rivet as his personal design trademark. The oak case of the Grove Park Inn clock features four pairs of half-inch pegs, but unlike the pegs found in Roycroft or Gustav Stickley furniture, these pegs were not sanded flush with the surface of the wood. Instead, each peg was meticulously rounded at one end, then deliberately left to protrude a quarter of an inch above the wood. Leaving the ends of these eight pegs exposed does not provide additional strength, but only serves as a decorative feature — a feature characteristic of Victor Toothaker, for they appear to be wooden rivets.

In addition, the hammered copper strap hinges, the smaller hinges and the two pulls are attached to the front of the clock using round-head copper screws. Each of the strap hinges is held in place with a total of fourteen screws — far more than structurally necessary. The screws, like the eight protruding pegs, look like raised rivets.

While Elbert Hubbard did not allow either his furniture craftsmen or his metalsmiths to affix a personal shopmark to their work, Victor Toothaker may well have devised his own signature — one which became an integral part not just of the Grove Park Inn lighting fixtures and the American Beauty vases, but of the Roycroft eight-foot tall clock as well — the raised rivet.

ROYCROFT METALWARE SHOPMARKS

Collectors of Roycroft metalware soon discover that the Roycroft mark, which was die-stamped into nearly each piece produced in the Roycroft Copper Shop, varied over time. The earliest known pieces, a letter opener and pen tray illustrated in their 1906 furniture catalog, feature a crude version with a letter "R" resembling that found on typewriters. Soon thereafter a more refined die was made, in which the letter "R" has curled tail and top serifs. At a later date, yet still prior to 1915, a second die was made, this one without the curled serifs on the letter "R."

While a few authors have attempted to assign dates of production to these two marks, referring to the curled "R" as the early (1906-1910) mark and the straight "R" as the later (1910-1915), this dating system has been proven inaccurate. The lighting fixtures made in 1912 and 1913 for the Grove Park Inn all display the curled "R" shopmarks, as do the special American Beauty vases made by the Roycroft Copper Shop for the Grove Park Inn beginning in 1913. In all likelihood, the craftsmen in the Roycroft Copper Shop utilized both styles of dies, using each one until it either broke or wore out. Little did they know that one hundred years later scholars would be scrutinizing their shopmarks with magnifying glasses, attempting to determine the precise date on which each piece had been completed.

In 1915, after the deaths of Elbert and Alice Hubbard aboard the *Lusitania*, the Roycroft Copper Shop underwent a reorganization, beginning with the return of master coppersmith Karl Kipp as foreman under the new manager, 33-year old Elbert "Bert" Hubbard, II. Around this time a new shopmark was created, this one featuring the straight letter "R" within the orb along with the word "ROYCROFT" spelled out in its entirety beneath the mark. Other more subtle variations of the Roycroft shopmark have appeared on Roycroft copper and brass items, many of which are more completely

explained and explored in the book *Head, Heart and Hand: Elbert Hubbard and the Roycrofters*. [*Head, Heart and Hand: Elbert Hubbard and the Roycrofters*, Marie Via and Marjorie Searl, University of Rochester Press, Rochester, NY, 1994, pg. 92-3].

While the workmen in the Roycroft Copper Shop remained diligent in their marking of each piece which left the shop, unsigned examples which, by their design, dimensions and hammering can be attributed to the Roycroft Copper Shop, do occasionally surface. Two theories help to explain their lack of a shopmark. While Elbert and Alice Hubbard were never noted for paying high wages, they did allow their employees to work on personal projects, especially during the holiday season. These pieces were either taken home for the employees' own use or given as gifts. In addition, but occurring less frequently, first attempts by a new apprentice deemed unworthy of the Roycroft shopmark may have been taken home. More often, these inferior pieces would have been tossed in the scrap box to be melted down and reused.

As evidence of what can happen in a busy workshop, note this letter from Fred Seely to Bert Hubbard written on June 10, 1924: "The candlesticks have just arrived. They are superb and simply perfect with one exception: I have looked everywhere on them and can't find the Roycroft mark. I know [shop foreman, Karl] Kipp won't believe it, but, really, if you could see them sitting in the alcoves at either end of the Dining Room, I believe you would have a Duck fit." [private collection]

Bert Hubbard wrote back on June 16, 1924: "It's a darn shame we didn't put the Roycroft mark on, but that was purely a matter of oversight. Kippy says that on the next ones we make there will be no extra charge for putting the Roycroft mark on. Now isn't that considerate of him?"

The Other Artisans

"Instead of deteriorating with age and wear it seems to get better, and I can say frankly that the furniture which you supplied us when the Grove Park Inn was built is practically in the same condition it was the day we received it — perfect.

FRED L. SEELY TO J. S. WHITE

January 6, 1927

The White Furniture Company

While the Roycrofters were Fred Seely's first choice in late 1912 to produce the Arts & Crafts furniture for the Grove Park Inn, it soon became apparent that their modest furniture workshop would not be able to complete the enormous order in time for the scheduled July 1913 opening. Given the choice, Elbert Hubbard and his son Bert opted to make the furniture for the public areas, including 400 "GPI" chairs, two massive sideboards, four corner servers and an assortment of miscellaneous pieces for the dining room; several settles, library tables and rocking chairs for the first floor Ladies' Parlor and Writing Room; the Arts & Crafts furniture for the various offices; and accessory pieces to compliment the wicker rockers in the Great Hall. In addition, the Roycroft Furniture Shop also produced bedroom furniture for approximately three of the guest rooms.

Grove and Seely's plan called for 150 guest rooms, the majority of which would feature two beds, two nightstands, a vanity and chair, a desk and chair, a chest of drawers and a rocker. Although the smaller rooms in the wings did not always have room for a complete bedroom suite, their order for bedroom furniture still totaled approximately 1,200 pieces. In order to maintain continuity throughout the hotel, Seely insisted that the firm he selected would be required to use the Roycroft bedroom furniture as their model and would have to attach Roycroft Copper Shop pulls to the drawers of the nightstands, chests of drawers, writing desks and vanities.

Rather than selecting one of the upstate New York Arts & Crafts furniture makers or one of the many firms

that produced Arts & Crafts furniture in Grand Rapids, Michigan, Seely awarded the contract to the White Furniture Company in Mebane, North Carolina. Founded in 1881 in a small village just west of Durham by two brothers, Will and Dave White, the company grew to become known as 'the oldest maker of fine furniture in the South.' The combination of a new railroad system, abundant tracts of both softwood and hardwood trees and a labor force skilled in manual labor, yet willing to work for far less than their Northern contemporaries provided the fuel for a profitable enterprise.

The brothers first produced oak wagon wheels and round oak tables, but as demand for household furniture grew in the burgeoning region, the White family, which by 1886 included all four brothers and their father, expanded their operation and their line to include chairs, tables and their specialty — bedroom suites. Unlike other North Carolina firms who manufactured low cost furniture for rural farmers, however, the White brothers offered a higher quality, more expensive line of furniture, which they marketed not only in the South, but in the North as well.

In 1906 the White Furniture Company convinced buying agents for the United States government that they could fill the contract for 58 train cars of oak furniture needed for the officers and workmen in the Panama Canal Zone. A dramatic photograph of a steam locomotive pulling a long train of White Company furniture appeared in newspapers across the country. Each boxcar proudly bore a banner proclaiming "The White Line Guarantees Satisfaction." The train, as one reporter noted, "served notice to the country that there was competition in North Carolina that counted; and it was that train which served as the announcement of what had hitherto been hidden in the ambition of the White Furniture Company of the tiny village of Mebane — that the best could be made at home." ["White Furniture Completes Its First Century" by Margaret Holmes, *The Enterprise Newspaper*, Mebane, NC, January 28, 1981, pg. A-3.] In the years following the Panama Canal contract, the White Furniture Company was awarded gold medals for furniture production at the North Carolina State Fair, the International Fair at San Antonio, Texas, and the 1907 national Jamestown Exposition.

In 1912, as the walls of the six-story Grove Park Inn were rising into the air, Arthur White called upon Fred Seely at the construction site. Seely's initial reluctance to consider the White Furniture Company may have been due to the fact that at that time "most Southern furniture makers specialized in low-cost furniture catering to the needs of Southerners." [*Closing: The Life and Death of an American Factory*, by Bill Bamberger and Cathy N. Davidson, W.W. Norton & Co., NY, 1998, pg. 25.] Stephen A. White V recounted the story of their meeting before the North Carolina Historical Society in Chapel Hill in 1982:

"Arthur did most of the selling, especially the sales of furniture for fine resort hotels. White Furniture Company shipped a sample dresser to Asheville to be shown as a typical piece of our quality. The gentleman who was in charge of buying furniture 'pooh-poohed' the idea of any furniture made in a little country town in North Carolina being even close to the standards, which were wanted for the Grove Park Inn. So, my Uncle Arthur uncrated the dresser and asked the potential buyer to select one of the drawers from the dresser and he would give a demonstration, which would prove that White Furniture Company produced furniture, which would stand the use and abuse to which it would be subjected. A drawer was selected and taken from the dresser and laid down on the floor upside down. Then Uncle Arthur jumped on the drawer and there was no sign of the abuse to which it was subjected. Arthur brought the order home in his pocket." [typed manuscript, private collection]

Fred Seely's initial reluctance to even consider offering a contract to the White Furniture Company may also have been influenced by their new 1912 catalog. He may have been impressed with the fact that, as the catalog forward stated proudly, "for six years Uncle Sam has been our steady customer and his rigid inspection before shipment and after arrival has exacted strength and quality in every pattern. Not a single piece has he rejected from over 150 carloads shipped. We have sold him thousands of pieces for use

One of the suites of bedroom furniture provided by the White Furniture Company for the Grove Park Inn.

COMPLIMENTS OF THE GROVE PARK INN RESORT & SPA

in the tropical Panama region and for officers' quarters in every state of the Union, Philippines, Porto Rico and Hawaii." [*The White Furniture Company Catalog*, Mebane, NC, 1927, pg. 2.]

However, of the 56 pages of furniture in the 1912 catalog only three pages featured Arts & Crafts furniture — and then only nine library tables. The vast majority of the furniture the White Furniture Company produced, while of extremely high quality, could only be classified as 'fancy oak,' featuring claw feet, curved drawer fronts, highly-figured veneers, stamped pulls and applied carvings. Once Arthur White demonstrated the quality of construction inherent in every piece of White furniture, he assured Seely that their craftsmen back at Mebane would certainly use a sample Roycroft bedroom suite as their model.

While the furniture produced by the White Furniture Company for the Grove Park Inn was modeled after that designed in the Roycroft Furniture shop, it was not identical. The tops of the White nightstands, vanities, dressers and desks are slightly thinner; the posts of the beds are not as massive; the slats in the beds, chairs and rockers are a little lighter. While the look is still definitely Arts & Crafts, it is not Roycroft. And unlike the Roycrofters, the craftsmen at the White Furniture Company were not as diligent about 'signing' their work. On occasion a one-inch circular metal disk bearing the words "The White Line — The Right Line" can be found on the interior of one of the drawers, but the majority of the pieces at the Grove Park Inn are unsigned.

Acting on Fred Seely's instructions, the White Furniture Company even made matching waste paper baskets from quartersawn oak for each of the orinigal guest rooms. Unfortunately, few remain with the hotel.

Each drawer in any piece of White furniture made for the Grove Park Inn, however, does bear a Roycroft hammered copper pull, each with the distinctive Roycroft orb-and-cross stamped in the center. The pulls were designed by Victor Toothaker, produced in the Roycroft Copper Shop and shipped to the White Furniture Company to be attached to the drawers. The presence of the Roycroft pulls on the drawers, combined with the lack of a White Furniture Company shopmark, has led many individuals to assume that what was actually made in Mebane, North Carolina had, instead, come from the Roycroft Furniture shop in East Aurora, New York. The difference in value between a White Furniture Company writing desk, nightstand or chest of drawers and the same form from the Roycroft Furniture Shop can amount to more than a thousand dollars.

This difference in value has less to do with quality of construction or relative scarcity than it has to do with the Roycroft mystique. By today's standards, the quantity of furniture which the White's produced for the Grove Park Inn was extremely low. Of the approximately 150 rooms in the original Main Inn, nearly

every one had a chest of drawers, nearly all of which is still in use today. Most of the larger rooms had two twin beds, while the smaller rooms had but one; however, nearly all of the beds were altered, first by being cut down, then, years later, by having the footboards removed and the headboards attached to the walls to accommodate larger mattresses. None of the original beds are still in use today in their original, unaltered form at the Grove Park Inn. Much of the original White furniture that was removed from the guest rooms has today been placed into service in the public hallways and the growing number of offices in the hotel. The few White pieces that do surface outside the Grove Park Inn are typically writing desks, straight chairs and an occasional rocker. Even when properly identified, the White pieces with Roycroft pulls do command higher than normal prices as a result of their connection with both the Grove Park Inn and the Roycrofters.

The quality of construction exhibited in White furniture needs to make no apologies to that of the Roycrofters or any other Arts & Crafts furniture manufacturer. The fact that the majority of pieces the White's made for the Grove Park Inn have been in continual service for nearly one hundred years speaks volumes. On January 6, 1927 Fred Seely wrote to J. S. White, "Instead of deteriorating with age and wear it seems to get better, and I can say frankly that the furniture which you supplied us when the Grove Park Inn was built is practically in the same condition it was the day we received it — perfect." [*The White Furniture Company Catalog*, Mebane, NC, 1927.]

Indicative of Fred Seely's respect for the quality of construction practiced by the White Furniture Company is the fact that in the spring of 1913 he selected them to make more than 400 solid oak doors for use in the Grove Park Inn. Despite being in the midst of producing more than 1200 pieces of furniture for Seely, the White Furniture company accepted the contract for the doors and delivered everything to the hotel on time for the July opening.

The Heywood Brothers & Wakefield Company

The heart of the Grove Park Inn is the Great Hall, an enormous lobby even by today's standards, but in 1913, as the first guests began arriving, it must have seemed astonishing. Flanked at either end by twin fireplaces capable of burning twelve-foot logs in fireboxes large enough for a man to stand upright, the 120-foot room was dominated by natural stone hauled down from the surrounding slopes: two granite fireplaces each more than thirty feet wide and nearly as high; rock walls on all four sides with boulders weighing as much as five tons;

and six towering rock columns rising up from the floor to support the poured concrete girders in the ceiling.

It was a room Fred Seely designed to provide his guests with comfort and quiet, a place where they could relax after a long day's journey to Asheville aboard the Southern Railway or listen to the Inn's five-piece orchestra each afternoon. It was a place where they could read or rest after a hike up Sunset Mountain, a horseback ride with Seely, or a game of billiards, some bowling or a swim in the lower level Recreation Room. The Great Hall could hold nearly one thousand people and Seely recognized that the furniture he selected for the lobby would need to serve two purposes: it would have to provide a soft contrast to the grey rigidity of the rock walls, tile floors and concrete ceiling, while at the same time offering flexibility in the arrangement of the furniture.

Neither the heavy Arts & Crafts furniture of the Roycrofters nor that of the White Furniture Company could meet these demands, so Fred Seely turned to a different furniture manufacturer and a different material — the wicker furniture of the Heywood Brothers & Wakefield Company.

While wicker furniture had been in existence for centuries, it remained for an enterprising young Boston businessman by the name of Cyrus Wakefield (1811-1873) to recognize the seemingly endless possibilities for inexpensive rattan. In the 1850's Wakefield cornered the American market for raw rattan, developed machinery for splitting and preparing the rattan into reed and cane, then adopted the material to a variety of furniture forms and styles. In 1868 the citizens of South Reading, a small town outside of Boston where Cyrus Wakefield built his first Wakefield Rattan Company factory, voted to honor their benefactor by changing the name of their town to Wakefield.

The immense popularity of wicker and rattan furniture during the Victorian era prompted the emergence of several competing firms, among them the Heywood Brothers & Company of nearby Gardner, Massachusetts. In 1897 these two leading manufacturers merged to form the Heywood Brothers & Wakefield Company under the direction of Henry Heywood. As the new company prepared for a new century, American tastes began to shift from the ornate Victorian look to the simple, straight-lined Arts & Crafts style. The Heywood Brothers & Wakefield Company adapted to the change in tastes, offering the public wicker furniture in the Arts & Crafts style that would be as suitable on lawns or the porches of bungalows as it would in their living room filled with Arts & Crafts furniture. Recognizing the both the popularity and suitability of wicker furniture, Gustav Stickley began promoting

his own line of Craftsman willow furniture, explaining that it "affords exactly the relief that is necessary to lighten the general effect of the darker and heavier oak pieces." [*The Early Work of Gustav Stickley*, by Stephen Gray, Turn of the Century Editions, Philmont, NY, 1996, pg. 140.]

Fred Seely and E. W. Grove undoubtedly agreed with what Stickley had written, for in 1913 they purchased a wide variety of wicker furniture for the Great Hall from the Heywood Brothers & Wakefield Company. While nearly all of it has since been dispersed, photographs taken shortly after the opening of the Grove Park Inn reveal what must have appeared to have been a Heywood Brothers & Wakefield Company showroom. Positioned throughout the room are at least two different styles of rocking chairs, each with tufted red leather upholstery, two styles of straight chairs, at least two long tables topped with newspapers, magazines and a wicker lamp, plus several wicker floor lamps. In total, the Great hall appears to have held more than two hundred pieces of Heywood Brothers & Wakefield Company furniture and accessories.

But as a letter written on April 20, 1920 from Fred Seely to the Heywood Brothers & Wakefield Company reveals, he was not entirely satisfied with what he received. "The two hundred and twenty-five chairs we purchased from you for our lobby are going to pieces rather badly. We are on track of a man who formerly worked in your factory, who will in all probability

An indentifying furniture tag from the White Furniture Company found on the interior of a vanity drawer.

come here and remake these chairs. We will have to weave in two rows of reinforcement across the back of every one of the rockers, and we will have to replace many hundreds of the up-and-down reeds. I should say that we will require 3,000 to 4,000 [feet of reed]." (private collection)

Soon after the death of owner E. W. Grove in 1927 and Fred Seely's departure at the end of that same year, Grove's widow and only son arranged for the sale of the hotel. Photographs taken in the 1930s, after the arrival of a new general manager, reveal that the Heywood Brothers & Wakefield Company furniture had all been replaced by new 'paddle arm' oak chairs and couches made by the Old Hickory Furniture Company. Of the more than two hundred examples of Heywood Brothers & Wakefield Company wicker furniture that once filled the Great Hall, only two wicker rocking chairs, both painted white, remain at the Grove Park Inn. Two similar rocking chairs, both from Asheville homes, have been identified by comparing them to the examples shown in vintage photographs. Both also still bear a Heywood Brothers & Wakefield Company paper label attached to one of the wooden supports beneath the seat. One maintains its original red leather seat cushion. The fate of the balance of the Heywood Brothers & Wakefield Company furnishings remains unknown, although an open wicker bookcase bearing the firm's paper label was purchased by the Grove Park Inn from an Asheville resident and is now on display.

The Great Hall originally featured Heywood-Wakefield wicker furniture, unaltered Roycroft copper chandeliers and granite columns. Today the columns are encased in oak, the wicker has been replaced by new Stickley furniture and the chandeliers have been opened, but the room is still impressive. COMPLIMENTS OF THE GROVE PARK INN RESORT & SPA

The Old Hickory Chair Company

A key element in the design of the Grove Park Inn were the outdoor terraces, for many of the early guests at the hotel came to enjoy the panoramic views of the Blue Ridge Mountains and to breath in the fresh, clean mountain air. In one of his early promotional brochures, manager Fred Seely extolled the virtues of the Grove Park Inn's five hundred feet of terraces, some roofed and others open to the sky, noting that "from the porches of the Inn one looks across the golf links upon an inspiring vista of mountain scenery — lofty peaks fading away in the distance — the most entrancing region and the most delightful climate to be found in America." [*Grove Park Inn brochure*, ca. 1919, private collection, pg. 1.]

Since neither the Roycroft Furniture Shop nor the White Furniture Company made outdoor furniture, designer Fred Seely and owner E. W. Grove turned to one of the makers of the popular outdoor rustic furniture — the Old Hickory Chair Company, known after 1921 as the Old Hickory Furniture Company. As author Ralph Kylloe has observed, "Ten different manufacturers, beginning in the late 1890s, produced tens of thousands of pieces from hickory saplings that grew in vast stands in Indiana. And no company had more influence on the styles and visibility surrounding the movement than did the Old Hickory Chair Company in Martinsville, Indiana." [*Rustic Artistry for the Home*, by Ralph Kylloe, Gibbs-Smith, Publisher, Salt Lake City, 2000, pg. 73.] The area surrounding Martinsville had also begun to attract tourists who came to relax in the abundant mineral water springs. A growing number of health spas soon were built around the springs, many of which were furnished with chairs and rockers made by the nearby Old Hickory Chair Company. Before long tourists were buying Old Hickory chairs for their own homes — and requesting additional pieces of furniture in the rustic style.

Rustic furniture fit comfortably under the philosophical umbrella of the Arts & Crafts movement, for its utilization of native materials, its unpretentious style, the craftsmanship it exhibited and, at least in the beginning, the fact that much of it was made in small workshops. It also dovetailed with Grove and Seely's stated intention to design a hotel "with the idea to build a big home where every modern convenience could be had, but with all the old-fashioned qualities of genuineness with no sham. Things made by Nature, assisted by artists, carry sentiment." [*Grove Park Inn brochure*, ca. 1919, private collection, pg. 11.]

Formed in 1892 and named in honor of former President Andrew "Old Hickory" Jackson, the Old Hickory Chair Company passed through several hands

This rare, early view of the Great Hall, first called the "Big Room," reveals the original location of the Roycroft clock against the center pillar. COURTESY OF THE FRED KAHN COLLECTION

until purchased in 1908 by Charles H. Patton, whose family maintained ownership of the firm for the next six decades. Although the company also originally sold log cabins, demand for their indoor and outdoor rustic furniture soon prompted the owners to concentrate solely on furniture. Quaint workshops were eventually replaced by a large factory, where, as Ralph Kylloe has determined, "peak production at the Old Hickory plant was about 2,000 pieces per week and records indicate that box cars of hickory furniture were sent to the Adirondacks to furnish the summer homes and retreats of New Yorkers. The company shipped so many items that both the Pennsylvania and the New York Central railroads had tracks leading to the warehouse doors at Old Hickory. Early newspaper records describe Old Hickory as doing 'an extensive business, employs hundreds of men and ships products to all parts of the United States, Canada and Europe.'" [*The Collected Works of Indiana Hickory Furniture Makers*, edited by Ralph Kylloe, Rustic Publications, Nashua, NH, 1989, pg. 2.]

Both Fred Seely and E. W. Grove are known to have vacationed in the Adirondack Mountains, where they may well have encountered examples of Old Hickory rustic furniture. In addition, the designers of the Old Faithful Inn at Yellowstone National Park, a major influence on the general design of the Grove Park Inn, had also purchased Old Hickory furniture that may have influenced Seely and Grove's choice of the rustic furniture for the Inn's porches.

The order for the Grove Park Inn called for two different styles of Old Hickory rocking chairs selected from the firm's 1912 catalog. The taller of the two, model #67, stood 44 inches high and featured a four-inch wide armrest. The second and smaller of the two, model #93, measured just 36 inches high and was distinguished by a hoop back. [*The Collected Works*, Kylloe, pg. 20-22.] Each style of chair would have been branded on one of the legs with the firm's mark, "Old Hickory Chair Company, Martinsville, Ind."

The pride Seely took in the Old Hickory rockers was soon revealed, for when he prepared the Grove Park Inn's first national ad for the *National Geographic* magazine in 1913, he selected for the illustration a photograph taken of the west terrace and a long row of more than thirty Old Hickory rocking chairs.

LEFT The current Old Hickory Furniture Company has reproduced this version of their original rocker using vintage photographs and catalog illustrations since none of the inn's 1913 order have surfaced.

ABOVE The Old Hickory Chair Company provided the rockers needed for the outdoor terraces. They proved so popular that guests could order them through catalogs at the hotel's News Stand. COMPLIMENTS OF THE GROVE PARK INN RESORT & SPA

Fifteen years later, in a letter written to William Patton, president of the Old Hickory Furniture Company, Seely remarked, "Incidentally, the Old Hickory chairs at Grove Park Inn are going into their fifteenth year sitting on the porch winter and summer and I can't see but what they are about as good today as when they came." [letter from Fred L. Seely to William Patton, May 1, 1928, private collection.] The Old Hickory rockers proved so popular at the Grove Park Inn that Fred Seely made it a point to distribute their catalogs to interested guests. In February of 1917 he placed an order for Mrs. Henry Ford "for one dozen large hickory rockers and one dozen of the smaller hickory rockers. Woven seats and backs stained brown. Frames dull var-

nished." [letter from Fred L. Seely to the Old Hickory Chair Company, February 1917, private collection.]

After a bitter and unsuccessful lawsuit with E. W. Grove, Fred Seely left the Grove Park Inn at the end of 1927. The hotel subsequently went through a series of owners until Charles Sammons, whose family still owns the property, purchased it in 1955. At some point in time between 1928 and 1955 the Old Hickory rocking chairs were removed from the Grove Park Inn's terraces. Their fate remains unknown. Unlike all of the other furniture purchased for the Grove Park Inn in 1913, not a single example of an Old Hickory rocking chair from the hotel is known to have surfaced in the Asheville area. This might be explained by the persistent rumor that all of the rustic rockers had been removed at one time and shipped to a hotel in Galveston, Texas, also owned by Charles Sammons. That hotel has since been demolished and its contents scattered.

In 1996 the Old Hickory Furniture Company, now located in Shelbyville, Indiana, released a new version of their 1913 model #67, aptly titled the Grove Park Rocker. An example of the rocker is currently in use in one of the lobbies at the Grove Park Inn.

THE NEWS STAND AT THE GROVE PARK INN

Photographs, sales records and early correspondence confirm that Fred Seely and E.W. Grove established a News Stand in the lobby of the Grove Park Inn soon after it opened in 1913. This, however, was not a typical newsstand that only sold newspapers, candy and tobacco products. Over the course of the next three decades the News Stand at the Grove Park Inn served as a marketplace for artisans and craftsmen working in the Arts & Crafts style, providing guests at the hotel with the opportunity to select from a wide assortment of handmade items.

Recognizing his guests' desire to stay abreast with both national news and news stories from their home territory, Fred Seely offered at the News Stand several major newspapers, including the *New York World*, the *Detroit Free Press*, the *Boston Globe* and the *Atlanta Journal*. In addition guests could purchase popular magazines and colorful postcards with various views of the interior and exterior of the Grove Park Inn, as well as nearby attractions in western North Carolina. Seely also sold souvenir plates manufactured by the Syracuse China Company featuring a drawing of the exterior of the Grove Park Inn and souvenir nickel-silver spoons by Wallace Silversmiths with an image of the hotel stamped into the bowl. Each of these were modeled after the same style and pattern as those used in the Grove Park Inn's dining room.

Stepping beyond the typical inventory of postcards, newspapers and cigars, however, Fred Seely introduced his guests to the handwork of area artisans, including willow and oak baskets woven by Cherokee Indians and local craftspeople, as well as coverlets, blankets and needlework. After he purchased Biltmore Estate Industries from Edith Vanderbilt in 1916, renaming it Biltmore Industries, he added to the News Stand homespun cloth woven on looms he installed in his workshops next to the Grove Park Inn. In addition, the hand-carved woodwork, including pictures frames, bowls, bookends and hearth brushes, made by his woodworkers at Biltmore Industries was also a main attraction at the News Stand.

Those guests wanting to take home a piece of sterling silver jewelry could select from an assortment produced by Stuart Nye, a World War I veteran who first learned the craft of silversmithing while recuperating at the nearby Oteen Military Hospital. Pottery lovers could find vases and bowls produced by the Nonconnah Art Pottery Company, later to be called the Pisgah Forest Pottery of Arden, N.C., the Newcomb College Pottery in New Orleans and the Roseville Pottery. An assortment of local crafts, including pottery, weaving, hooked rugs, carvings and metalware, distributed by the Treasure Chest (1926-1931), an Asheville business founded by Hugh Brown, Edwin Brown and W. H. Lashley, and later known as Three Mountaineers (1931-1992), was also sold through the News Stand.

Fred Seely also kept at the News Stand furniture catalogs from the Roycroft Furniture Shop, the Old

This rare photograph of the original News Stand in the Great Hall reveals a variety of Arts & Crafts items offered for sale: Roycroft lamps and books, local crafts, art pottery and Cherokee baskets. COURTESY OF THE FRED KAHN COLLECTION

Hickory Chair Company and the Heywood Brothers & Wakefield Company, and assisted his guests in placing orders through them.

Undoubtedly, though, the Arts & Crafts enterprise whose merchandise dominated the display at the Grove Park Inn News Stand for several years was the Roycroft Shop. Although Elbert Hubbard preferred to sell directly to his customers through his catalogs, magazines and East Aurora sales shop, his son, Bert, recognized the value of a national network of retail outlets distributing Roycroft products. As he wrote, "We do business with our friends — and we would count you as one. So to that end we have made a selection of hand-wrought copper gift articles made by Roycroft workers 'in joyous animation' at the famous Roycroft Shops. This selection we term 'Our Get Acquainted Offer' and it is made up of thirty-two items. It is a rich, dignified and colorful display that attracts attention and sells quickly." [*The Book of the Roycrofters*, catalogs 1919, 1926, edited by Linda Hubbard Brady, House of Hubbard, East Aurora, NY, 1995, pg. 64.]

Among the first Roycroft items which Fred Seely sold through the News Stand were Bibles bound in hand-tooled leather by the Roycrofters. In a letter written to the Bible House in New York in 1921, Seely explained, "As you must know, we simply send these Bibles to the Roycroft Shop and have them re-bound in hand-tooled leather in a most luxuriant way, and re-sell them here at the Inn. This sale sprung up out of the fact that we equipped all of the rooms in the Grove Park Inn with these Roycroft bound testaments when we built the building." [private collection, March 12, 1921]

In 1918, as the war in Europe was finally drawing to a close and Americans, including Bert Hubbard, were anticipating a relaxation on the restrictions placed on such valuable metals as copper and brass, Karl Kipp and Bert Hubbard developed a new marketing plan. In a letter dated March 8, 1918, Hubbard wrote to Fred Seely:

"Our Artists are always getting out new designs in Copper and Leather things and right now they have completed some very excellent pieces. We think the best way to find out whether these things are really as good as we think they are is to send them to a few of our very best representatives and have them put on display and sale — so with that idea in mind we have sent four new pieces to you, as per enclosed invoice. I wish that you would display these prominently and put a little extra attention on them, showing them to your customers and making a strong endeavor to sell them. I hope you can sell them, and that you will order more, but, of course, in the event they do not sell and after a reasonable try-out you want to send them back, you are privileged to do so."

A mainstay at the News Stand, this shoe shine station is still dutifully attended at GPI.

At the end of the letter Burt hand-wrote this personal note:

"Dear Fred: A new scheme. Am trying it out on a dozen stores. You included. — Bert"

In a letter dated September 30, 1920 Bert Hubbard again wrote to Fred Seely, "By the way, ask the girls up at the News Stand to look over the Roycroft stuff and see what they are going to need for Christmas, and let us hear from them about it. If there is any place I want to keep supplied with the good stuff, it's the G. P. I." [private collection]

And on November 22, 1924 he commented, "You see I am mighty proud of the fact that you folks sell so much of our stuff down there, and I have heralded the information to other stores selling our stuff. I have used it as a whip to show them what they could do. We will do our best to fill your orders and would rob our own salesroom for you any time." [private collection]

Although Fred Seely left the Grove Park Inn at the end of 1927, he continued to lease the News Stand from the new owners until his death in 1942. Throughout those years the News Stand sold thousands of examples of Roycroft books, motto cards, leather purses, lamps, bookends, desk sets, candlesticks, letter openers, flower holders and American Beauty vases. And while a few of those items remained in Asheville, the majority traveled home with each guest, explaining, in part, why Roycroft items have continued to surface in nearly every part of the country.

The Final Years

"Victor Toothaker has come back to East Aurora to join The Roycrofters. Inasmuch as he is an artist and designer of national reputation, we are glad to have him back with us again. It was during the time that he was with us that he designed and supervised the installation of all the lighting fixtures that decorate the magnificent Grove Park Inn built by Fred Seely at Asheville, N.C. He comes back to put that experience to work for us in the designing and in the making of beautiful things which he is well qualified to do.

    Elbert "Bert" Hubbard, II
    February 1931

The Roycroft Shops: 1915-1938

All work at the Roycroft Shops came to a halt when word reached East Aurora of the deaths of Alice and Elbert Hubbard aboard the Lusitania on May 7, 1915. Little more than a week earlier, as he and Alice were about to depart for New York, Elbert Hubbard had called all of his Roycrofters together in what would be his final meeting with them. The risk he and Alice were taking by sailing aboard the Lusitania had been well publicized; he had unsuccessfully attempted to dissuade her from going with him on what he had hoped would be a mission of peace. Both agreed, however, that none of their children should accompany them. At that meeting Elbert Hubbard announced that if he did not return, his eldest son, Elbert 'Bert' Hubbard II, would take charge of the Roycroft Shops.

At age thirty-three, Bert Hubbard had spent more than half his life working along side his father and stepmother in the Roycroft Shops. Elbert Hubbard had trained his oldest son for this very day, rotating him through the various shops and departments in order that he might know first-hand what was expected from each of the Roycroft employees. The challenges Bert Hubbard faced in 1915 were daunting, for not only would he be expected to assume the roles of his charismatic father and business-minded stepmother, he also had to guide the Roycroft Shops into a future that would not be driven by the public's captivation by the Arts & Crafts movement. Rumors had filtered down from Syracuse that the Arts & Crafts empire assembled

by Gustav Stickley was teetering on bankruptcy. Leopold Stickley and Charles Limbert were both preparing to introduce furniture lines which were dramatically lighter in color and form than the dark, massive furniture they and the Roycrofters had been making for nearly two decades. The pace of the economy had slowed as talk turned from automobiles, bungalows and furniture styles to the real threat of war.

Most accounts of the Roycroft Furniture Shop conclude with the Grove Park Inn commission, for Herbert Buffum and his woodworkers never again achieved the fame or fortune which came with that 1913 commission. After the final railcar of furniture was sent off to North Carolina in June of 1913, many of the extra men who had been hired to work in both the Roycroft Furniture Shop and the Copper Shop were laid off, most never to be hired back again. When war broke out in Europe in the summer of 1914, Americans began to curtail their spending in anticipation of the United States' involvement in the hostility. The economic stagnation continued into 1917, when in April America declared war on Germany. Although the war ended in November of 1918, the American economy was slow to rebound; when it did, Arts & Crafts was no longer the popular style of the day.

The first Roycroft casualty of the cutbacks necessitated by the economic slowdown, the deaths of Elbert and Alice Hubbard and diminished interest in the Arts & Crafts style was the Roycroft Furniture Shop. On May 22, 1920 Bert Hubbard wrote to Fred Seely, who had just requested some additional Roycroft furniture for one of the cottages on the grounds of the Grove Park Inn, "I am very sorry about the situation regarding furniture, but I don't see how it can possibly be helped. It would be impossible for the boys to get out anything under three months. We haven't a blooming sideboard or table except those that are sold and in process of making now. I am going to tell you confidently that we are only going to maintain a small carpenter shop where an occasional piece of Roycroft furniture can be made for special Roycrofters. We are not going to advertise this fact at all." [private collection]

By November 20, 1920 business at the Furniture Shop had slowed even more, prompting Bert Hubbard to report to his friend Fred Seely, "The furniture business is just like this: We have had to use the furniture shop floor for the bindery and were unable to get our new little furniture shop ready for occupancy in time to do the work this winter. We have therefore cleared out the furniture shop and won't be in a position to make any more furniture for probably six months.

"We never could make it in a volume large enough to make it to make it pay, and the other branches of our work are growing to such as an extent that they must be given first consideration, so our furniture shop is out of business temporarily." [private collection]

The Roycrofters final foray into furniture production came in 1925 when they produced 1,200 two-shelf, open-back, oak bookstands specifically designed to hold a complete 14-volume set of Elbert Hubbard's *Little Journeys* and *The Selected Writings of Elbert Hubbard*. It represented their first — and last — attempt at mass production. The small bookstand was designed to be disassembled and shipped flat in a carton along with a set of Hubbard's books. It was signed not with the familiar carved orb-and-cross, but with a metal plate tacked onto one of the legs.

Ironically, just as the Roycroft Furniture Shop had been formed in 1897-98 to provide work tables and furniture for the printing, illuminating and binding of Roycroft books, their final furniture project was driven by the need in 1925 for a bookstand for a collection of Elbert Hubbard's books.

Upon the death of his famous father in 1915, Bert Hubbard had taken stock not only of the strengths and weaknesses of the Roycroft business, but of the changing taste of the American public and of his own skills as well. Rather than attempt to become the prolific writer his father had been, Bert Hubbard instead re-issued many of his father's earlier works, including the popular and highly successful fourteen-volume sets of Elbert Hubbard's *Little Journeys* (1916) and his *Selected Writings* (1928). Both sets were mass-marketed

The final form produced by the Roycroft Furniture Shop was this oak two-tiered bookstand designed to hold a special edition of Elbert Hubbard's writings. PHOTO COURTESY OF TREADWAY GALLERY, WWW.TREADWAYGALLERY.COM.

by the William L. Wise Company of New York, while the Roycroft Printing Shop produced a limited number of sets in special Roycroft bindings. He also suspended publication of his father's two magazines, *The Philistine* in 1915 and *The Fra* in 1917, replacing them with a smaller and more economical publication called *The Roycroft* (1917-1926). It was subsequently replaced by the *Roycrofter* (1926-1932), but like its predecessors, it, too, struggled to maintain the readership — and advertisers — who had been so loyal to Elbert Hubbard.

In 1915, for reasons yet unknown, Victor Toothaker left the Roycroft Copper Shop, where he had served as foreman since 1911 (See separate entry.). Bert Hubbard then convinced both Karl Kipp and Walter Jennings, who had left the Copper Shop in 1911, reportedly after a dispute over their wages with Alice Hubbard, to return to Roycroft. Hubbard approached the two metalsmiths, who had been working for themselves in East Aurora since leaving Roycroft, with an idea, which ran counter to his father's lifelong aversion to middlemen. As Roycroft historian Kevin McConnell noted, "His first business decision was a brilliant one, which involved a system by which Roycroft books, copper and leather items were sold to department and gift stores throughout the country. This had multiple repercussions since these items had previously been available to the public only through the mail or by visiting the campus itself. In all likelihood, it was this new distribution policy that helped to stabilize the Roycroft Community and keep it in business long after the Depression had ravaged other business enterprises." [*Roycroft Art Metal*, by Kevin McConnell, Schiffer Publishing, West Chester, PA, 1990, pg. 15.]

TOP After an extensive remodeling, the Roycroft Inn has reopened with a combination of authentic antiques and quality Arts & Crafts reproductions.

ABOVE Like the Grove Park Inn, the Roycroft Inn has again drawn visitors and Arts & Crafts enthusiasts eager to relax amid Arts & Crafts furnishings in an Arts & Crafts environment.

PHOTOS BY ROB KAROSIS, COURTESY OF THE ROYCROFT INN

Through his cost-cutting measures, by correctly gauging the changing tastes of the American public and by marketing the celebrity status of his notorious father and his writings, Bert Hubbard was able to maintain the Roycroft Shops for a remarkable twenty-three years — three more years than the reign of his father. But as the Great Depression tightened its grip on the American public, interest in the Roycroft campus, the Roycroft Inn and Roycroft products dwindled until even these measures proved unable to stave off bankruptcy. In 1938, a disheartened Bert Hubbard was forced to walk away from the workshops which his father had first built forty-three years earlier and which had been his home — and that of his children — his entire life.

While a few vain attempts were made to keep the Roycroft campus intact, eventually the buildings were sold off individually. The Roycroft Inn remained open until 1987; soon thereafter it was purchased by the Landmark Society of Western New York with the assistance of the Margaret L. Wendt Foundation.

After an extensive eight million dollar renovation, the jewel of the Roycroft Campus re-opened in 1995 with 22 suites offering a harmonious blend of historical accuracy and modern facilities. In 1989 a group of concerned individuals formed the Roycroft Revitalization Corporation, which since 2004 has been known as the Roycroft Campus Corporation (RCC) and has taken as its motto: "The Roycroft Campus: As if Elbert Hubbard and the Roycrofters never left." It is the goal of the RCC "to preserve and promote the ideals, traditions, architectural legacy and business skills of Elbert Hubbard and the Roycrofters through the acquisition and restoration of the Roycroft Campus buildings and grounds, in a manner consistent with their National Historic Landmark status." In 2005 the RCC acquired the Roycroft Copper Shop and the Power House, two of the surviving fourteen buildings on the campus, and have undertaken their restoration. In the years since then the RCC, private property owners and the Town of East Aurora have been working together to coordinate their efforts to restore, preserve and sustain the Roycroft Campus.

Another group, the Roycrofters At-Large Association, is a non-profit organization of artists, artisans and friends of Roycroft, which was formed in 1976 to preserve not only the Arts & Crafts philosophy and heritage at Roycroft, but also the skills evident in the work of the original Roycrofters. Among the many goals, achievements and accomplishments of the Roycrofters At-Large Association is the juried recognition of a select number of individuals who have been awarded the title of Roycroft Artisan and given the privilege of signing their work with the Roycroft Renaissance mark — back-to-back "Rs" signifying the Roycroft Renaissance. These artists and artisans have achieved Roycroft Artisan status through the quality of their workmanship, their contributions to the field, their innovation and originality of expression, and their professional recognition.

Members of the Roycrofters At-Large Association and the Roycroft Campus Corporation, as well as the staffs at the Roycroft Inn, the volunteers at the Elbert Hubbard Roycroft Museum and the owners of various buildings on the Roycroft Campus, have again given Arts & Crafts enthusiasts the inspiration and the motivation to travel to East Aurora, where the spirit of Elbert Hubbard lives on.

Victor Toothaker: The Years After the Grove Park Inn Commission

As previously mentioned, the year 1915 marked a crucial turning point at the Roycroft Shops. The deaths of Elbert and Alice Hubbard and the uncertainty

Beginning in 1917 Fred L. Seely built five workshops for his Biltmore Industries, an Arts & Crafts enterprise which still flourishes today as the Grovewood Gallery, a cafe and artisan studios. The buildings still retain their Arts & Crafts detailing, including Seely's inspirational mottos, hand-carved doors and a collection of Roycroft antiques.

hovering over the silent shops may have prompted thirty-three year old Victor Toothaker to resign his post as foreman and chief designer for the Roycroft Copper Shop. This assumption is based on two known facts. In 1915 Victor Toothaker formed his own metal-smithing business in East Aurora. That same year, after the deaths of Elbert and Alice Hubbard, Bert Hubbard assumed the role of general manager of the Roycroft Shops and persuaded both Karl Kipp and Walter Jennings to return to the Roycroft Copper Shop. Obviously, their return would have been unnecessary had Victor Toothaker remained as foreman of the Copper Shop, a position he had held and had managed successfully since 1911.

Victor Toothaker's first attempt at his own business in East Aurora may have been short-lived, for when on September 12, 1918, thirty-six year old Victor Toothaker registered for the draft he was then living in Detroit, working as a "Chandelier Designer" for the C.J. Welling Company. [Scarab Club archives, Detroit, MI, information provided by curator Patricia Reed] In 1919 he was designing lights for the Charles V. Daiger Company of Boston. Over the course of the next twelve years it appears that Victor Toothaker moved fre-

quently, working at various times in Detroit, Grand Rapids and Michigan as a lighting designer. During this time period his name has been associated with the lighting fixtures of the Mastercraft Novelty Lighting Company of Cleveland, Ohio, which produced lighting fixtures for churches; the Drake Hotel in Chicago; the Marshall Field stores in Oak Park and Evanston, Illinois; the Elks Club in Cleveland; and the Wardell Apartment Hotel in Detroit.

On October 9, 1923, the United States Patent Office approved Victor Toothaker's application for a patent for an adjustable wrought-iron lamp. The floor lamp featured a two-piece sliding shaft secured with a hand-screw at the mid-point. Toothaker's invention enabled users to adjust the height of the shade to suit their needs by loosening and tightening the hand-screw. It is not known if the floor lamp was ever placed into production. His patent application, #63,126, indicates that in 1923 Toothaker was again living in East Aurora, as he was in 1924 when, as evidenced by a letter written on April 18 in which Bert Hubbard states that Victor Toothaker "is in business for himself here in East Aurora and is not connected with us at all." [private collection]

Today the historic Main Inn looks much as it did when it opened its doors in 1913, due to a large part to the diligence of the Charles Sammons family, owners since 1955, who have carefully protected and preserved its Arts & Crafts heritage.

By November of that same year, however, it appears Victor Toothaker had moved to Grand Rapids, Michigan, to work for Albert Stickley, brother of Gustav Stickley and owner of the Stickley Brothers Company. According to author David Cathers, as far back as 1914, "while still working In East Aurora, he was also drawing model rooms for the Grand Rapids furniture firm run by Gustav Stickley's brother Albert; they appear that year in Stickley Brothers' advertisements for its 'Quaint Furniture' in Good Furniture magazine." [*Gustav Stickley*, Cathers, pg. 215.] Toothaker may have revived his connection with Albert Stickley, perhaps as demand for his metalware slowed. On November 20, 1924 Fred Seely wrote to Victor Toothaker, "Care of Stickley Brothers Company, Grand Rapids, Michigan: 'The copper stuff which you designed for the Grove Park Inn is somewhat out of repair. That is to say it needs going over. The shade supports [on the table lamps] need strengthening and straightening and a good deal of the stuff ought to be cleaned up and re-waxed. Do you happen to have any man who could be spared after Christmas and could you send one here to go over the stuff? We cannot spare many pieces at a time and could not ship it away, but we believe it would be a simple matter to let a man

come right here in our wood carving shop [next door at Biltmore Industries, that Seely owned] and clean the stuff up.' " [private collection] It is not known whether or not Victor Toothaker received or responded to Fred Seely's request.

In 1928 Victor Toothaker was again in Detroit, designing Art Deco style chandeliers for the Scarab Club, "a truly unique building," according to historian Patricia Reed, "that has miraculously survived. Every aspect of the interior and exterior décor was designed, painted, or crafted by Scarab Club members in 1928 when the building was built." [letter to author from Patricia Reed, May 7, 2008] The Scarab Club has traced its beginnings back to 1907, when a group of Detroit men formed an organization "to promote the mutual acquaintance of art lovers and art workers… and to maintain a clubhouse for entertainment and social purposes as well as to provide working and exhibit facilities for artist members." [Scarab Club web site] When in 1928 the members voted to construct a three-story brick building for their clubhouse, they turned to fellow member and architect Lancelot Sukert, who designed it in the Northern Italian Renaissance style. The Art Deco glass and mica chandeliers for the main gallery on the first floor, the stairwells and the second floor lounge were all designed by Victor Toothaker, possibly a member of the Scarab Club, and produced by the C.J. Welling Company.

Victor Toothaker's name has also been linked to the Kokoon Arts Club of Cleveland, an avant-garde art organization noted for its unconventional activities. It had been founded in 1911 by a group of Cleveland artists seeking means of allowing their members to express their creative talents. In 1930 the group moved its headquarters to a new location in Cleveland, leaving open the possibility that Victor Toothaker, either as a member or as a hired craftsman, may have designed the lighting for the club. Toothaker, along with his wife, Anne, is listed in the Cleveland City Directory in both 1929 and 1930; his stated occupation was that of a designer.

Back in East Aurora, problems had arisen at the Roycroft Copper Shop. Declining sales had forced Bert Hubbard and Karl Kipp to begin laying off Copper Shop workers in 1928 and in April of 1929 Hubbard presented Kipp with a difficult choice: either buy the Copper Shop from Hubbard or leave. The following month Karl Kipp resigned; three weeks later his replacement, Arthur Cole, whom Kipp had trained, resigned as well. The Copper Shop struggled through the remainder of 1929; in 1930 Bert Hubbard may well have begun looking for a new shop foreman. Thinking that his former shop manager might be available, Bert Hubbard may well have contacted Victor Toothaker in Cleveland. It may also be that Toothaker and his wife, Anne, who grew up in East Aurora, may have heard about the problems at the Roycroft Copper Shop through their longtime friends and may have contacted Hubbard.

Regardless of the connection, in January of 1931, Victor Toothaker returned to East Aurora. His arrival was announced quite proudly by Bert Hubbard in the February 1931 issue of *The Roycrofter* magazine:

In 1913 Fred Seely built "Overlook," a 30,000 square foot castle on the top of Sunset Mountain. PHOTO COURTESY E.M. BALL PHOTOGRAPHIC COLLECTION (1918-1969), SPECIAL COLLECTIONS, D.H. RAMSEY LIBRARY, UNIVERSITY OF NORTH CAROLINA AT ASHEVILLE.

"Victor Toothaker has come back to East Aurora to join The Roycrofters. Inasmuch as he is an artist and designer of national reputation, we are glad to have him back with us again.

"In the years that Mr. Toothaker was with The Roycrofters his great talent in design and skill in workmanship was demonstrated in the Copper Things that he made for us.

"Mr. Toothaker's influence helped us to create the prestige enjoyed by the Roycroft Copper Line down through the years.

"It was during the time that he was with us that he designed and supervised the installation of all the lighting fixtures that decorate the magnificent Grove Park Inn built by Fred Seely at Asheville, N.C.

"While away from The Roycrofters Mr. Toothaker has grown and progressed. He has enjoyed a broad experience in the making of Art Objects and Lighting Fixtures. He comes back to put that experience to work for us in the designing and in the making of beautiful things which he is well qualified to do.

"Mr. Toothaker is now at work on new designs. In fact, a few of these designs are now being executed by the dexterous hands of Roycroft artisans." [*The Roycrofter*, February 1931, volume 5, no. 4, pg. 112-113.]

A few weeks earlier, having learned of Victor Toothaker's return to the Roycroft Copper Shop, Fred Seely had written to Bert Hubbard, "I am more than pleased to see Toothaker coming back home. You know I have sort of an inborn feeling that people ought to stick at what they undertake in life, and I am not so very soft on tramps — even respectable ones. 'Tooth' probably thought he would conquer a few new worlds, but it certainly is good business when he makes up his mind to come back to the parental roof at East Aurora. Any man who can't work out a good mousetrap with you fellows at the atmosphere of Roycroft isn't likely to do it anywhere else." [Letter dated January 26, 1931, private collection.]

When Victor Toothaker arrived back in East Aurora he was about to turn forty-nine and brought with him more than thirty years' experience working for and alongside such men as Paul Elder, Gustav Stickley, Elbert Hubbard, Karl Kipp and Walter Jennings; designing lighting fixtures for homes, hotels, churches and commercial buildings; and illustrating magazine covers, articles, model rooms, advertisements, catalogs and architectural renderings. He had demonstrated his ability to work in a variety of metals, from hand-forged iron to brass and copper; and he had shown that he could adjust to changing tastes, making the transition from massive Arts & Crafts chandeliers to more refined Art Deco. But one year later Victor

LEFT The rock walls of the Grove Park Inn reflect Fred Seely's instructions to his workmen in 1913 that neither the mortar nor the marks of the mason's tools were to be visible when the inn was completed.

ABOVE The most recent addition to the hotel has been the award-winning spa, built completely underground in 2001 so as not to detract from the historic Main Inn. It, too, features Arts & Crafts lighting and detailing. COMPLIMENTS OF THE GROVE PARK INN RESORT & SPA

RIGHT Once largely ignored, today the famous Roycroft clock receives daily care and regular attention from the staff at the Grove Park Inn. The original works by the E. Howard Clock Company still keep good time.

Toothaker died unexpectedly just a few weeks after his fiftieth birthday. His friends Karl Kipp and Bert Hubbard led his funeral service, after which Victor Toothaker was buried five miles from East Aurora in South Wales, New York.

The Grove Park Inn, Edwin W. Grove and Fred L. Seely

Like the Roycroft Shops, the Grove Park Inn struggled through the years surrounding World War I. When owner Edwin Wiley Grove announced his decision to temporarily close the hotel in 1914, just months after it had opened, son-in-law Fred Seely stepped forward with a proposal: although he had no experience in the hotel business, he would lease the Grove Park Inn from Grove for a percentage of the gross revenues. Bemused, perhaps, but realizing this would insure that his daughter and grandchildren would remain in Asheville where Grove had maintained a summer home for nearly fifteen years, the owner agreed. A first lease was signed by the two men that year; a revised lease was agreed upon in 1917, extending Fred Seely's contract to operate the hotel through the end of 1927. [For more information,

see *Built for the Ages: A History of the Grove Park Inn*, by Bruce Johnson, The Grove Park Inn Resort and Spa, Asheville, NC, 2003.]

Despite Grove's misgivings and his own inexperience, Fred Seely ran the Grove Park Inn successfully throughout his thirteen-year tenure. With each passing year, however, relations between the two men deteriorated. Throughout their adult lives they had always competed for the attention and approval of Evelyn Grove Seely — E. W. Grove's only daughter and Fred Seely's wife. In his letters to her, Grove boasted openly of the vast sums of money he was generating through the Paris Medicine Company and his various real estate investments in Florida, Texas, Virginia and North Carolina. In 1917, announcing he no longer needed the rental income from the Grove Park Inn, he directed Fred Seely to pay it instead to his daughter Evelyn.

Although Fred Seely, through his shrewd financial skills and his dictatorial management style, produced a respectable income from the Grove Park Inn, he also poured much of it back into the hotel and, starting in 1916, into the five large workshops he built for his weavers and woodworkers at Biltmore Industries. In 1920 Grove further irritated Seely by purchasing The Manor, an English-style inn a few blocks from the Grove Park Inn. Then, in 1922 Grove purchased the 36-year old Battery Park Hotel in downtown Asheville and, to the dismay of the citizens of Asheville,

demolished it to make way for a modern 14-story hotel. Finally, the 75-year old Grove publicly announced that he had re-written his will, removing any reference to Fred Seely in his latest version.

Incensed over the move, Fred Seely filed a lawsuit against his father-in-law, claiming that Grove had earlier promised him upon Grove's death his choice of either the Paris Medicine Company or the Grove Park Inn. The suit attracted national attention and was still underway when on January 27, 1927, E.W. Grove died in his suite atop the new Battery Park Hotel. After months of delay, the court finally ruled that since Fred Seely had no written proof of a prior agreement promising him the Grove Park Inn upon Grove's death, the final will of the multi-millionaire would stand as written.

On the final day of 1927 Fred Seely turned management of the Grove Park Inn over to the trustees of Grove's estate, who soon thereafter sold it to a group of investors. Fred Seely retreated to his office at Biltmore Industries, where he guided his homespun weaving and woodworking business safely through the ensuing Great Depression. During the 1930s Fred Seely continued to

work closely with the different managers who operated the Grove Park Inn, advising them on various issues, leasing the News Stand space in the Great Hall and serving as unofficial ambassador of Asheville for visiting dignitaries and public officials. In 1942, at the age of 70, Fred Seely died in his home atop Sunset Mountain.

Despite Fred Seely's efforts to assist them, the new owners of the Grove Park Inn eventually declared bankruptcy and the Inn struggled to remain in business for the next twenty-five years. Each of a succession of new owners and general managers made feeble and often horrendous attempts to update the aging Arts & Crafts hotel, including removing the copper bottoms from the Roycroft chandeliers in the Great Hall and from the ceiling lights in the guest rooms, discarding many of the original Roycroft, Old Hickory and Heywood-Wakefield furnishings and covering the granite walls with plasterboard.

In 1955 yet another new owner arrived on the scene. Charles Sammons (1898-1988) of Dallas, Texas, had made his first fortune in the insurance business, then, through several wise investments, had founded

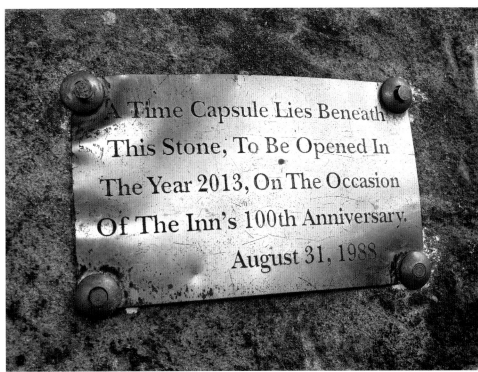

LEFT The grounds of the Grove Park Inn, while considerably smaller than in 1913, still contain walking trails and stone bridges for the enjoyment of its guests.

ABOVE A time capsule was imbedded in the granite wall of the Vanderbilt Wing addition upon its completion in 1988, awaiting opening when the inn celebrates its one hundredth birthday.

the Jack Tar chain of hotels. His staff of decorators descended on the hotel and began the slow and costly journey toward re-establishing the Grove Park Inn as one of the country's premier resort hotels. That first year they made many mistakes, but by 1964, when Sammons undertook his second major remodeling of the hotel, they took the first steps toward emphasizing rather than disguising the Grove Park Inn's heritage. By 1984, the year that marked the completion of the Sammons Wing, Charles Sammons and his staff recognized the important role the Arts & Crafts movement had played in the original design and furnishing of the Grove Park Inn. They took their inspiration for the lighting fixtures, wall and floor coverings and the furnishings, both new and antique, from original photographs of the Great Hall, the Palm Court and the guest rooms. When in 1988 they completed the Vanderbilt Wing, the Arts & Crafts style had achieved national recognition and along with it so had the Grove Park Inn. Additional Arts & Crafts antiques by Gustav Stickley, Charles Limbert, Albert Stickley, L. & J.G. Stickley, J.M. Young and others were purchased, along with many original pieces of Roycroft furniture that had in previous years passed into private collections.

In 1912 Gustav Stickley predicted that Arts & Crafts furniture "in fifty or a hundred years will be worth many times its first cost, for the time is coming when good oak furniture will be valuable on account of its permanent worth and of its scarcity." Even Stickley could not have envisioned the recognition and appreciation which the American people have demonstrated for the Arts & Crafts style.

No where is that more evident than in the hallways, the guest rooms and the Great Hall of the Grove Park Inn, where the spirit and the philosophy of the Arts & Crafts movement have come alive through a careful blending of original antiques and quality reproductions. As word gradually spread of the inn's collection of Arts & Crafts furniture, lighting, pottery and textiles, a steady stream of collectors, editors, publishers, architects and authors began making the journey to Asheville to experience for themselves what it would have been like — and still is — to stay in an authentic Arts & Crafts resort.

THE MORRIS GALLERY

No single piece of furniture represents the Arts & Crafts movement better than the classic Morris chair. Named in honor of the British philosopher, writer, publisher and designer William Morris (1834-1896), the first adjustable back armchair represented a collaboration between Morris and his partner architect Philip Webb (1831-1915). Although their first armchair was decidedly Victorian in flavor, Arts & Crafts designers and manufacturers from Frank Lloyd Wright to Gustav Stickley to Elbert Hubbard introduced their interpretation of the Morris chair.

Ironically, although it does not appear that any Morris chairs were among Fred Seely and E. W. Grove's initial order for the furnishings of the Grove Park Inn, today the hotel's collection of Arts & Crafts Morris chair is without equal anywhere in the world. The majority were purchased on behalf of the inn in 1984 by John Jung, a Florida-based antiques dealer and collector hired by the management to assemble a collection of Arts & Crafts antiques for the new Sammons Wing.

Visitors to the Grove Park Inn have the unparalleled opportunity not only to view and compare Morris chairs by Gustav Stickley, L. & J.G. Stickley, J.M. Young, Stickley Brothers and others, but to also relax in them as they watch the sun set behind the Blue Ridge Mountains in the distance.

Arts & Crafts furniture designers experimented with various elements, including the arrangement of slats under the arms, the means of allowing the back to pivot between the rear legs and the method of securing the back into a preferred position. This particular Morris chair is a rare, early design from the workshops of Gustav Stickley.

An oak bar in Arts & Crafts Morris chairs often replaced the brass rod of nineteenth century Victorian models.

The Quaint Art Furniture Company, a Syracuse-based competitor of Gustav Stickley, produced this magnificent example during their brief existence. Its designer borrowed Stickley's adjustable pin system behind the pivoting back.

What a difference a slat can make: Compare this four-slat version with the five-slat model next to it. The similar dimensions and proportions, the arrangement of the corbels under the arms, the exposed tenons in the legs and the brass hinges beneath the adjustable back seem to indicate that both of these Morris chairs were produced by the same firm. Customers could also choose between the adjustable bar or the adjustable pins to support the back.

BILTMORE INDUSTRIES, FRED SEELY AND THE ROYCROFTERS

In 1916, keenly aware of the tenuous nature of his relationship with Edwin W. Grove — his father-in-law, landlord and rival for the attention of Evelyn Grove Seely — Fred Seely purchased from Edith Vanderbilt a small Arts & Crafts enterprise known as Biltmore Estate Industries. [For more information see "Eleanor Vance, Charlotte Yale and the Origins of Biltmore Estate Industries," by Bruce Johnson, *May We All Remember Well*, Vol. 2, edited by Robert Brunk, Brunk Auction Services, Asheville, NC, 2001, pg. 241-266.]

Begun in 1901 as a woodcarving club for the sons of workers on the Biltmore Estate, the group was led by Eleanor Vance (1869-1954) and Charlotte Yale (1870-1958), two Presbyterian missionaries from Chicago who had come to Southern Appalachia to teach woodworking, woodcarving and weaving skills to members of the mountain community. Their salaries and that of

their mentor, Reverend Rodney R. Swope, rector of the All Souls Church in Biltmore Village, were paid by George Vanderbilt, who had moved to his 125,000-acre estate south of Asheville in 1895. He and his wife, Edith Vanderbilt, supported and encouraged Vance and Yale to develop the woodcarving club into an Arts & Crafts enterprise known, beginning in 1905, as the Biltmore Estate Industries.

The cottage business provided young men and women with the opportunity to learn the skills of woodworking, woodcarving and weaving, then to apply those skills in the making of objects to be sold to local residents and tourists. They began by carving walnut and mahogany bowls, picture frames, bookends and letter openers designed by Eleanor Vance, who had studied woodcarving under William Fry. Their finest pupil, George Arthur, evolved into the shop foreman and demonstrated his ability to both design and build furniture as well. By 1909 their shop had been equipped with a number of power tools, including a lathe, circular saw, band saw and scroll saw; among the publications they subscribed to was Gustav Stickley's magazine, *The Craftsman*. In 1913 George Arthur exhibited their work

LEFT Located on a wooded knoll adjacent to the hotel, the 1917 workshops provided the craftsmen and craftswomen of Biltmore Industries with an idyllic setting. COMPLIMENTS OF THE GROVE PARK INN RESORT & SPA

BELOW Now carefully restored and maintained, the workshops at Biltmore Industries are home to an antique automobile collection, an Arts & Crafts museum, the nationally-ranked Grovewood Gallery, a café and a number of artisans, making it a destination of its own distinction.

Outdoor sculpture and artwork greet visitors as they stroll up the flagstone path leading from the Grove Park Inn to the Grovewood Gallery, the centerpiece of buildings and grounds that Fred Seely designed, constructed and directed beginning in 1917, even while he was still leasing and managing the Grove Park Inn.

at the National Conservation Exposition in Knoxville, TN, where they were awarded a gold medal.

In 1914, however, George Vanderbilt died unexpectedly, leaving his widow with the enormous responsibility of raising their fourteen-year old daughter and managing his entire estate. Unfortunately, George Vanderbilt had spent most of his inheritance, placing Edith Vanderbilt in the position of having to reduce their staff, sell portions of their forestlands and divest herself of many of her charitable commitments. In 1916 she began conversations with Fred Seely regarding the future of Biltmore Estate Industries, which she sold to him in 1917. From that point on it would be known as Biltmore Industries.

That year Fred Seely began construction of the first of five buildings styled after English cottages on land he leased from E. W. Grove next to the Grove Park Inn. George Arthur continued to supervise the workers five miles away in the workshops in Biltmore Village, but in August of 1917, however, just as the first of the workshops was nearing completion, George Arthur resigned, citing differences in management styles with his new employer.

In either 1917 or 1918 Fred Seely placed an order for additional Arts & Crafts furniture from the Roycroft Furniture Shop. Most of what he required consisted of desks, file cabinets, straight chairs and swivel desk chairs, many of which have remained at Biltmore Industries and are now on display in their museum. Included is an example of the Roycroft Magazine Pedestal, model #080, which Fred Seely either ordered from the Roy-

crofters in 1917-1918 or may have ordered earlier and moved from his office at the Grove Park Inn.

Several of the straight chairs which Fred Seely purchased from the Roycrofters for his office at Biltmore Industries were the same model as the dining room chairs which he had ordered in 1913 for the Grove Park Inn. Unlike the Grove Park Inn chairs, however, the chairs intended for Biltmore Industries did not have either the letters "GPI" or any other special designation inscribed on them.

From 1917 until his departure from the Grove Park Inn in December of 1927, Fred Seely divided his time between his two offices and his two businesses — the Grove Park Inn and Biltmore Industries. By the close of 1927 he and the trustees of E. W. Grove's estate had agreed that his lease on the hotel would not be renewed. From 1928 until his death in 1942, Fred Seely managed Biltmore Industries, where he gradually decreased the emphasis on woodworking and woodcarving, preferring, instead, to build the weaving of homespun cloth into a business with a national reputation for quality. Among the clients for his homespun cloth were Eleanor Roosevelt, Harvey Kellogg, President and Mrs. Herbert Hoover and President and Mrs. Calvin Coolidge. Today the buildings Fred Seely constructed for his woodworkers and weavers have been meticulously restored and now serve as a restaurant, an automobile museum, workshops and studios for artisans and the nationally known Grovewood Gallery.

The Arts & Crafts
Tradition Continues

*"We talked to several designers until we found someone who appreciated the Inn as much as we did.
Mr. Sammons and I wanted them to make the new wings look as much like the old as possible by
duplicating the Roycroft furniture and by using authentic antiques."*

ELAINE D. SAMMONS

MAY 3, 1991

When Fred Seely left the Grove Park Inn at the close of 1927, little had changed in the furnishings of the hotel since the Saturday it had opened in July of 1913. The Heywood Brothers & Wakefield Company wicker furniture still filled the Great Hall, though the fragile nature of the woven rattan was beginning to become more evident. The Roycroft furniture in the dining room and public areas, as well as the White Company furniture in the guest rooms, had held up far better, as Fred Seely often noted in his correspondence.

With the arrival, beginning in 1928, of a series of new owners and general managers came many changes to the furnishings of the hotel. The first casualty was the Heywood-Wakefield wicker furniture in the Great Hall, which was replaced by oversized 'paddle arm' sofas and chairs made by the Old Hickory Furniture Company. This durable, but outdated line of 'distressed' oak furniture remained in service at the Grove Park Inn for more than seventy years before it was replaced by more appropriate Arts & Crafts reproductions from the Stickley Company of Manlius, New York. Numerous examples still exist and can be seen in several of the Inn's alcoves and seating areas. At some point in the 1930s workmen lowered the six massive Roycroft chandeliers to the floor of the Great Hall and used hacksaws to unceremoniously cut off the riveted copper bowls which had reflected the light of the bulbs up against the ceiling. In its place they

installed flat, frosted glass panels and fleur-de-lis better suited for a French castle.

In 1955 the decorators hired by new owner Charles Sammons to make some necessary improvements to the hotel deemed the Arts & Crafts style outdated. In their defense, it must have seemed totally alien during an era of bleached blond Danish modern furniture, as well as chrome and glass tables, beanbag chairs and Harvest Gold kitchen appliances. In addition, the American public had just begun a love affair with the automobile and the new 'automobile hotels', i.e. motels, which sprung up along old two-lane roadways and the new interstate highways. In comparison, the stately queen of Sunset Mountain looked like an aging monarch dressed in tattered robes.

Her first facelift came at great expense. What remained of the weathered Old Hickory porch rockers and the brittle Heywood-Wakefield wicker furniture was shipped to an undetermined destination. The majority of the 400 Roycroft 'GPI' chairs were gathered up and sold to the general public for five dollars apiece. For decades afterwards they could be seen in local bars, at flea markets, on porches and even lining the hallway of one nursing home. Victor Toothaker's hammered copper ceiling lights in the guest rooms suffered the same fate as the chandeliers in the Great Hall; several others were dismantled, fitted with stubby legs and filled with sand to become Roycroft ashtrays. Tall Arts & Crafts headboards and footboards were first cut down, then discarded and replaced by Hollywood beds on metal frames and rollers.

Once an eclectic conglomeration of styles of furniture, the Great Hall has recently been refurbished using accurate reproductions of Arts & Crafts furniture manufactured by the current Stickley Company.

Fortunately, there were survivors. Those pieces considered too heavy to move — the eight-foot Roycroft clock in the Great Hall, plus the four corner servers and the two eight-foot sideboards in the dining room — stayed safely in place. Other pieces survived simply because they were out of public view: several Roycroft "GPI" chairs were left in the basement recreation room and the six-foot Roycroft clock remained tucked away in Charles Sammons' private suite for more than thirty years. The White Furniture Company's chests of drawers, vanities and writing tables remained in the guest rooms, but were sanded and refinished to change their color from dark Fumed Oak to light Golden Oak.

In 1964, long before the Arts & Crafts era had even begun to receive any widespread recognition, the first steps were taken to correct many of the mistakes made in 1955. Tongue-and-groove oak boards, stained a medium brown, replaced the blue vinyl wallpaper the first decorators had wrapped around the concrete columns in the Great Hall. Native granite flagstone was laid on the floor of the lobby and public hallways. Original Arts & Crafts furnishings, while still being refinished, at least were no longer being sold; instead, many were brought out of storage, repaired and placed back into service.

During this era the designers in charge of the Grove Park Inn's dining room commissioned scores of new oak dining room chairs loosely modeled after the original Roycroft chairs. These mass-produced chairs do bear the "GPI" letters across the top, but in a different typestyle from the original. These chairs were used in the hotel until 2005, when they, along with other non-antique furnishings, were donated to the Asheville Habitat for Humanity store, where they were sold to an eager Asheville public. When compared to an original Roycroft chair, it is difficult to imagine that someone could mistake a late 20th-century reproduction for an original 1913 Roycroft antique, but it has happened. In at least one instance a later chair was refinished and reupholstered to look like the original Roycroft chair, then offered on-line with a less-than forthcoming description.

The education of the American public to the significance and the value of the Arts & Crafts movement began in earnest with the 1972 Princeton exhibition entitled "The Arts & Crafts Movement in America." The catalog for this exhibit represented the first comprehensive attempt to tie together the furniture, art pottery, metalware, textiles and artwork that had been designed and created by craftsmen and craftswomen striving to achieve the ideals first promoted by John

This three-legged half-round table seems identical to one produced by the Roycrofters around 1906, but is actually an accurate replica signed and dated by two woodworkers using an original as a model.

authentic antiques by Gustav Stickley, Charles Limbert, J.M. Young, L. & J.G. Stickley, Lifetime, Stickley Brothers and, of course, the Roycrofters.

Four years later, as the Vanderbilt Wing was nearing completion, increasing the Grove Park Inn's total number of guest rooms to 512, the architects and decorators continued to recognize the importance of the Arts & Crafts style. In addition to commissioning new Arts & Crafts pieces, they purchased more antiques and artwork from the Arts & Crafts era. The management of the hotel contributed to the effort by, whenever possible, purchasing original Grove Park Inn antiques from individuals, antiques shops and at auction. Elaine Sammons, the widow of Charles Sammons, who had died in 1988 at age 90, commissioned the writing of the first full-length history of the Grove Park Inn, *Built for the Ages: A History of the Grove Park Inn*, which further documented the role of the Roycrofters and of Fred Seely in making the Grove Park Inn a true Arts & Crafts resort.

In recent years the Grove Park Inn's management has taken additional steps to insure not only that the Inn's collection remains intact, but that it grows along with the hotel as well. In 2007 and 2008 the last of the non-Arts & Crafts furniture in the Great Hall was removed and replaced with oak settles, rocking chairs, arm chairs, end tables and coffee tables produced by the Stickley Company of Manlius, N.Y.

The current Stickley Company can trace its lineage back to Gustav and Leopold Stickley. When Gustav declared bankruptcy in 1916, Leopold bought his brother's business assets and in 1918 they formed the short-lived Stickley Handcraft Craftsman firm. By 1922 Leopold had assumed control of the company and had begun diverting orders for Arts & Crafts furniture to the J. M. Young Furniture Company so that he could concentrate on a new line of quality Colonial reproductions marketed as "Cherry Valley" furniture. After a long and successful career, Leopold Stickley died in 1957; shortly thereafter the firm, which had dwindled to 22 workers, was purchased by Alfred Audi (1938-2007), whose father had worked with Leopold Stickley. Audi continued to produce the Cherry Valley line, but in 1989, with the rising popularity of the Arts & Crafts movement, began issuing reproductions of classic Gustav Stickley and L. & J.G. Stickley designs, along with new pieces, such as entertainment centers and coffee tables. Today the company, which is managed by Alfred

Ruskin and William Morris. The Princeton exhibition and catalog inspired authors, collectors and antiques dealers to publish books and articles on Gustav Stickley, Elbert Hubbard, mission oak furniture, American art pottery, Prairie School architecture, rustic furniture and other components of the Arts & Crafts movement.

By 1984, when the latest team of decorators hired by Charles Sammons was preparing to furnish the new Sammons Wing, Arts & Crafts was no longer considered alien. Rather than hiding the Inn's heritage under another coat of paint or wallpaper, they sought to enhance it. Lighting fixtures in the bedrooms, meeting rooms and hallways were modeled after original Roycroft chandeliers and wall sconces. Carpeting and draperies proudly revealed their influence by English Arts & Crafts designers. Woodwork, trim and doors were made of stained oak; the furniture for the public hallways represented a pleasing combination of new Arts & Crafts furniture alongside recently purchased

Audi's widow, Aminy, and his son, Edward Audi, has become the largest and most respected of the Arts & Crafts furniture manufacturers, with a work force of 1600 craftsmen and craftswomen. Among the many examples of Arts & Crafts furniture that the firm has reproduced is the eight-foot tall-case clock the Roycrofters made in 1913 for the Grove Park Inn.

As the host site of the annual Arts & Crafts Conference, which features more than 130 exhibitors selling antiques and new works in the Arts & Crafts style, the Grove Park Inn has also recognized this opportunity to meet craftsmen and craftswomen who design and produce new Arts & Crafts furniture.

In 1989 the management commissioned Ben Little and Tom Harris, two Roycroft Renaissance craftsmen who own and operate the Schoolhouse Gallery in East Aurora and whose work was exhibited at the Arts & Crafts Conference, to make two, half-round Roycroft tables for the Grove Park Inn. This particular 48" table, model # 011, referred to in the 1906 Roycroft furniture catalog as a Serving Table, had not been included in the original 1913 order for the Roycroft Furniture Shop, but seemed appropriate for the hotel. The two craftsmen were fortunate to have access to an original version of this table, as well as to drawings made by artist Rixford Jennings (1906-1996), who, along with his father, had formerly worked at the Roycroft Shops. Their example proved so convincing — even down to

the Roycroft shopmark on the center leg — that the following year at the Arts & Crafts Conference a Grove Park Inn staff member proudly led them to two of the Inn's original, antique Roycroft half-round tables. Not until Little and Harris showed the employee their own incised shopmark inside the apron did he believe that the tables were reproductions. Today, with more than two decades' wear, the two half-round tables look even more authentic than they did when they were first made.

Among other conference craftsmen whose work is now a part of the Grove Park Inn collection is Robert Hause of Wilmington, N.C. His version of a Gustav Stickley hexagon table, model #624, was selected to remain at the Grove Park Inn after the 2007 Arts & Crafts Conference. In addition, the Inn also purchased from Hause a three-panel folding screen inspired by Gustav Stickley's model #84, with chamfered boards joined by butterfly keys serving both a functional and decorative purpose. Hause had also designed a three-panel screen which incorporated three inserts by Atlanta stained glass artist Susan McCracken. In the lower portion of the center panel Hause carved a popular Elbert Hubbard motto: "Blessed Is That Man Who Has Found His Work."

Before the following year's conference the Inn's management approached Robert Hause with the idea of reproducing one of the original Roycroft furnishings which has never been found: a large, three-panel

One of the great mysteries at the Grove Park Inn remains the fate of the original three-panel folding screen (above) made in the Roycrofter Furniture Shop around 1913. Using this single photograph and dimensions found in a Roycroft furniture catalog, woodworker Robert Hause, an exhibitor at the annual Grove Park Inn Arts & Crafts Conference, created the replica seen here (right) for use at the inn.

folding screen with three modeled leather inserts. Seen only in a vintage photograph, the Roycroft screen disappeared decades ago, but using the photograph and his knowledge of Roycroft joinery, Hause was able to duplicate the custom screen for the Grove Park Inn. The handmade leather inserts, also reproduced from the original photograph, were executed for Hause by Roycroft Renaissance craftsman Gordon Galloway. In this model, Hause includes the original Roycroft motto carved into the center panel: "All Men Can Not Be Heroes, But All Men Can Be Men."

More recently, Hause took on the challenge of duplicating the famous Roycroft "GPI" chair (see separate section). With an original 1913 chair in his personal antiques collection, Hause was able to study the Roycroft joinery closely, including the means by which the craftsmen at Biltmore Industries had in 1920 attached the demi-arms. Hause made the decision to also use the same exposed square-headed bolts to attach the arms to the rear posts on the four chairs that he made in 2008. He utilized a router and a chisel to duplicate freehand the "GPI" letters across the back of each top rail, but to avoid any confusion between his chairs and the originals he omitted the Roycroft orb-and-cross shopmark. Each chair he made is branded

with his personal mark on the underside. Two of his reproduction chairs are now in the Grove Park Inn's collection, while the other two are in the homes of Arts & Crafts collectors.

In 2008, Stuart Crick, a woodworker in Manassas, Virginia, and exhibitor at the annual Arts & Crafts Conference, created what he calls his 'Blue Collar' table for the Grove Park Inn. As Stuart explained, "the Blue Collar table speaks to the sometimes perplexing philosophy that is the American Arts and Crafts movement. With Charles and Henry Greene catering to high-end Arts and Crafts aficionados, Gustav Stickley sought to bring that same quality of craftsmanship to working families across America. It is within this spirit that the Blue Collar Table was created...its design embraces and blends traditional influences from Charles and Henry Greene, Gustav Stickley and Frank Lloyd Wright, while also integrating a contemporary style that creates the illusion that the table's lower shelf is floating between the two sides. The table's construction stretches from traditional to contemporary. It features an ebony splined, bread-board top, pegged mortise and tenon joints with ebony plugs, and a unique table-top button system that indicates when the solid-wood top has expanded or contracted." [www.stuswoodworks.com.]

PHOTO COURTESY OF GREG STALEY,
STALEY PHOTOGRAPHY

Woodworker Stuart Crick also added a piece to the Grove Park Inn's collection, but rather than making a reproduction of an earlier piece, Stuart designed his own interpretation of an Arts & Crafts library table, combining quartersawn oak with square ebony pegs.

THE RETURN OF THE GROVE PARK INN POOL TABLE

Included in Fred Seely's original plans for the Grove Park Inn was a lower-level Recreation Room, which included a forty-foot long swimming pool, a pool table, a billiard table and a three-lane bowling alley. The pool table and the billiard table, as well as the equipment for the three-lane bowling alley, were all purchased from the Brunswick-Balke-Collender Company of Baltimore. In addition, guests could also take advantage of the adjacent barbershop, a small pharmacy stocked with products from E. W. Grove's Paris Medicine Company and a game room. A ceiling made from twelve inches of poured concrete muffled any sounds rising from the Recreation Room toward the guests directly overhead in the Great Hall.

The expansion program begun in 1955 by new owner Charles Sammons required additional office space for a growing staff of accountants, sales managers, meeting planners and related personnel. The addition of an outdoor pool and tennis courts prompted the demolition of the aging indoor pool and manual bowling alley, leading to the conversion of the original Recreation Room into offices. At some point in the 1960s, as a former employee recalled, the original 1913 pool table was last seen being loaded onto the back of a pickup truck. The fate of it and the billiard table remained a mystery for more than forty years.

Then, in 2007, an Arts & Crafts pool table manufactured by the Brunswick-Balke-Collender Company and marked with a metal tag indicating it had once belonged to the Grove Park Inn suddenly appeared in an Internet auction. With little time to thoroughly research or document the pool table, the Grove Park Inn entered the bidding, but was beat out in the closing seconds. Fortunately, the winning bidder failed to make payment and the Grove Park Inn was offered the chance to buy back their pool table.

As it turned out, the furthest the pool table had traveled in forty years was to Charlotte, just two hours away. It still retained its original finish and only required new cloth before it could be put on display back at the Grove Park Inn.

Furniture of the
Arts & Crafts Movement

While Gustav Stickley, long considered the spokesman for the Arts & Crafts movement in American, stressed the creation of a total home environment consisting of handcrafted furniture, rugs, textiles, curtains, artwork and art pottery, a deeper appreciation for the design and craftsmanship which went into each piece of furniture can best be gained by a close inspection of individual pieces.

The Grove Park Inn's collection of Arts & Crafts furniture is unique not only for its sheer number, but for the opportunity it offers each visitor to closely inspect nearly every piece in the hotel. Their Morris chairs, settles, sideboards and dressers are used each day by their guests, lining the hallways, tucked into alcoves and filling the Great Hall — even remaining in the 142 original guest rooms.

The pieces selected for close examination in this book reflect an intention to include a number of different Arts & Crafts furniture manufacturers, from such well-known firms as the Craftsman Workshops of Gustav Stickley, the Roycroft Furniture Shop of Elbert Hubbard and the Charles Limbert Furniture Company to lesser known companies, including Lifetime Furniture, the White Furniture Company, the Quaint Art Furniture Company and a company yet to be identified.

While all of these firms and individuals adhered to the basic principles of the Arts & Crafts movement, namely an emphasis on handcraftsmanship, the utilization of native materials (i.e. oak), the elimination

Although the hall seat is more often associated with Victorian furniture, one manufacturer produced this Arts & Crafts example using highly-figured quartersawn oak. This hall seat, which came to the Grove Park Inn from the Midwest, was selected by woodworker Norm Abrams to be reproduced on his television show, *The New Yankee Workshop*.

of unnecessary ornamentation and the achievement of a simple, yet elegant design, the interpretation of these principles varied from firm to firm, often from designer to designer. Only through close inspection can we examine the various construction techniques each employed, compare them to one another and draw our own conclusions as to which Arts & Crafts firms deserved our recognition and appreciation.

Armed with the objectivity only time can provide, future historians are apt to look back on the first hundred years since the introduction of the Arts & Crafts movement to America around 1900 and declare that, despite the intrusion of two world wars and a national depression, the Arts & Crafts movement persevered throughout the entire twentieth century.

That news will come as no surprise to those of us in Asheville, for we have long known that here and at the Grove Park Inn, the Arts & Crafts movement never really ended.

TOP The adjustable peg on this Morris chair is a functional and simple answer to adjust the back to a comfortable angle.

RIGHT The carving and hardware on this server door sets the piece apart as a likely British Arts & Crafts construction.

Two-Door Bookcase with Drawers

LIFETIME FURNITURE
GRAND RAPIDS BOOKCASE & CHAIR COMPANY
CA. 1911

This handsome Arts & Crafts bookcase was added to the Grove Park Inn's collection in 1988. Although unsigned, the unusual positioning of the three drawers over the two doors represents a design favored by the Grand Rapids Bookcase & Chair Company formerly located in Hastings, Michigan. This particular bookcase is nearly identical to model no. 7274 illustrated in their 1911 catalog. (*Lifetime Furniture: Grand Rapids Bookcase & Chair Company*, ca. 1911, reprinted by Turn of the Century Editions, New York, 1981, pg. 53.].

That year two neighboring furniture companies — the Barber Brothers Chair Company and the Grand Rapids Bookcase Company — merged to form the Grand Rapids Bookcase & Chair Company and began producing a line of Arts & Crafts furniture under the Lifetime label. Included in the Grove Park Inn's collection is a similar bookcase bearing a brass tag from the Grand Rapids Bookcase & Chair Company and a sideboard bearing the firm's Lifetime decal. (For additional historical information see *The Official Price Guide to American Arts & Crafts*, 3rd ed., David Rago and Bruce Johnson, House of Collectibles, New York, 2003, pg. 200-205.]

This bookcase is typical of much of the Arts & Crafts furniture produced in Grand Rapids, for it incorporates quality materials and respected construction techniques, yet pays but shallow homage to the ideals of the Arts & Crafts philosophy. For example, what appear to be several individual panes of glass in each of the doors is actually one large sheet of glass set behind a thin oak latticework. This technique provided the appearance of extensive handwork but at a small fraction of the cost. In a similar manner, the two exposed tenons at the lower front corners of the bookcase are actually false tenons — strips of wood cut and inserted into a slot mortised in the front legs to give the appearance of a structural through-tenon. Their purpose is purely ornamental.

That having been said, the quality of construction needs no apologies. This bookcase consists of quality oak,

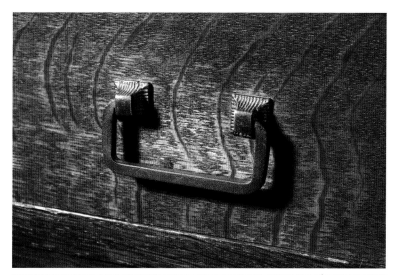

The simple brass pull compliments the grain of the quartersawn oak on the drawer front. The evenly spaced dovetails at the back of the drawer are a sign of quality construction, for some manufacturers reduced costs by simply nailing the back joints together. The addition of the runner beneath the drawer strengthened and insured the durability of the piece.

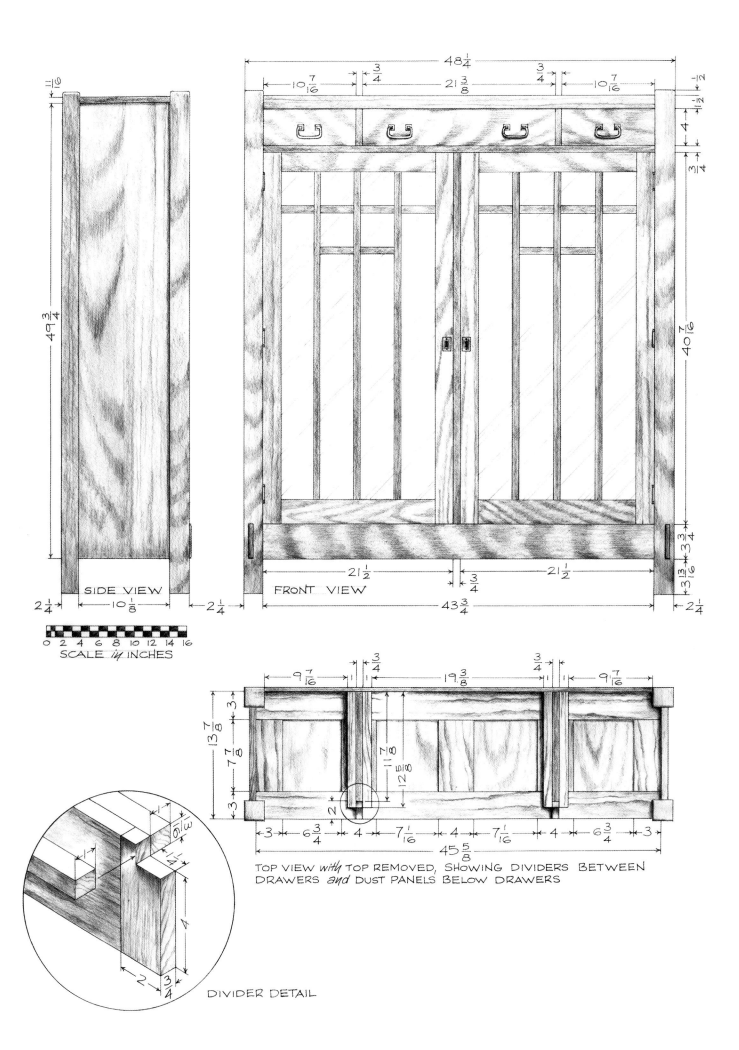

SIDE VIEW

FRONT VIEW

SCALE *in* INCHES

TOP VIEW *with* TOP REMOVED, SHOWING DIVIDERS BETWEEN
DRAWERS *and* DUST PANELS BELOW DRAWERS

DIVIDER DETAIL

The lamp on top of this bookcase is of recent vintage manufactured by the Arroyo Craftsman lighting company. The pottery pictured inside the bookcase is an assortment of molded art pottery produced by various firms during the 1920s and 1930s.

including quartersawn oak on the doors and drawer fronts. The sides and bottoms of the drawers are also constructed of oak and employ machine cut dovetails at the joints. The hardware is original to the bookcase and appears similar to that manufactured by the Grand Rapids Brass Company and utilized on several signed pieces of Lifetime furniture. [*Arts & Crafts Furniture Design: The Grand Rapids Contribution*, 1895-1915, Don Marek, Grand Rapids Art Museum, Grand Rapids, MI, 1987, pg. 63.]

The design of this bookcase is well proportioned, beginning with the four sturdy corner posts that provide a strong functional and visual framework for the case. The eye is immediately drawn to the row of drawers across the top, each perfectly accented with hardware, which is neither too heavy for their upper location nor too light for such a large bookcase. The symmetrical arrangement of the three drawers was

carefully considered by the designer, who aligned the dividers between the two small drawers and the larger center drawer with one of the vertical mullions of the grillwork in each of the doors. The center drawer straddles the center post between the doors, providing a visual balance point, not unlike the trunk of a tree and its spreading branches. The base of this bookcase is firmly rooted to the ground by the sturdy corner posts, the two tenons and by the wide toeboard providing support for the center post and the three upper drawers. Finally, the removable shelves on either side of the center post provide the homeowner with the capability to adjust the shelves to accommodate their various books or, as in this case, their collection of art pottery.

The result is a well-built Arts & Crafts bookcase that is as functional as it is attractive, yet is far more affordable than similar bookcases produced by either L. & J. G. Stickley or their brother Gustav Stickley.

Tall Case Clock

ROYCROFT FURNITURE SHOP
CA. 1914-1918

In 1986, when I first visited the Grove Park Inn to begin researching its Arts & Crafts heritage, a few members of the staff would occasionally make vague references to "the other clock." At first I assumed they were referring to the eight-foot tall clock the Roycrofters had made for the Grove Park Inn in 1913 and which had for decades stood in the Great Hall. But as I asked more questions it became apparent that a second clock had been — and might still be — somewhere in the Grove Park Inn.

The mystery of the second clock was not solved until the completion of the Vanderbilt Wing in 1988. That year the owners of the Grove Park Inn, Charles and Elaine Sammons, moved their permanent suite from Rooms 220 and 221 in the original Main Inn to new quarters atop the Vanderbilt Wing. The Sammons, who had purchase the Grove Park Inn in 1955, lived in Dallas, but a suite had always been kept ready for them in the event they would make an unannounced visit to the hotel. Only the housekeeping staff had access to their suite. In 1988, as the hotel staff was preparing their new rooms, Mrs. Sammons decided that one item in their former suite should go on public display. That item was this rare, six-foot Roycroft clock.

While the existence of the second clock is no longer a mystery, its origin and its history remain so. Of the hundreds of photographs taken of the Grove Park Inn since 1913, this second Roycroft clock does not appear in any of them. Given its more modest six-foot frame, it undoubtedly had been intended for a normal-sized room, perhaps one that had never been photographed in its entirety. Among the possibilities are the Ladies' Parlor, the Writing Room, the Recreation Room and Fred Seely's personal office. All of these rooms were originally decorated with Arts & Crafts furniture in 1913 and remained relatively intact until 1955, when Charles Sammons purchased the hotel and embarked on a major remodeling program. At that time or soon thereafter, the clock, had it been in one of these rooms, could have been moved to the Sammons's

new suite, where it remained virtually unnoticed for more than thirty years.

A comparison of the two Roycroft clocks made for the Grove Park Inn would seem to indicate that the clocks were neither designed by the same person nor made at the same time. The earlier 1913 eight-foot tall clock features exposed keyed tenons, pegged joints, over-sized strap hinges and a sweeping arch — all design elements associated with early Arts & Crafts furniture [see separate entry for more details]. In contrast, this six-foot tall clock has been scaled down, something every major Arts & Crafts designer and furniture manufacturer, including Gustav Stickley, L. & J.G. Stickley and Charles Limbert, began doing by 1914. Gone are the two, long strap hinges and the three butterfly hinges; the two door pulls are modest by Roycroft standards; the sweeping arch has been diluted and the exposed tenons eliminated. Only the thick, overhanging top — a familiar Roycroft design element — has been retained, along with the orb-and-cross carved into the front.

While no correspondence has surfaced to confirm the purchase of this clock by the Grove Park Inn, we do know that between 1917-1918 Fred Seely ordered additional furniture from the Roycrofters for his new business, Biltmore Industries (see separate entry). Seely had purchased the weaving and woodworking enterprise from Edith Vanderbilt in 1917 and had soon thereafter begun construction on five buildings for his workshops, showrooms and offices adjacent to the hotel. Once his office had been completed, he purchased a number of chairs and desks, each bearing the Roycroft orb-and-cross. Although the business, buildings and contents were sold several years after Fred Seely's death in 1942, many of the Roycroft pieces remained in the buildings and are currently on display at the Biltmore Industries Museum on the grounds next to the Grove Park Inn.

Although by 1917 the Roycroft Furniture Shop had nearly ceased to exist, having been moved out of their

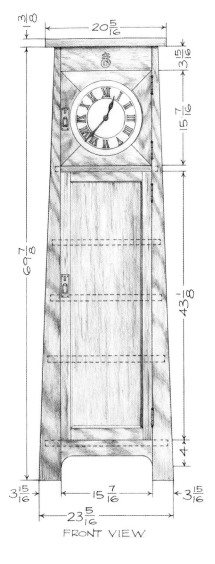

FRONT VIEW

SCALE *in* INCHES

DOTTED LINES INDICATE
LOCATIONS *of* SHELVES

EACH GRID SQUARE
REPRESENTS 1 INCH

BOTTOM SIDE DETAIL

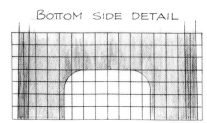

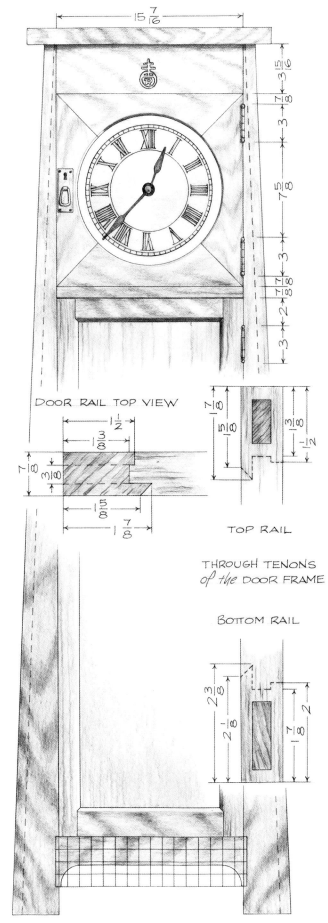

DOOR RAIL TOP VIEW

THROUGH TENONS
of the DOOR FRAME

BOTTOM RAIL

TOP RAIL

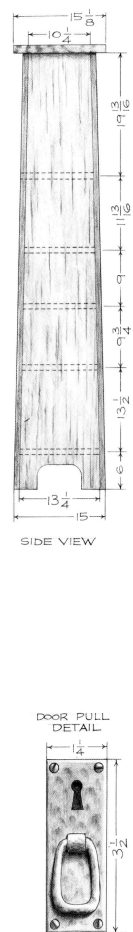

SIDE VIEW

DOOR PULL
DETAIL

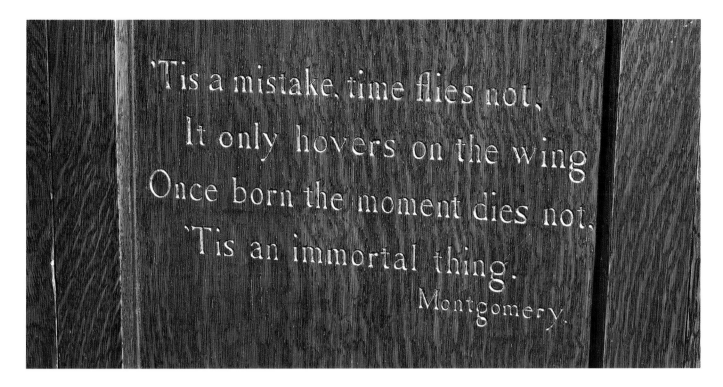

original building by Elbert "Bert" Hubbard II as furniture orders declined dramatically, they apparently were able to complete Fred Seely's order. It is possible that at the time Fred Seely placed the furniture order for his office at Biltmore Industries he may also have ordered this six-foot clock for either that office, his office at the Grove Park Inn or one of the other rooms at the hotel. Given the gradual departure of many of the craftsmen and designers who had worked on the 1913 commission, including Victor Toothaker [see separate entry], this theory would explain why the six-foot Roycroft clock differs substantially in design, although not in quality, from the eight-foot clock constructed in 1913.

One unusual element, which both clocks share, is the presence of a carved verse on the panel of the front door. Inspired by Elbert Hubbard's passion for inspiration mottos, Fred Seely had several epigrams painted on the rock walls in the Great Hall in 1913 as well as on the walls in the workshops of Biltmore Industries in 1917, many of which still survive (see pages 46-47). Given the fact that he owned a woodworking and woodcarving enterprise, it is likely that Fred Seely selected and personally supervised the carving of the verses of each of the two clocks.

The stanza on the eight-foot tall clock which greeted guests as they arrived through the front doors of the Grove Park Inn came from a poem entitled "A Psalm of Life" (1838) and written by Henry Wadsworth Longfellow (1807-1882):

Not enjoyment and not sorrow,
Is our destined end or way;
But to act that each tomorrow,
Find us further than today.

For the second clock Fred Seely selected a quotation (shown above) from "Time: A Rhapsody" (1850), a poem by British poet James Montgomery (1771-1854).

The case of this six-foot clock is strikingly similar to a standard Roycroft form — their #080 Magazine Pedestal. Standing 63" high (just eleven" shorter than this clock), their magazine stand had remained in production since nearly the beginning of the Roycroft Furniture Shop, becoming a form every craftsman in the workshop knew quite well. In 1917 or 1918, in fact, it appears they built a model #080 Magazine Pedestal for Fred Seely's new office at Biltmore Industries — and may have relied on it for the inspiration for this particular clock. Both pieces feature a thick, overhanging top, tapering sides of solid wood rather than panel construction, and an abbreviated arch on the sides. Behind the lower door of this custom made clock are four original shelves — the same number as are found on the Roycroft Magazine Pedestal.

Since the Roycrofters are believed to have only made five tall-case clocks during their entire history, it is very likely that this particular clock was their final one. Coming at a time when the Roycroft Furniture Shop was nearly closed, Fred Seely's order may have found the shop without the services of an experienced furniture designer. Without any blueprints, plans or patterns to fall back on, the Roycrofters — or Fred Seely — may have decided to build a clock which incorporated many of the same design elements as their Magazine Pedestal. The result is one of the finest examples of a tall-case clock known to Arts & Crafts collectors and rivals those designed and crafted in the workshops of either Gustav or L. & J.G. Stickley.

The "GPI" Chair

ROYCROFT FURNITURE SHOP
1913

As Fred Seely and E.W. Grove worked on the plans for the Grove Park Inn during the summer of 1912, they decided that they would need 400 chairs for the dining room, all of which had to be in place for their official opening banquet, which took place on Saturday evening, July 12, 1913. The chairs were arranged around unusual tables that, in all likelihood, were designed by Seely. Each consisted of an extremely heavy cast iron base formed in the shape of the bell of a trumpet. On top of each pedestal was a separate, twelve-inch circular disk of iron, designed to spin on a center bolt attached to the top of the slender shaft of the circular base. A wooden top was then attached to this circular disk, enabling the diners or waiters, if they wished, to rotate the tabletop. The iron table bases, like the gigantic andirons in the twin fireplaces in the Great Hall, were produced not by the Roycrofters, as has often been presumed, but by the nearby Asheville Supply and Foundry Company.

The chairs Fred Seely selected to accompany these dining tables came directly from the 1912 *Roycroft Hand Made Furniture* catalog, which Bert Hubbard had mailed him in July of that same year. On October 30, 1912 Seely and Hubbard signed a contract calling for 700 pieces of Roycroft furniture to be delivered by July 1, 1913. Of those 700 pieces, 400 were to be the chairs for the dining room. The chair, model #030 ½, was a variation on the model #030 dining room chairs Seely had selected for his personal use in 1906. While nearly all of the Roycroft furniture Seely had ordered between 1904 and 1909 had been of mahogany, all of the furniture destined for the Grove Park Inn was to be constructed of white or red oak. As listed in the 1912 catalog, this particular chair would have cost $13.50 in mahogany and just $11.00 in oak, a detail that would not have escaped the frugal Fred Seely.

It is interesting to note that chair model #030 which Fred Seely had earlier selected for his home was still available in 1912 at the same price as the model #030 ½ which he selected for the Grove Park Inn. There were only three subtle differences between the two chairs:

1. The earlier model #030 had the bulbous Mackmurdo-style feet often found on Roycroft furniture.

2. The tops of the back posts were rounded rather than square.

3. The center back slat had been formed in the shape of an hourglass rather than a straight rectangle found in #030 ½.

Since the price for the two slightly different styles of chairs was identical, Seely seems to have found the more austere, plainer version more appropriate for his plans for the Grove Park Inn.

The model #030 ½ chair features a standard Roycroft arrangement of just four stretchers between the legs, each sturdy, yet rather narrow, especially when compared to the extremely wide stretchers often incorporated into the dining chairs of Gustav Stickley. The leg stretchers were not pegged, but, in the Roycrofters' defense, this does not seem to be an inherent weakness, for despite their constant use — and occasional abuse — in the dining room from 1913 until 1955 and elsewhere afterwards, these chairs rarely suffer from loose joints.

The chair seats consisted of a thick piece of black sole leather wrapped around the four seat rails and notched for the front and rear legs. Although the opening page of the introduction to the 1912 catalog states, "the seats on all chairs not upholstered are a heavy sole-leather, strongly supported underneath with heavy webbing," this was not the case with the model #030 ½ chairs made for the Grove Park Inn. The leather, supplied to the Roycrofters by the Ashtabula Hide & Leather Company of Ashtabula, Ohio, while quite thick and secured with half-inch steel tacks spaced closely together, had no support other than its own inherent strength. Today, when a Roycroft "GPI" chair does surface with its original leather seat, the dry, brittle leather typically has cracked or torn.

Credit for the strength of these chairs is due to a great extent to the width and construction of the seat rails. Each is cut from highly figured, quartersawn

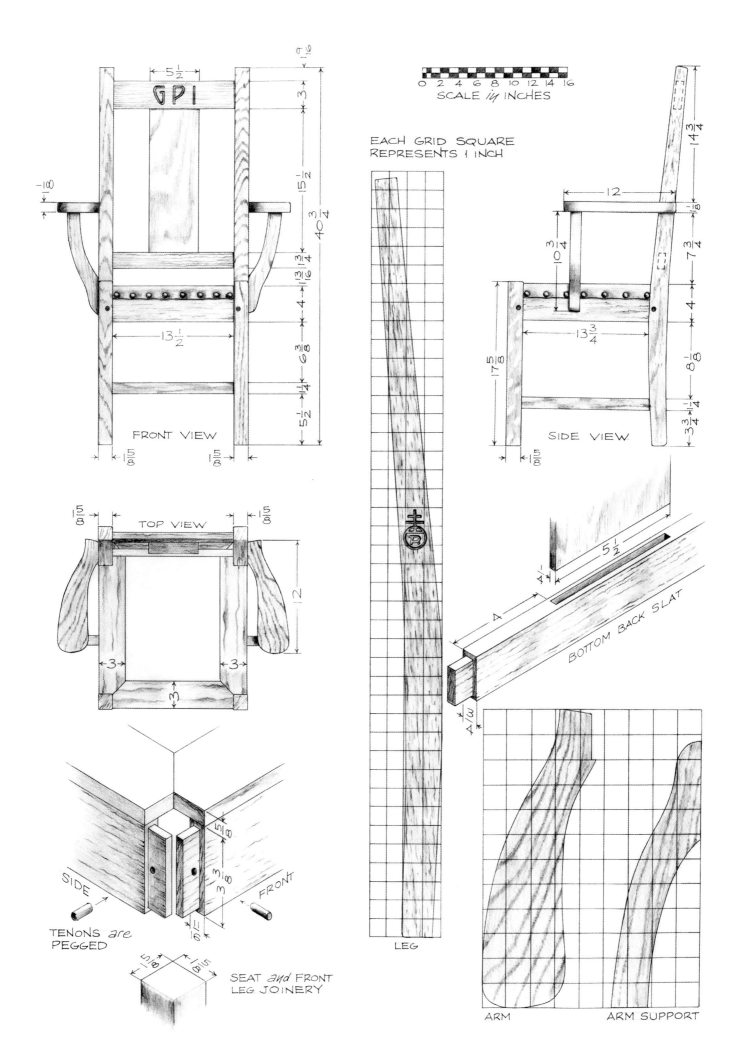

FRONT VIEW

GP1

TOP VIEW

SIDE VIEW

SCALE in INCHES

EACH GRID SQUARE
REPRESENTS 1 INCH

BOTTOM BACK SLAT

TENONS are
PEGGED

SEAT and FRONT
LEG JOINERY

LEG

ARM

ARM SUPPORT

The craftsmen at the Roycroft Furniture Shop were kept busy the spring of 1913 building, staining and finishing 400 oak dining rooms chairs, each with two inscriptions: the initials of the hotel and the Roycroft shopmark.

oak and measures four inches in width. In addition to being deeply mortised into the front and back posts, each joint is pinned with a ⅜"- diameter oak peg.

Care was also taken in selecting highly figured oak boards for the back slat in each of the chairs, as well as for the top and bottom rail securing it in place. The Roycrofters did not pin the top or bottom rails to the back posts either for additional strength or, as was often the case with some Arts & Crafts workshops, to provide a decorative element.

Unlike most Arts & Crafts furniture shops and factories, the Roycrofters relied on their own trademark to provide a key element of decoration. Whereas Charles Limbert, L. & J.G. Stickley, Albert Stickley and Gustav Stickley each directed their craftsmen to attach their firm's unique paper label, decal, metal tag or brand in an unobtrusive place, Elbert Hubbard took the opposite approach. As with his books, magazines, motto cards and metalwork, Hubbard insisted that the Roycroft orb-and-cross or, in some cases, the entire word "Roycroft," not only be permanently carved into the wood, but also carved in a prominent location. Every chair pictured in the 1912 *Roycroft Hand Made Furniture* catalog features either the orb-and-cross or the word "Roycroft" carved into the front seat rail. There would be no mistaking who made any piece of Roycroft furniture.

Yet while Fred Seely had earlier demonstrated in his correspondence that he, too, prized the Roycroft shopmark on his personal furniture, he may well be the only person who ever persuaded Elbert Hubbard to move the Roycroft shopmark to a less visible location. With rare exception, the Roycroft dining chairs made for the Grove Park Inn will have the Roycroft orb-and-cross on the side of the right rear post. In only a few instances does the Roycroft orb-and-cross retain its original location on the front of the chair. It seems safe

to presume that since the model #030 ½ chairs were a standard Roycroft design, some chairs had already been made prior to the signing of the Grove Park Inn contract. In all likelihood, these chairs — with their Roycroft mark on the front of the seat rail — were pulled from the small inventory of furniture that the Roycrofters had amassed and were then included among the 400 chairs Seely had ordered.

Seely's motive for moving the Roycroft shopmark may have had less to do with the mark itself than it did with an additional feature he had requested. Across the front of each of the top rails Seely instructed the Roycroft craftsmen to carve the letters "GPI" in an Arts & Crafts typeface. It only stands to reason, then, that Seely believed the addition of the Roycroft shopmark on the front of each chair would either confuse his guests or would detract from the Inn's own trademark. Given the size of the Grove Park Inn commission and its importance to the revitalized Roycroft Furniture Shop, it is doubtful Elbert Hubbard had any problem with Fred Seely's request.

On occasion, an example of a Roycroft chair model #030 ½ without the "GPI" carved lettering will surface, prompting the question: could it have been made for the Grove Park Inn?

At least three possible origins of such a chair should be considered:

1. The chair may be one sold to a Roycroft customer with no connection to the Grove Park Inn.

2. The chair may be part of an order of Roycroft furniture which Fred Seely placed in 1917 or 1918, when he purchased an Asheville Arts & Crafts woodworking and hand-weaving enterprise called Biltmore Industries from Edith Vanderbilt. When Seely needed additional furniture for the workshops and offices he had built on land adjacent to the Grove Park Inn, he again turned to his friend Bert Hubbard and the few

remaining craftsmen at the declining Roycroft Furniture Shop. Included in his order were several model #030 ½ chairs, but without the "GPI" initials. Examples of these chairs and other Roycroft office furniture that Fred Seely purchased are on display in the Biltmore Industries Museum next to the Grovewood Gallery on the grounds by the Grove Park Inn (see Grovewood.com).

3. The chair may be one of the original Grove Park Inn chairs which were sold to the public or given to employees after the Inn began a series of major remodeling projects starting in 1955. In one known case, several of the Roycroft chairs were purchased by the owner of an Asheville nursing home, who had the chairs refinished and the letters "GPI" completely sanded off. Such chairs are easy to recognize simply by feeling the depression left by the belt sander across the front of the top rail. A more recent owner of a pair of these former Grove Park Inn chairs commissioned a woodcarver to duplicate the "GPI" letters in these chairs, but they can still be recognized by the depression left in 1955 by the sander.

While the Roycrofters completed all 400 of the chairs by Fred Seely's deadline of July 1, 1913, they

As it first appeared in 1913, each Roycroft chair featured a leather seat and the hotel's initials across the back, but no arms. Of the 400 chairs produced, only four are known to have retained their original appearance.

were not yet finished with them. Early guests at the Inn complained to Fred Seely, who had remained in Asheville to manage the hotel, that the Roycroft chairs were uncomfortable. Several must have suggested that the chairs needed arms, for in a letter dated July 3, 1920, Seely wrote to Bert Hubbard:

"You remember that you cut out four hundred dining room chairs for us when the Inn was built.

"I have an idea, as our people are usually well along in life, we could make these chairs more comfortable if we had a nice little arm on them, and I wish you would have the boys see what they can do about working out a sample pair of arms for the chair such as you made for the dining room.

"I would not want them to come very far to the front and would want them to be quite stocky to be in keeping with the chair; for instance, I would like for the arm itself to be made of about 1¾" stuff and not of ⅞'s. Then I think the little riser, which would go from the side board of the chair to the arm would be mortised into it, should be about as big in section as the upright which carries the back.

"I am making a little sketch of it, and am wondering if you could get out a sample or two ready to screw onto the chair, and if you could give me a figure on about 350 chairs, ready for us to put them on here. I simply want to make them that much more comfortable." [private collection]

Activity at the Roycroft Furniture Shop had slowed in 1920 [see separate section], prompting Seely to write on November 3, 1920, "Are the boys doing anything about the chair arms for dining room requested some time ago?" [private collection]

The 350 pairs of oak demi-arms, each measuring twelve inches from front to back, arrived from the Roycroft Furniture Shop a few weeks later and were sent across the road to the workshop Seely had constructed for the woodworkers and woodcarvers of Biltmore Industries. Then, in 1921, as he could spare them, the Roycroft "GPI" chairs from the dining room were carried over to Biltmore Industries a few at a time to be fitted with arms. The process required that the woodworkers remove one or two of the steel tacks before cutting out a small section of the leather seat wrapped around the side rails. Each riser was then screwed to a side rail, with each screw head recessed and hidden beneath an oak plug sanded flush with the surface of the wood.

The means of attaching the back of each arm to one of the rear posts, however, proved less satisfactory. Rather than recessing the screw as had been done on the risers, each arm is generally, although not always, attached to a rear post with a square-headed lag bolt,

In 1921, after complaints from diners, Fred Seely had the Roycrofters make 350 pairs of demi-arms for the chairs in the dining room. A refinished orginal, 1913 Roycroft chair with 1921 Roycroft arms stands on the left; the reproduction on the right by woodworker Robert Hause (his shopmark replaces the Roycrofter's to avoid any confusion) has been added to the Grove Park Inn's collection.

with the black head of the bolt left exposed. Given Fred Seely's proven penchant for details and his insistence on such matters being handled perfectly and precisely, it is difficult to imagine that these exposed bolts met his standards, especially given his high regard for both his Roycroft furniture and the opinions of his guests. It is possible that the recessed screw technique used for the risers simply did not provide the required strength for the backs of the arms. If that were the case, then Seely might have ordered his woodworkers to replace the original screws with longer and stronger lag bolts, despite their obtrusiveness.

The fifty Roycroft-G.P.I. chairs that were not fitted with pairs of demi-arms had, as seen in early photographs, been pressed into service in other parts of the hotel, including the Recreation Room in the lower level where several armless Roycroft "GPI" chairs had been arranged for spectators next to the three-lane bowling alley. The 400 Roycroft "GPI" chairs continued to be used at the Grove Park Inn until 1955, when decorators hired by new owner Charles Sammons removed them

from the dining room. While several of the chairs, all with arms, survived the purge and remain at the Grove Park Inn, the majority were sold to the general public, along with other original Arts & Crafts furnishings, reportedly for as little as five dollars each. In 1988 the Grove Park Inn was able to purchase from a private individual four of the original Roycroft "GPI" chairs that had not been fitted with the demi-arms. Each of the fours chairs, however, had been painted and required a total restoration.

Estimating how many of the original 400 Roycroft "GPI" chairs still exist remains a matter of speculation. The Grove Park Inn has approximately twenty of the chairs in its collection; the author knows of approximately eighty more which have either passed through local and national auction houses or have been added to the inventories of museums and Arts & Crafts collectors. Beyond that, calculating how many of the undocumented 300 Roycroft "GPI" chairs have either been destroyed since 1913 or are quietly sitting in an Asheville home or private collection is anyone's guess.

Single Drawer Library Table

CHARLES LIMBERT
CA. 1906-1910

One of the inspirations for the architectural design of the Grove Park Inn was the Old Faithful Inn at Yellowstone National Park, an inn which had been furnished in part in 1906 by Charles P. Limbert (1854-1922), a well-known American Arts & Crafts furniture manufacturer. Ironically, although both E.W. Grove and Fred Seely studied photographs of the interior of the Old Faithful Inn, which included numerous examples of Limbert furniture, none of the furniture from this Grand Rapids, Michigan manufacturer made its way into the Grove Park Inn until the furnishing of the Sammons Wing in 1984.

Although his furniture excels in design, materials and construction, Charles Limbert is not as well known today as Gustav Stickley and Elbert Hubbard, primarily because Limbert had little interest in writing about the Arts & Crafts movement, in flagrant self-promotion or in publishing his own magazine, as was the case with both Stickley and Hubbard. Limbert was born in 1854 and by age 35 had settled in Grand Rapids, where he established a reputation as a successful furniture salesman and manufacturer. Among the companies he represented was the Old Hickory Furniture Company [see separate entry], whose rustic furniture he enjoyed in his home on Fisk Lake, where the lifelong bachelor lived with his sister.

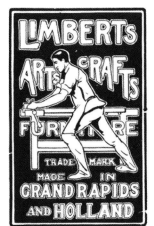

Charles Limbert's first line of Arts & Crafts furniture appeared in 1902 and for the next fifteen years his designers and craftsmen produced a wide variety of forms in a complete line of household furnishings. His early work, like that of Gustav Stickley, tends toward the more massive, heavier Arts & Crafts style, as evidenced by this library table. From 1904-1910 Limbert furniture reflects a range of influences, including Prairie School and Frank Lloyd Wright, the Glasgow School and Charles Rennie Mackintosh, and the Vienna School and Josef Hoffmann. His later Arts & Crafts designs, which he phased out around 1917, is marked by inlaid woods, lighter frames and colors, and the use of fabrics rather than dark leather upholstery. Charles Limbert died in 1922, but the firm he founded remained in business until 1944.

As Limbert collectors are quick to point out, especially in examples such as this 48" library table, model #1129, Charles Limbert often combined the best of Stickley and Roycroft in a single piece. [*Limbert Furniture Catalog No. 119*, reprinted by Turn of the Century Editions, New York, 1981, pg. 39.] In this example we find the massiveness of the Roycrofters in the four stout legs balanced by the sweeping arch and overhanging top more often found in the furniture of Gustav Stickley. The result is the finest example of an Arts & Crafts library table in the Grove Park Inn's collection.

Although Charles Limbert is often praised for his use of splines — thin strips of oak inserted into slots cut the entire length of two boards being glued together — to provide more strength and stability on tabletops, this particular library table proves to be an exception. Instead, the boards in this top are joined together with a shallow tongue-and-groove joint, much like that found in the furniture of Gustav Stickley. The top and long single drawer are firmly supported by four large legs, each three inches square and punctuated by wide exposed tenons. The legs are constructed of three 1" × 3" boards glued together. The thick lower shelf is secured to the side stretchers with exposed tenons, each of which is pinned into place with oak pegs located on top of each of the stretchers.

The massiveness of this low, stout table might have left it looking like a block of oak had it not been for the decision to cut an arch not only in the front of

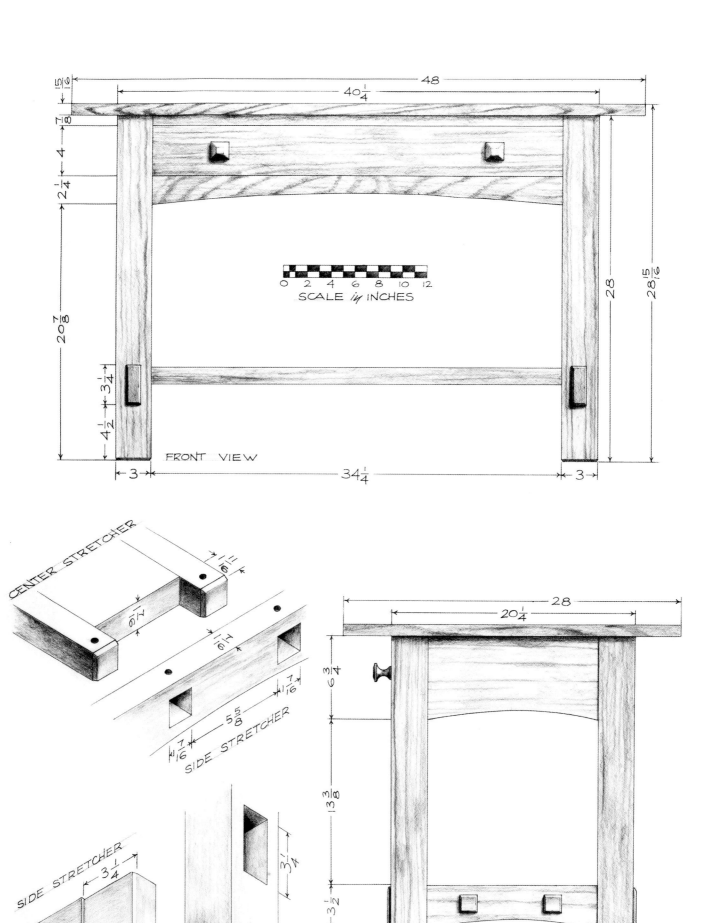

CENTER STRETCHER

SIDE STRETCHER

SIDE STRETCHER

FRONT VIEW

SIDE VIEW

SCALE in INCHES

The arched aprons, overhanging top, brass hardware and exposed tenons combine to make this Charles Limbert library table one of the finest examples of a simple, yet elegant form.

the table, but in the upper side stretchers as well. These sweeping arches, along with the overhanging top, add the drama and lightness, which this table needed to make the leap from a workbench form to a sophisticated library table.

The single drawer deserves attention as well, for it, too, speaks for the quality of design and construction inherent in most Limbert furniture. Like the rest of the table, the front of the drawer is quartersawn oak. Unlike Gustav Stickley and the Roycrofters, who preferred large, heavy drawer pulls, the designer of this table opted instead for simple, square brass knobs with

chamfered facets. Rather than adding to the weightiness of this piece, the chamfered knobs compliment the exposed tenons near the base of the legs — and don't compete with the arch for our attention. The sides and bottom of the drawer are also made of oak and the joints are dovetailed for additional strength. Finally, the piece is signed with Limbert's brand on the inside of the drawer. [For additional information, see *Kindred Styles: The Arts & Crafts Furniture of Charles P. Limbert*, edited by A. Patricia Bartinique, Published by Gallery 532, New York, 1995.]

Slant Arm Morris Chair

QUAINT ART FURNITURE COMPANY
CA. 1909-1915

To most Arts & Crafts collectors, the name "Quaint" conjures up images of the Arts & Crafts furniture produced by Albert Stickley in Grand Rapids, Michigan, and signed with a brass tag marked "Quaint Furniture." Arts & Crafts researchers Dr. Michael Clark and Jill Thomas-Clark discovered, however, that Albert Stickley was not the only manufacturer to adopt the name "Quaint." In 1909, not far from the Craftsman Workshops of Gustav Stickley in Syracuse, four men formed a new enterprise known as the Quaint Art Furniture Company to begin manufacturing and marketing a line of Arts & Crafts furniture. ["The Quaint Art Furniture Company of Syracuse, New York" by Dr. Michael Clark and Jill Thomas-Clark, *Style 1900*, vol. 9, no. 3, August 1996, pg. 12-14.].

The name "Quaint" had been borrowed from the British, who used it to identify what in America was commonly called either Mission or Arts & Crafts. It may have been suggested by George Perin, the new firm's general manager and chief designer, who for several years had worked in Syracuse as a cabinetmaker, furniture designer and woodworker. Perin undoubtedly knew of Gustav Stickley and his furniture, either through Stickley's retail store, his magazine *The Craftsman* or one of the Arts & Crafts expositions Stickley sponsored in Syracuse. In 1910, the year after George Perin and his partners had begun manufacturing Arts & Crafts furniture in Syracuse, Gustav Stickley attacked in print "an army of imitators [who had] at once began to turn out large quantities of furniture which was designed in what seemed to them the same style." [*Stickley 1910 Craftsman Furniture Catalogs*, Dover Publications, NY, 1979, pg. 8.] Among those

whom Gustav Stickley singled out were both the Roycrofters and the name "Quaint," which we now suspect referred not to his brother Albert but to his nearby competitor — the Quaint Art Furniture Company.

This five-slat, slant arm Morris chair may explain Stickley's irritation with the Quaint Art Furniture Company, for it bears an uncanny resemblance to one of Stickley's most popular forms, his #369 Morris chair. Similar to Gustav Stickley's version, this Quaint Art Furniture chair features a slant arm over five wide slats with the front and rear legs protruding through the quartersawn oak arm. Each of the major joints are pinned with oak pegs, although some of the pegs on the Quaint Art Furniture Company chair are slightly smaller than those Stickley's craftsmen used. The adjustable back of this chair is quite similar to that designed by Gustav Stickley: The two back posts pivot on a pair of oak pins in the rear legs while the back rests against a second pair of oak pins placed into one of four holes drilled into the rear portion of the arms.

Collectors who encounter an unsigned Quaint Art Furniture Company Morris chair can distinguish it from similar chairs made in the Craftsman Workshops of Gustav Stickley one of two ways. First, whereas the Stickley Morris chair featured corbels on both the front and rear legs, the Quaint Morris chair only has corbels under the arms on the front legs. Second, the exposed tenons on the Quaint Morris chair are only a half-inch wide, compared with Stickley's tenons, which are nearly three-quarters of an inch in width.

What sets this particular Morris chair apart not only from those of Gustav Stickley, but other designers as well is the triangular space purposely left vacant beneath each of the arms. By lowering the top rail into which the five side slats are mortised, George Perin created an eye-catching, dramatic space, which frames and accents the slanted arm in a way even Gustav Stickley would have appreciated.

While this particular Morris chair has lost its original paper label, possibly during an early refinishing, it

LEFT The pair of table lamps and the two tile-topped coffee tables are reproductions purchased in recent years by the Grove Park Inn for the Sammons Wing (1984). Visible in the background are the original Main Inn (1913), the Vanderbilt Wing (1988) and the stone steps leading to the Inn's underground spa (2001).

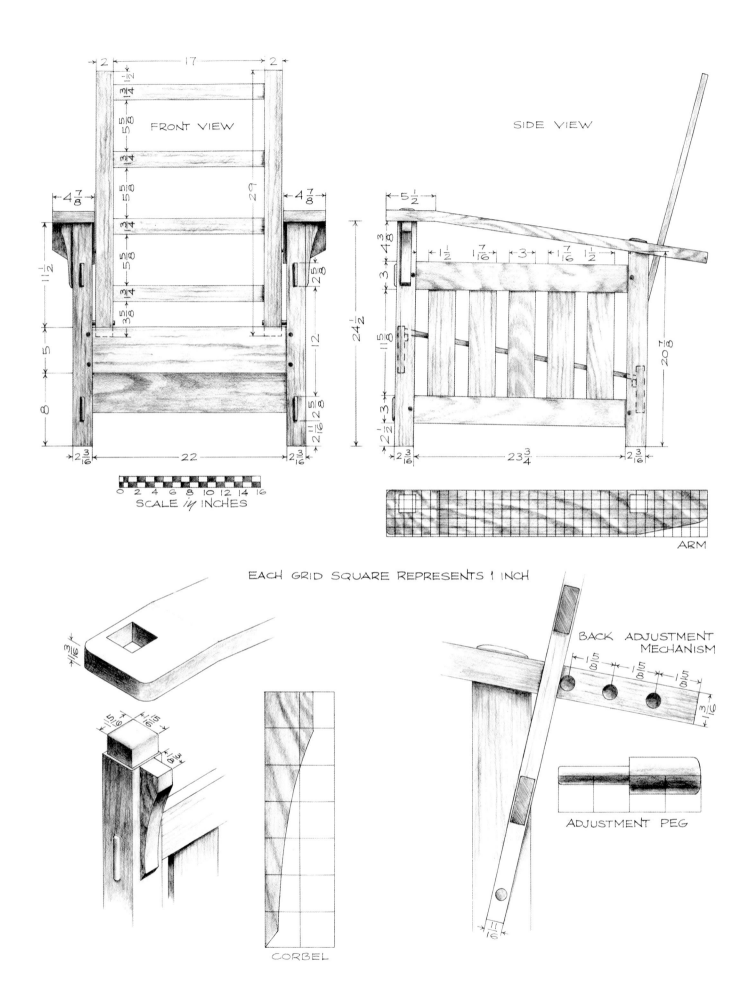

FRONT VIEW

SIDE VIEW

SCALE *in* INCHES

EACH GRID SQUARE REPRESENTS 1 INCH

ARM

CORBEL

BACK ADJUSTMENT
MECHANISM

ADJUSTMENT PEG

In a bold departure from the traditional arrangement of slats beneath the arm of a Morris chair, the designer of this Quaint Art Furniture Company chair created a dramatic and desirable version that garners praise from every collector who views it. Perfectly proportioned and evenly-spaced quartersawn slats, an adjustable back and a comfortable slanted arm makes this Morris chair design second to none.

can readily be identified by its unique arm design and narrow exposed tenons. When they survive, Quaint Art Furniture Company labels are typically paper, either oval or rectangular, approximately one to three inches wide and were only attached with either one or two small tacks, which may account for their high mortality rate. This example — and its identical mate — were purchased by the Grove Park Inn in 1984 for the new Sammons Wing.

Although the Quaint Art Furniture Company produced high quality Arts & Crafts furniture, by 1915 the firm was struggling to stay in business. That year — the same year Gustav Stickley declared bankruptcy — they dropped their line of Arts & Crafts furniture to concentrate on school desks, but by 1920 had closed their doors. Yet as Michael Clark and Jill Thomas-Clark have noted, "Even though the Quaint Art Furniture Company of Syracuse was in existence for only six years, the company created some of the better constructed and designed Arts & Crafts furniture. Although mostly derivative in design, their construction surpassed many of their competitors." [Clarks, Style 1900, pg. 14.]

While the Grove Park Inn has nearly two dozen Arts & Crafts Morris chairs in its collection (see the chapter on the Morris Chair collection on page 98), including examples by Gustav Stickley, J. M. Young and L. & J.G. Stickley, none are more attractive than the matched pair of Morris chairs made by Quaint Art Furniture Company.

Nightstand

ROYCROFT FURNITURE SHOP
1913

This simple, straightforward oak nightstand may have been a new design for the Roycroft Furniture Shop, for it does not appear in the 1912 *Roycroft Hand-Made Furniture Catalog* published just a few months before their craftsmen undertook the Grove Park Inn commission. Since the Roycrofters only produced an estimated three sets of bedroom furniture for the hotel's guest rooms, these nightstands are extremely rare. They served as the model for a similar nightstand design produced by the White Furniture Company (see separate entry) for nearly all of the 150 guest rooms. This particular example bears the Roycroft shopmark carved into the side of the front leg (not visible).

The nightstand design is based on practicality and efficiency, with each of four sections providing a different service. The thick overhanging top offered each guest ample room for a book or magazine beside the reading lamp produced by the Roycroft Copper Shop (see separate section). While the lamp pictured on this particular nightstand is original to the Grove Park Inn, the shade is not. When they arrived at the hotel in 1913, each of the Roycroft table lamps was equipped with a hammered copper shade. While attractive, the copper shades directed the light from the single bulb down upon the table rather than over the bed. After listening to innumerable complaints from his guests, Fred Seely had the copper shades removed and replaced with the parchment shade shown in this example. The copper shades were shipped back to the Roycrofters in East Aurora, where they were re-used.

The single drawer with the hammered copper pull bearing the Roycroft orb-and-cross stamped in the center sits above an open alcove. The drawer provided guests with a safe place for medicines, reading glasses and papers, while the alcove held books and magazines. The lower door relies on the flaking of the quartersawn oak for its only decoration. The modest wooden knob represents a departure for the Roycrofters, one which might have been directed by Fred Seely, for the Roycrofters typically attached brass or copper knobs to the doors on their case pieces. Historically, this compartment would have held a chamber pot in most nightstands, but since the Grove Park Inn provided a bathroom for each bedroom, it most likely served other purposes.

As was customary, the Grove Park Inn placed a Bible in each room, typically in the nightstand. Under Fred Seely's management (1913-1927), each of the Bibles in the guest rooms had first been sent to the Roycrofters for a custom, tooled-leather binding, making this ensemble — nightstand, hardware, lamp and Bible — totally Roycroft.

The Roycroft Nightstand shown at left was photographed in room 441 at the Grove Park Inn. This room bears the plaque, shown above, identifying one of its most famous tenants, author F. Scott Fitzgerald.

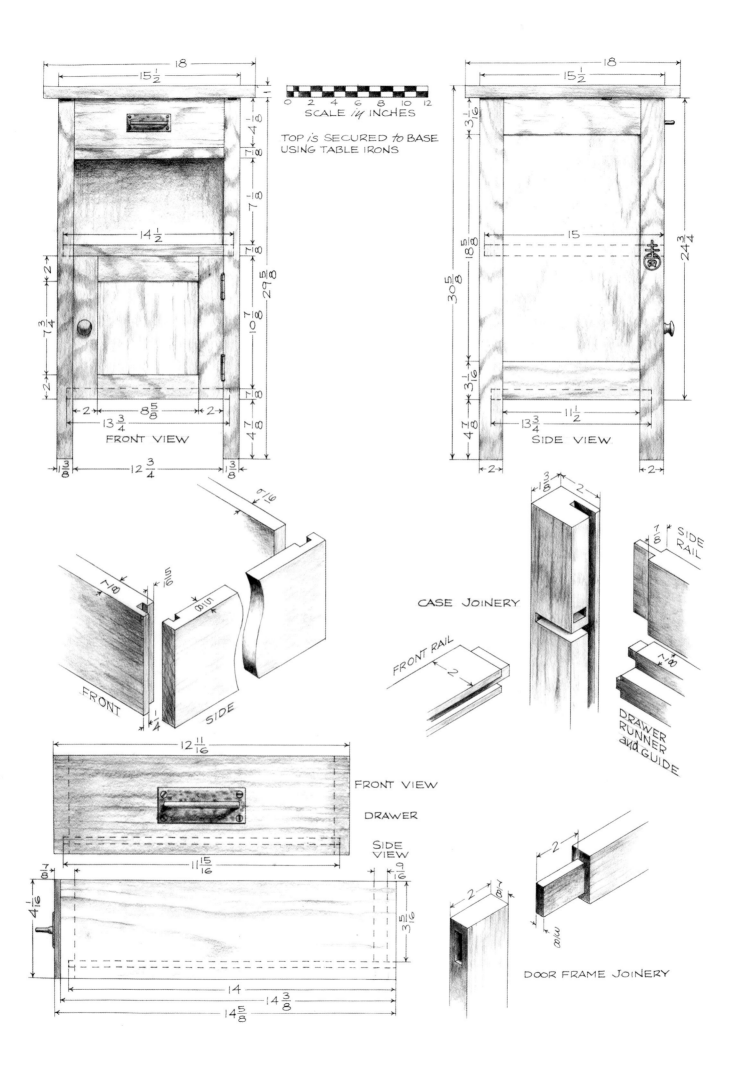

TOP *is* SECURED *to* BASE USING TABLE IRONS

SCALE *in* INCHES

FRONT VIEW

SIDE VIEW

FRONT

SIDE

CASE JOINERY

FRONT RAIL

SIDE RAIL

DRAWER RUNNER *and* GUIDE

FRONT VIEW

DRAWER

SIDE VIEW

DOOR FRAME JOINERY

ONE OF MANY FAMOUS GUESTS

From its first event — the opening night banquet held on July 12, 1913 — the Grove Park Inn has always attracted popular celebrities, including presidents, dignitaries, governors, senators, politicians, entertainers and businessmen. That first night's keynote address was delivered by William Jennings Bryan, the three-time candidate for the White House and Secretary of State under President Woodrow Wilson. As general manager of the hotel until 1927 and one of Asheville's most ardent supporters until his death in 1942, Fred L. Seely worked to attract the rich and famous to the Grove Park Inn, for he knew that where celebrities traveled, the press invariably followed.

That belief was born out in August of 1918 when his good friend Henry Ford brought his group of campers to the Grove Park Inn for a few days of luxury away from trail. They included businessman Harvey Firestone, naturalist John Burroughs and inventor Thomas A. Edison. A photograph taken of the group standing front of the hotel, along with Fred Seely, appeared on front page of newspapers across the country.

Although their names are not as familiar as they were to earlier generations, the list of celebrities, entertainers and businessmen who came to the Grove Park Inn for several days of rest and relaxation included Harry Houdini, Al Jolson, Enrico Caruso and Will Rogers, as well as General John J. Pershing, Eleanor Roosevelt and Presidents Herbert Hoover, Calvin Coolidge, Franklin Roosevelt and Dwight Eisenhower. The list continues to grow as the reputations of both Asheville and the Grove Park Inn continue to draw the rich and the famous to western North Carolina.

Perhaps the most infamous guest to have stayed at the Grove Park Inn, however, came not upon the urging of Fred L. Seely. In 1935 the celebrated novelist and prince of the Jazz Age — F. Scott Fitzgerald — moved into rooms 441 and 443. Fearing he might have contracted tuberculosis, Fitzgerald had fled New York, coming to Asheville in hopes of restoring his health, reviving his writing career and replenishing his depleted finances. Ironically, Fitzgerald's literary rival, Thomas Wolfe, had taken the opposite course, leaving his mother's boarding house in Asheville as he sought his fame in New York City. Though both writers died tragic deaths, it was Wolfe who succumbed to tuberculosis at the age of 38. Fitzgerald died at age 44 from a heart attack brought on by a lifetime of alcohol addiction.

With the onslaught of the Great Depression, Fitzgerald's novels chronicling the Roaring Twenties and their lives of decadence, *The Great Gatsby* (1925) and *This Side of Paradise* (1920), had little relevance to the plight of typical Americans. With his only daughter enrolled in a series of private boarding schools and his celebrated wife, Zelda, now interred indefinitely in a Baltimore mental hospital, Fitzgerald arrived in Ashville broke, in debt and with few friends. Borrowing against advances his literary agent would loan him, Fitzgerald lived at the Grove Park Inn for much of 1935 and 1936.

Forced to write short stories strictly for the money his reputation could still command, Fitzgerald complained his literary talents were being siphoned away before he could complete his next major novel. His efforts to revive his career were short-circuited by his two life-long addictions: women and alcohol. A disastrous affair with a young married woman staying at the Grove Park Inn for the summer left Fitzgerald even more depressed and insecure. Afterwards he transferred Zelda to Asheville, placing her in Highlands Hospital where she remained even after Fitzgerald had left Asheville for Hollywood, where he floundered as a screenwriter.

When a diving accident in 1936 while on an outing with Zelda left Fitzgerald in a cast for several weeks, he hired a secretary to whom he dictated his short stories in his room at the Grove Park Inn. As she later recalled, "His usual pattern was to start out having pots of black coffee served to us at intervals, but as the morning progressed into afternoon and the pain and stress increased, he would advance to stronger stuff. At the end of the session he would slump over, overcome by exhaustion and drink."

Fitzgerald checked out of the Grove Park Inn near the end of 1936, moving to Hollywood in 1937, where he died three years later. Zelda remained in Asheville, a patient at Highlands Hospital, where a fire in 1948 swept through the wooden structure, killing seven patients on the top floor. Zelda Fitzgerald, who had been scheduled to be released the following week, was among the dead.

Photo by Carl van Vechten, June 4, 1937

Rocking Chair

WHITE FURNITURE COMPANY 1913

While recent visitors to the Grove Park Inn have been accustomed to seeing these oak rocking chairs on the covered terraces, in truth they were originally intended to be used in the largest of the guest rooms, as well as in the first floor Ladies' Parlor and the public Writing Room. When these two rooms were later remodeled into a new kitchen — and when entertainment centers and larger beds were added to the sleeping rooms — the staff at the Grove Park Inn began to move the rocking chairs to other areas in the hotel, including the covered terraces.

These sturdy oak rockers were produced for the Grove Park Inn in 1913 by the White Furniture Company in Mebane, North Carolina [see separate entry]. While similar to rocking chairs crafted by the Roycroft Furniture Shop, they are not identical to any illustrated in the 1912 Roycroft Hand-Made Furniture Catalog, leaving open the possibility they may have been come from the drafting table of one of the designers at the White Furniture Company.

The chairs exhibit many standard Arts & Crafts design elements, including the three vertical slats in the back, wide seat rails and thick arms. Subtle differences between these rocking chairs and those designed by the Roycrofters and other Arts & Crafts firms are worth examining. Unlike Gustav Stickley, L. & J. G. Stickley and Charles Limbert, the White Furniture Company did not attach corbels beneath the arms of their chairs or rockers. Evidently they believed — correctly so — that the mortise and tenon joints connecting the arms to both the front and rear legs would provide sufficient support to bear the stress placed on the arms.

The seats of the White Furniture Company rocking chairs are made of woven rattan, a departure from the leather seats the Roycroft Furniture Shop and other Arts & Crafts firms favored. Photographs taken soon

OPPOSITE   These chairs are on the front terrace near the main entrance to the hotel. In the background hangs an original lantern made in 1913 by the Roycroft Copper Shop.

after the Inn opened confirm that the rattan seats are original to the rocking chairs and may reflect Fred Seely's personal preference.

As a study of the Roycroft Furniture Shop catalogs reveals, the Roycrofters included four stretchers between the legs of their regular chairs, but opted to omit stretchers from their rocking chairs. Unfortunately, from a design standpoint this omission leaves many Roycroft rocking chairs looking top-heavy. Either Fred Seely or one of the Whites may have noted this, for the White Furniture Company rocking chairs shown here do utilize stretchers between the legs. In addition to providing extra strength, the horizontal stretchers compliment and balance the three vertical slats in the back.

The stretcher arrangement the Whites selected for the Grove Park Inn rockers is rather unique, for they included only three rather than four stretchers, omitting the rear support. The rocking chairs have not suffered for a lack of a rear stretcher and the unusual configuration provides collectors with a means of identifying those rocking chairs made for the Grove Park Inn. The dimensions and arrangement of the White stretchers is similar to that found on the Roycroft

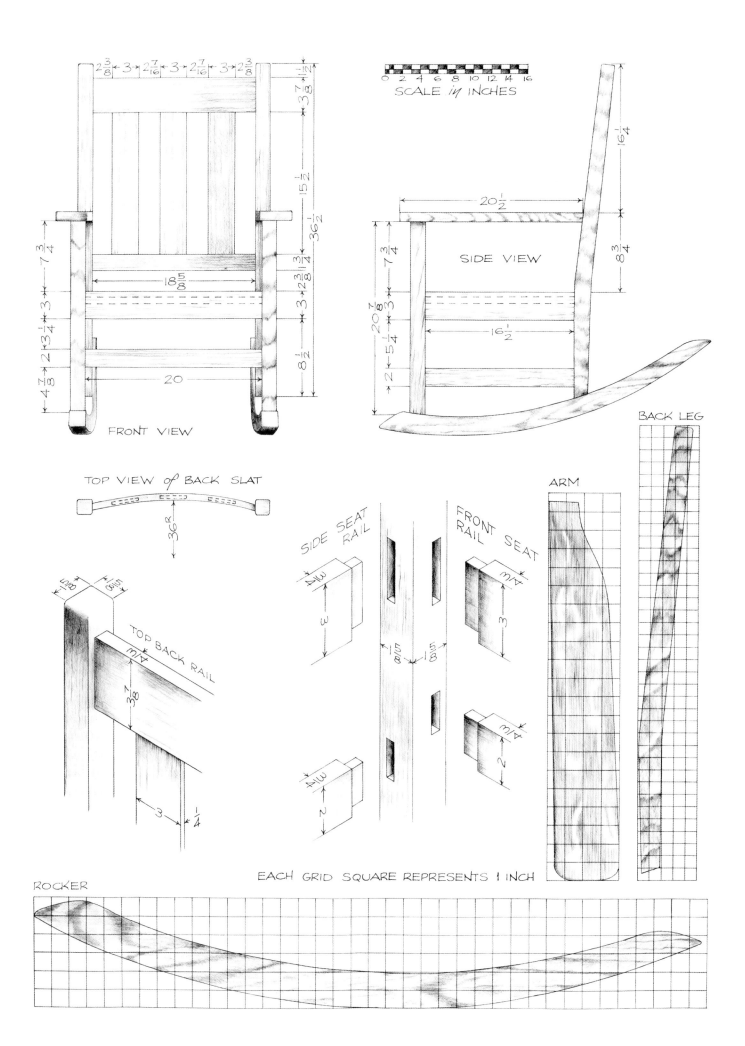

SCALE *in* INCHES

FRONT VIEW

SIDE VIEW

TOP VIEW *of* BACK SLAT

BACK LEG

ARM

TOP BACK RAIL

SIDE SEAT RAIL

FRONT SEAT RAIL

EACH GRID SQUARE REPRESENTS 1 INCH

ROCKER

"GPI" dining room chairs [see separate entry], with the front stretcher positioned slightly higher than the two side stretchers.

The result is a rocking chair that has demonstrated its attractiveness and its durability, as well as its comfort and its balance — and one that can be identified through its unique design elements. Unlike the desks, vanities and chests of drawers made by the White Furniture Company for the Grove Park Inn, these rocking chairs were generally not signed with the firm's round metal tag. As a result, collectors must rely on careful comparisons to those rocking chairs still remaining at the Grove Park Inn or pictured in vintage photographs for a positive identification.

Drop-Arm Settle

MANUFACTURER UNDETERMINED
CA. 1910

Furniture historians often have to play the role of furniture detectives, and, as in the case of this particular drop-arm settle, the results are often frustrating. While not an outstanding example of Arts & Crafts furniture, this respectable settle exhibits some unique characteristics, which should, quite deservedly, serve as clues to whom the designer and manufacturer were.

Three identical Arts & Crafts settles and two matching armchairs were purchased by the Grove Park Inn in 1988 from a private school in Raleigh, North Carolina. At that time it was reported the settles and chairs had been made by a furniture company formerly located in High Point, North Carolina. That assumption had been based on a recollection by an antiques dealer of a paper label on the underside of the upholstered seat, a label that subsequently had been lost or destroyed by a careless upholsterer.

It should be noted that while the original Arts & Crafts furniture companies generally did not made any distinction between the different types of settles in their catalogs and sales material, collectors today classify them into various categories. Those with arms and backs of equal height are referred to as 'box' settles; examples with a flat arm located at a height lower than the back, like the example pictured here, are labeled 'drop-arm' settles. Although found less frequently, 'slant-arm' settles, 'V-back' settles and 'spindle-back' settles can also be found.

Within each of these various categories, settles without any slats beneath the arms are identified as being 'open-arm' settles and those with slats under the arms are considered 'closed-arm' settles. All other criteria being equal, closed-arm settles are considered more desirable than open-arm settles, for they required additional material and labor, are found less often, are associated with higher-quality construction and are considered more pleasing to the eye.

This particular closed-arm, drop-arm settle features a rather unique design and construction detail, which may eventually identify the manufacturer.

Rather than extending over the front leg, as is normally the case in Arts & Crafts drop-arm settles, each arm is notched around the front leg. The top of the leg has been beveled, much like the top of an exposed tenon in other examples of Arts & Crafts furniture, and the wide arm is supported by a long, graceful corbel. One furniture manufacturer known to have used a similar notched-arm design is the Harden Furniture Company of Camden, New York. Harden is not, however, believed to have made these settles, for other design and construction elements typically associated with Harden's line of Arts & Crafts furniture, such as exposed tenons, arched seat rails, pinned joints and thicker materials, are lacking in these three settles and two matching arm chairs at the Grove Park Inn.

This settle does exhibit several design elements which Arts & Crafts collectors appreciate, beginning with the three wide slats under each arm. The back features twelve three-inch slats, each spaced one-inch apart in a proportion which is visually very pleasing. The slats are crowned with a wide crest rail of quarter-sawn oak which provides the strength needed to prevent the slats from bowing under pressure and which also provides a balance to the wide seat rail spanning the distance between the front legs.

The wide seat rail on all four sides of this settle provides strong support for the drop-in spring cushion, but the designer provided additional support in the form of stretchers positioned on both sides and the front of the settle. These stretchers help to brace the four legs and, from a visual perspective, fill in what would otherwise be a negative space between the seat rails and the floor.

It is interesting to note both the presence and the absence of two construction details. Whereas most Arts & Crafts manufacturers lightly sanded the inside edge of each arm to eliminate any sharp edges, the craftsmen building these settles took the time to pass each arm over the rotating blade of a shaper. The shaper blade rounded the top edges of each arm, insuring that

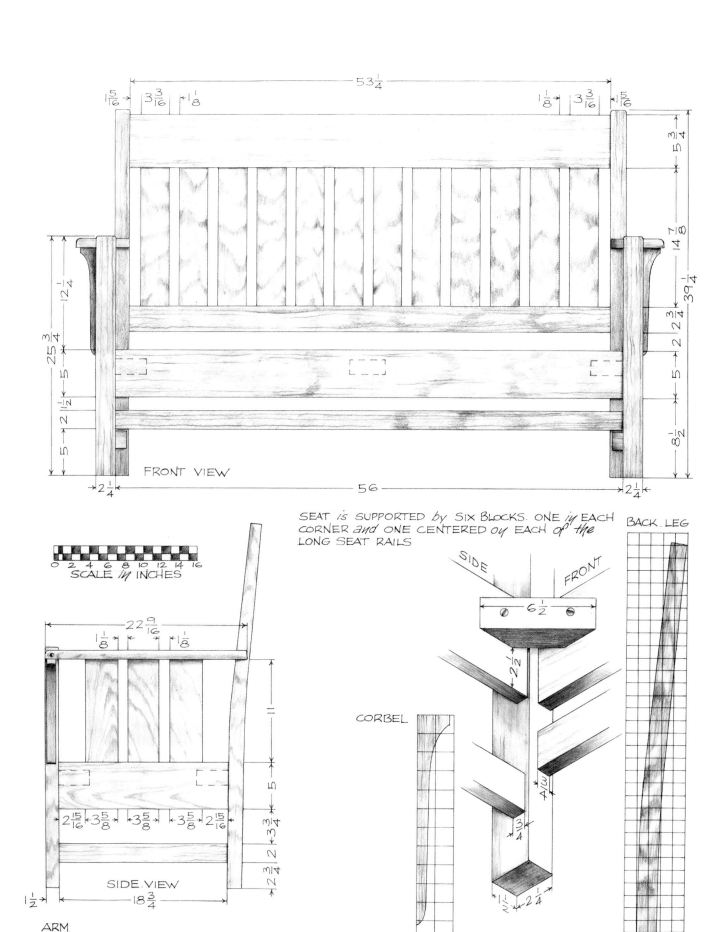

FRONT VIEW

SCALE in INCHES

SEAT is SUPPORTED by SIX BLOCKS. ONE in EACH CORNER and ONE CENTERED on EACH of the LONG SEAT RAILS

SIDE   FRONT

BACK LEG

CORBEL

SIDE VIEW

ARM

EACH GRID SQUARE REPRESENTS 1 INCH

ABOVE The wide crest rail and matching seat apron combine to provide this Arts & Crafts settle with the necessary framework to support both the slats and the spring seat cushion.

RIGHT The unique notched arm-and-post detail may someday identify the manufacturer of this settle and its matching armchair, neither of which bears a shopmark.

they would cause no discomfort to anyone pressed against them.

This attention to detail makes it all the more difficult to explain the absence in each of these settles of a prominent Arts & Crafts detail — the pegged joint. Nearly every designer, craftsman and manufacturer of Arts & Crafts furniture recognized the dual purpose served by pinning the major joints in a piece of furniture. The pins provided far more strength to each joint than could any amount of glue and, when the hide glues did lose their effectiveness, the oak pins prevented the tenons from sliding out of the mortises. Despite being aware of the dual benefit of the practice of pinning the major joints, especially on a piece as long and subject to as much stress as a settle, the

designer and manufacturer of this particular settle elected not to employ pegs in any of the joints.

Despite this minor disappointment, one which could easily be corrected when constructing a new version of this design, this settle has proven to be a comfortable and respectable addition to the Grove Park Inn's collection of Arts & Crafts furniture.

Sideboard with Plate Rail

CRAFTSMAN WORKSHOPS OF GUSTAV STICKLEY
CA. 1909-1912

In his 1909 furniture catalog Gustav Stickley offered homeowners three versions of his Arts & Crafts sideboard. Each of the three represents a different era in the development not only of Stickley's Arts & Crafts style, but of the movement as it matured in America. The earliest and most massive, model #817 (ca. 1902), often referred to as the eight-legged sideboard, measures nearly six feet in length and features a chamfered board back, large drawer and door pulls and medieval strap hinges on the doors. Model #814, introduced during the middle period (1904-1909) of Stickley's career, is slightly smaller, the hardware has been scaled down and the legs are thinner.

The final version, model #816, is shown here in the Grove Park Inn's dining room, for which it was purchased in 1984. First offered in 1909, its design reflects Stickley's intention of offering the American people an alternative to his earlier, more massive Arts & Crafts furniture. The most obvious omission are the long, strap hinges on the two doors, which now rely only on the hammered pulls and the highly-figured grain on the oak veneered doors for their ornamentation. The center drawers have been shortened and now require only one pull each. The long drawer, which in the previous version had been positioned across the bottom of the sideboard, now has been moved to the top (which has been planed down to just three-quarters of an inch). The plate rail, which Gustav Stickley preferred over a mirror, has also been lightened, in keeping with the prevailing theme of the piece.

In an additional move to make the sideboard appear lighter than earlier versions, in 1909 the straight toeboard was replaced with a sweeping arch. By raising the arch higher off the floor, the designer did achieve a lighter feel, but left the front legs looking rather spindly for a piece as heavy as a sideboard. Unfortunately, this arch loses much of its dramatic impact when stretched the entire length of the 48-inch sideboard. It proves far more effective on more slender pieces, such as Stickley's 42-inch and narrower china cabinets, serving tables

The copper and mica lamp on the Gustav Stickley sideboard is a reproduction of a lamp designed by famed San Francisco coppersmith Dirk van Erp (1860-1933).

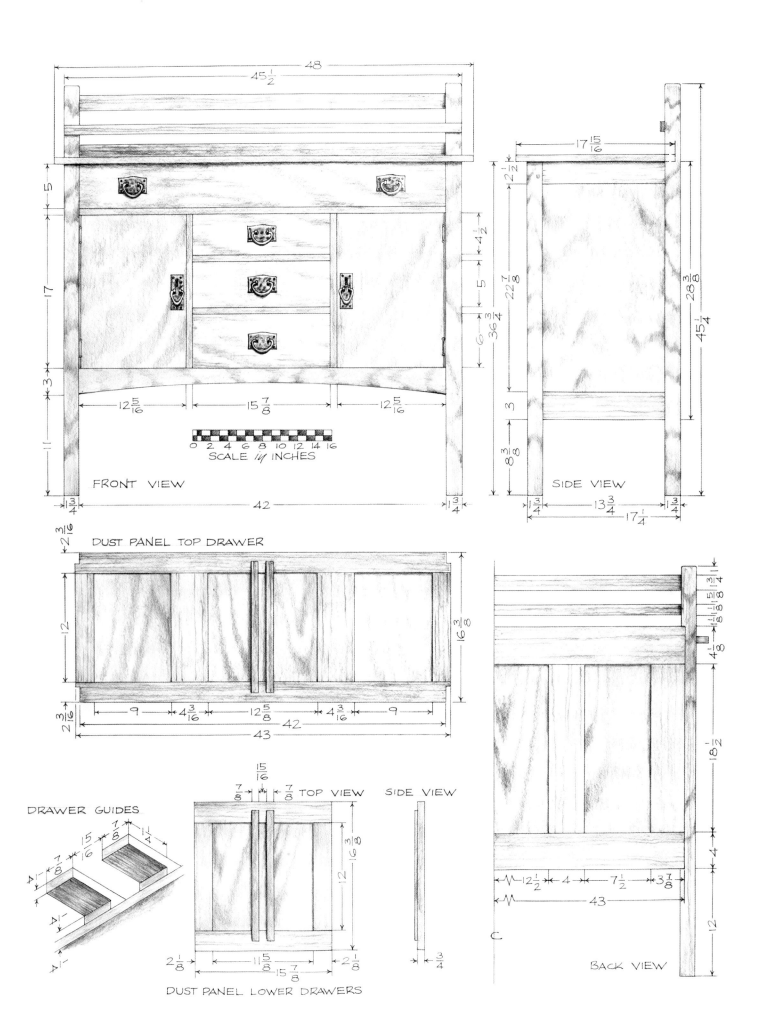

48

45½

5

17

3

11

¾

42

¾

FRONT VIEW

0 2 4 6 8 10 12 14 16
SCALE in INCHES

4½

5

6

36¾

12 5/16

15 7/8

12 5/16

17 15/16

2½

22 7/8

3

8 3/8

28 3/8

45¼

¾

13¾

17¼

¾

SIDE VIEW

2 3/16

DUST PANEL TOP DRAWER

12

16 3/8

2 3/16

9

4 3/16

12 5/8

4 3/16

9

42

43

1 3/8
1 5/8
1¼

4 1/8

18½

4

12 1/2

4

7½

3 7/8

43

12

C

BACK VIEW

DRAWER GUIDES

15/16

7/8

7/8

TOP VIEW

SIDE VIEW

15/16
1/8
1¼

7/8
1/8

1

1

12

16 3/8

2 1/8

11 5/8

2 1/8

15 7/8

¾

DUST PANEL LOWER DRAWERS

ABOVE Gustav Stickley and Elbert Hubbard shared the distinction of having their craftsmen design and produce their own furniture hardware, whereas most manufacturers elected to purchase cast or stamped pulls from other metal shops. The simple iron pulls on this sideboard serve a necessary function while providing a critical decorative feature.

RIGHT As a final touch, his shopmark — a red decal of a joiner's compass over his full signature — appears inside the top drawer.

and bookcases. Stickley may have also come to this conclusion, for in his 1912 catalog the model #816 re-appears with a straight rather than arched toeboard.

While he may have felt that to meet the changing tastes of the American public he had compromise on many of the Arts & Crafts design elements he had introduced between 1900-1902, Gustav Stickley did not sacrifice the construction techniques for which he had always been noted. The top boards are strengthened with tongue-and-groove joinery, the major joints are pinned with oak pegs and the drawers are all constructed with dovetail joints.

#603 Round Tabouret

CRAFTSMAN WORKSHOPS OF GUSTAV STICKLEY
CA. 1907-1908

Between 1900 and 1902 Gustav Stickley issued a series of catalogs of his earliest Arts & Crafts furniture, including several experimental forms of small tables which he referred to at various times as tea tables, plant stands, chalet tables, bungalow tables, cottage stands and drink tables. By 1904 he had settled on the name tabouret (from the French, meaning 'small drum') and a standard form: A circular top supported by four legs joined by arched cross stretchers. Clients could select from one of three sizes: 14-inch diameter (16 inches high), 16-inch diameter (18 inches high) or 18-inch diameter (20 inches high).

The three sizes of tabourets remained a standard Stickley offering the remainder of his Arts & Crafts career with only three subtle changes in design. The earliest version, offered in 1904, featured exposed through-tenons on the outside of the legs and sweeping arches culminating at the inside of the legs. In the second version, which appeared around 1907-1908 and is pictured here, the sweeping arch remained, but the exposed tenons had been eliminated. As illustrated in Stickley's 1909 catalog, the tabourets reached their final form: No exposed tenons and the sweeping arch had been shortened so that it ended prior to meeting the leg. The final version remained in production until Gustav Stickley declared bankruptcy in 1915.

The version shown here in front of the fireplace at the Grove Park Inn represents the second of these three designs and is not original to the hotel. It is model #603 with a top diameter of 16 inches and a height of 18 inches. It is signed on one of the stretchers with a one-inch red decal bearing Gustav Stickley's name beneath a joiner's compass. While not visible in the photograph, the top of this table is attached to the base using what collectors refer to as a 'figure-8 fastener.'

Cast from iron rather than stamped from a thin sheet of steel, these fasteners were designed with beveled holes for two screws: One going down into the top of the leg, the other going up into the bottom of the table. The fasteners could pivot slightly on the screws, permitting the top to expand or contract with changes in humidity without splitting. Arts & Crafts collectors have learned to look closely for these cast iron fasteners, for they were favored by Gustav Stickley and can help confirm a piece of furniture made in his Craftsman Workshops but without a red decal, paper label or brand identifying it.

There are two other notes of interest regarding furniture produced in the Craftsman Workshops of Gustav Stickley. In nearly every case the edges of the bottom of each leg will have been beveled. As anyone who has ever slid a piece of furniture across a floor will attest, legs which have not been beveled are more apt to snag and splinter than those which have had their sharp edges softened. On a less positive note, furniture made in the Craftsman Workshops generally will only reveal either a very shallow tongue-and-groove joinery on the top boards or only a butt joint between boards. In both cases the strength of the joint is nearly totally dependent on the adhesive. In contrast, both Charles Limbert and L. & J.G. Stickley often incorporated a wooden spline inserted into slots cut into the face of each board before they were glued together. The spline provided more stability and gluing surface than Gustav Stickley's shallow tongue-and-groove joinery. The Roycroft Furniture Shop also relied on glue and butt joints, but they compensated for the lack of a spline by making their tops thicker than any other Arts & Crafts furniture workshop, which created additional gluing surface.

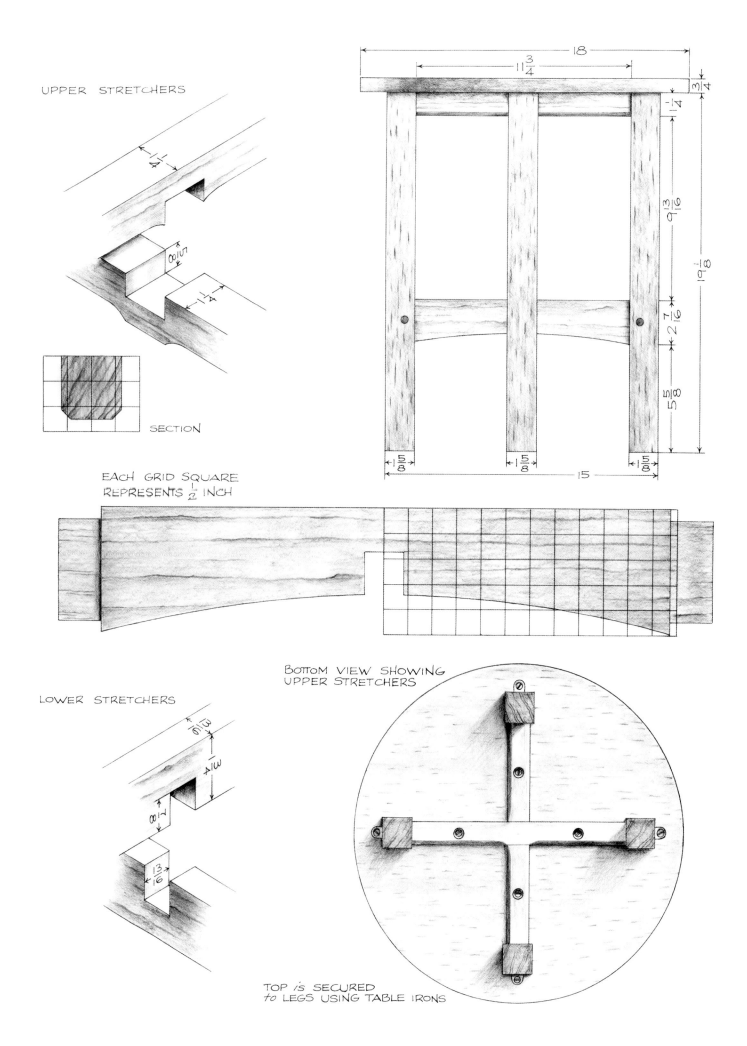

UPPER STRETCHERS

SECTION

EACH GRID SQUARE
REPRESENTS $\frac{1}{2}$ INCH

LOWER STRETCHERS

BOTTOM VIEW SHOWING
UPPER STRETCHERS

TOP is SECURED
to LEGS USING TABLE IRONS

The twenty-two inch hammered copper American Beauty vase (see separate entry) that Victor Toothaker designed for the Grove Park Inn serves as a compliment to any Arts & Crafts table, sideboard or mantle.

Three-Mirrored Vanity

WHITE FURNITURE COMPANY
1913

Modeled after an oak vanity designed and produced in 1913 by the Roycroft Furniture Shop for the Grove Park Inn, this version produced by the White Furniture Company appeared in nearly every sleeping room at the hotel, typically with a low-back White Furniture Company chair (not shown) featuring a woven rattan seat. Although the original plans called for the Roycrofters to produce all of the furniture for the public areas, the dining room and the 150 guest rooms, it became apparent that their small workshop would be unable to meet Fred Seely's deadline. The contract for the sleeping rooms furniture, including beds, nightstands, rocking chairs, library tables, a chest of drawers and a mirrored vanity for each room, then went to the White Furniture Company [see separate entry]. Seely did stipulate, however, that the White Furniture Company would have to use one of the Roycroft sets of bedroom furniture as their prototype — and would be mounting Roycroft pulls on each of the drawers.

This design for a three-mirrored vanity does not appear in the 1912 *Roycroft Hand-Made Furniture Catalog*, but may have been inspired by a five-drawer desk, model #059, pictured in that year's catalog. The unique three-panel beveled mirror arrangement, with two hinged outer mirrors, cannot be found in any of the White Furniture Company literature prior to 1913 either, leaving in question the designer of this mirrored vanity. Since we know that Fred Seely played an active role not only in the selection of the furniture for the Grove Park Inn, but in the design of several of the pieces, it may be that the idea for the pivoting outer mirrors originated with him.

The White Furniture Company craftsmen remained true to their Roycroft model, starting with the thick (1⅛") oak top and continuing through to the paneled sides and the dimensions of the five drawers. Although most of the White vanities bear a one-inch circular identification plate inside the central drawer, it is possible to distinguish an unsigned White vanity from furniture made by the Roycrofters. For starters, the White Furniture Company used a tongue-and-groove joint between each pair of boards that they glued together; the Roycrofters only utilized butt joints and glue, making for a weaker joint. Rather than utilizing dovetail joints on their drawers, the White craftsmen relied on an interlocking joint which proved to be both easier to cut by machine and stronger than even a dovetail joint (see lower left photo page 155). In a departure from the Roycroft Furniture Shop, the White craftsmen used oak for

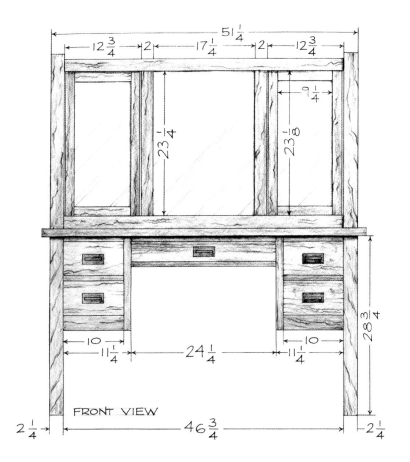

FRONT VIEW

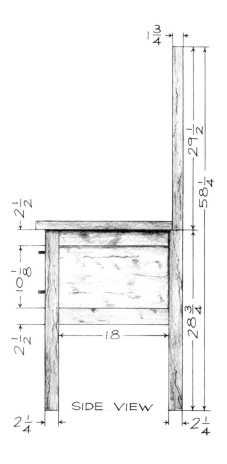

SIDE VIEW

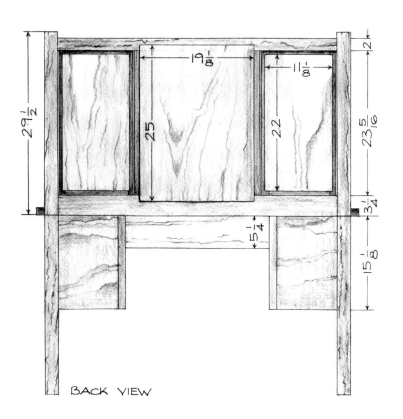

BACK VIEW

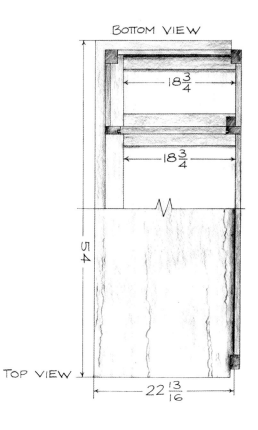

BOTTOM VIEW

TOP VIEW

their drawer sides and bottoms; in the Roycroft vanity at the Grove Park Inn the sides and bottom are made of a dark-stained gumwood.

The Roycrofters typically pinned the major joints in their furniture with oak pegs, but for whatever reason none of the joints in the existing Roycroft vanity, nor any of the White Furniture Company vanities at the Grove Park Inn, exhibit any pegs. While none of the vanities appear to have needed the pegs for additional strength, the decorative impact of the pegs is lacking.

On the one Roycroft model of this vanity which still exists at the Grove Park Inn, the Roycroft craftsman carved the orb-and-cross shopmark into the center of the middle drawer, assuming that the drawer would later have two pulls attached to it, one on either side of the orb-and-cross. Instead, the drawer pull was attached in the exact center of the middle drawer, effectively covering the Roycroft shopmark.

When several of these antique vanities in the guest rooms were replaced with new Arts & Crafts entertainment centers, the staff at the Grove Park Inn removed some of the mirror attachments so that the vanities could then be used as desks. Distinguishing an original Roycroft or White Furniture Company desk from an altered vanity is not difficult, for the vanity top was notched the entire length of the back to provide a ledge to support the framework and the mirrors. An Arts & Crafts 'desk' with a missing strip of wood across the back or with a new strip of wood across the back is, in all likelihood, a vanity which has been altered — and is worth less to a collector than an original desk.

The drawer joints made by the White Furniture Company were strong and have lasted for generations. This is a drawer from the three-mirrored vanity, showing the machine-cut locking rabbet joint.

The 1913 Roycroft "GPI" dining room chair shown in this photograph is one of only four chairs known to exist which did not have arms added to them in 1920-1921 (see separate section). The original order called for 400 of these chairs; 350 had arms added to them in 1920-1921 to make them more comfortable for the diners in the hotel dining room. The fifty which did not have arms added to them are assumed to have been in use in other parts of the hotel. When this chair returned to the Grove Park Inn in 1987, it had been painted gray and the original black leather seat had been removed. It has subsequently been refinished and the seat recovered with green leather. The positioning of the Roycroft carved orb-and-cross on the right side of the rear post of the chair is unique to the chairs, which Fred Seely ordered for the Grove Park Inn and for his office at Biltmore Industries (see separate entry).

Postcards from the Roycroft Campus

Possibly the most-gifted designer to work for Elbert Hubbard was Dard Hunter (1883-1966). Born into a newspaper family, Hunter's father was an advocate of hand craftsmanship and the emerging ideals of the Arts & Crafts movement. In 1904 the twenty-one year old illustrator left their Ohio home for East Aurora, NY, where he went to work for Elbert Hubbard at the Roycroft Shops. All images compliments of The Roycroft Campus Corporation.

Although he intended to be a furniture designer, it soon became apparent that Hunter's skills could more profitably be put to use at the Roycroft Print Shop, where Dard Hunter designed book covers and title pages for Roycroft books and periodicals. He also collaborated with craftsmen in the Leather Shop, the Copper Shop and the Furniture Shop on various items, including a carved oak chair, stained glass table lamps, metalware and the windows in the Roycroft Inn. By 1910, however, Dard Hunter felt the draw of distant lands and new challenges, leaving the Roycrofters to embark on a noted career of papermaking and printing.

POSTCARDS AT RIGHT

The 1904 peristyle in this Dard Hunter drawing connected the original Roycroft Inn (shown here) with a nearby three-story addition. This 200-foot veranda created the courtyard seen here and provided guests seated on Old Hickory rockers with a view across the street to the workshops on the Roycroft campus.

The Roycroft Chapel (1899) was not, as its name implies, a place of worship, but instead served as a meeting hall for the Roycrofters and as a showroom for items they had for sale.

Although Elbert Hubbard did not make it a practice to allow his craftsmen to sign their work with any mark other than the Roycroft orb-and-cross, Dard Hunter was permitted to incorporate his moniker, a reversed "DH", into many of his illustrations, seen here in the lower right hand corner of his illustration of the Roycroft Inn.

The Roycroft Print Shop (1900) always had an Old English feel to it. It housed modern printing presses for Hubbard's magazines, tables in brightly lit rooms for illustrators and designers, facilities for binding and shipping and administrative offices, including those for Alice and Elbert Hubbard.

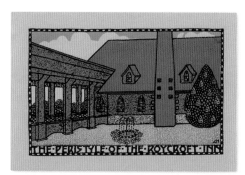

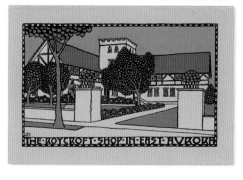

Postcards based on photos were used to promote the Roycroft Campus.

APPLE-BLOSSOM TIME AT ROYCROFT, EAST AURORA, N. Y. 115247

THE COPPER SHOP (ROYCROFT-TOWN), EAST AURORA, N. Y. 115251

Campus at Roycroft, East Aurora, N. Y.

THE ROYCROFT SHOPS, EAST AURORA, ERIE COUNTY, NEW YORK.

The Roycroft INN

ROYCROFT CHAPEL, FRONT VIEW, EAST AURORA, N. Y

Rear View of Roycroft Chapel. East Aurora, N. Y

Main Building, Roycroft Shops, East Aurora, N. Y.

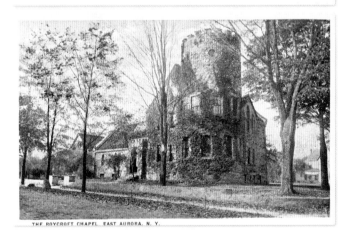

THE ROYCROFT CHAPEL, EAST AURORA, N. Y.

The first Print Shop later was remodeled to become the Roycroft Inn after completion of the existing Print Shop across the street in 1900.

As his business expanded from a small hand press in a drafty barn in 1895 to one which by 1913 employed nearly five hundred townspeople, Elbert Hubbard continued to purchase land, move houses and build workshops for his various branches. Many were constructed of fieldstone hauled in by the wagonload by local farmers. As the numbers of visitors increased, Hubbard constructed the Roycroft Inn and later additions to house them. Today the majority of the original buildings still survive and are in various stages of restoration, much under the guiding hand of the Roycoft Campus Corporation. Elbert Hubbard was first and foremost a writer, so he depended on other talented people, most notably designers, artists, managers, craftsmen and craftswomen to accomplish the daily tasks and routines required within the various departments. Most of these individuals achieved little recognition during their time or after, as is often the case when a leader casts a shadow as large as that of an Elbert Hubbard, a Gustav Stickley, a Fred L. Seely or a Frank Lloyd Wright. While never noted for generous paychecks, Elbert Hubbard provided his employees with pleasant working conditions, entertainment, educational lectures and the opportunity to play a role in the creative process. *Photos compliments of The Roycroft Campus Corporation.*

Young women from East Aurora were employed to hand illuminate title pages in some of the more expensive Roycroft books.

Hubbard provided his illuminators, artists and designers with pleasant working conditions, as evidenced in this photograph of East Aurora women working on pages brought over from the Print Shop.

Two unidentified blacksmiths are seen here in the original Blacksmith Shop, a wooden structure that was torn down after the Copper Shop was built in 1902.

St. Jerome of E.Aurora.

Irish artist Jerome Connor (1876-1943) worked at Roycroft for Elbert Hubbard from 1898-1903 before leaving to pursue fame as a sculptor.

In the Bindery.

The Roycrofters took pride in their custom bookbindings, which ranged from heavy paper to handtooled and embossed leather.

Ali Baba & the Book.

A Roycroft Artist.

A young Elbert "Bert" Hubbard II posed for this photograph of him breaking rocks for the stonemasons building one of the Roycroft workshops.

The Red One

Unidentified young man. Could have been a guest at the Roycroft Inn.

"Ali Baba," more correctly known as Albert Danner (ca. 1843-1913), an East Aurora carpenter and cabinetmaker, was one of Elbert Hubbard's earliest woodworkers.

Old Uncle John
Woodworker & Horse Trainer

"Uncle John" and Elbert Hubbard shared a love for horses, one reason for Hubbard's move from Buffalo to the small town of East Aurora. In addition to helping Hubbard care for his horses, Uncle John also worked with Albert Danner in the Furniture Shop.

All Good Roycrofters

Handyman Albert Danner is shown here giving one of the children a ride in his wheelbarrow in front of what is now the Roycroft Inn.

Gallery of Grove Park Inn Furniture

Whenever I visit the Grove Park Inn, I'm amazed by how many wonderful pieces of furniture are on public display. On the previous pages of this book we've highlighted many historically significant, and important pieces of furniture, but there are literally dozens of other beautiful pieces of furniture that would, in and of their own qualities, be considered significant pieces, if there weren't so many to look at. These pages are a look at some of the other significant pieces scattered throughout the hotel.

ABOVE   The Grove Park Inn also owns several examples of Arts & Crafts sideboards by Charles Stickley (another brother of Gustav), Lifetime, the Grand Rapids Bookcase Company, Stickley Brothers and other notable manufacturers.

OPPOSITE TOP   While not every example of Arts & Crafts furniture can be superbly designed and crafted, this unsigned library table with false tenons and a laminated top is certainly striking.

OPPOSITE BOTTOM   Wandering through the Blue Ridge Dining Room, my attention was drawn to two beautiful servers that are in daily use by the hotel staff, and are also amazing pieces of Arts & Crafts craftsmanship.

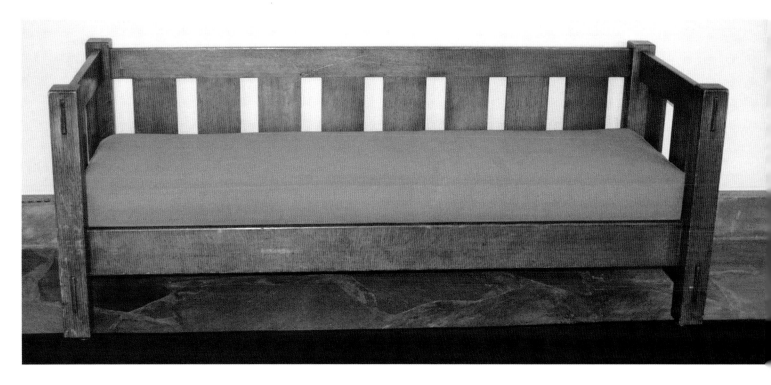

LEFT AND BELOW In case we forget that the Arts & Crafts movement started in England before making its way to the U.S., there are a nice selection of some interesting English Arts & Crafts pieces also displayed in the hotel.

OPPOSITE Two of dozens of settles that are scattered throughout the hotel — each interesting in design, and different from each other.

RIGHT Though almost certainly refinished, the lines on the china cabinet (and the original hardware) make a great location to display some of the historic artifacts collected by the hotel.

Other Views of the Grove Park Inn

During the course of creating this book, many photos were taken that don't have a logical place. Luckily we have enough space to share some of those "other views" of the Grove Park Inn.

Although I have walked through the Grove Park Inn hundreds of time over the course of the past twenty-three years, I never fail to discover a small detail that I either had missed or had forgotten from an earlier jaunt. While at first glance the inn itself can seem over-whelming, the details are really what set it apart and makes it special. Whether it be a stained glass scene above the wine rack in the Blue Ridge Dining Room, the stencils in the third floor Palm Court or the addi-tion of new spindle-back Arts & Crafts chairs to the Sunset Terrace restaurant, the Grove Park Inn never fails to amaze or impress me.

Arts & Crafts furniture collectors invariably rush to the Great Hall to study the examples, both antique

and contemporary, inspired by the Arts & Crafts movement and its philosophy of "Head, Heart and Hand." Also, let's not forget the architecture which provides the perfect setting for this fabulous collection. Local stone hauled down from Sunset Mountain and from E.W. Grove's 1200 acres of land provided the perfect building material for an Arts & Crafts hotel, and for the nearby cottages which were built a few years later.

Today the Grove Park Inn represents a delightful blend of the old with the new, from ivycovered walls and contemporary garden art to shiny automobiles parked where less than one hundred years ago horse-drawn buggies stood.

It was, as William Jennings Bryan declared on opening night, "built for the ages."

Final Thoughts

Historians with the benefit of an additional hundred years of research, discovery and analyzation will no doubt smile at many of the assertions made in this and other books written by those of us so deeply and personally involved with what has been called the Arts & Crafts Revival. Many, including myself, made the mistake of declaring that the original Arts & Crafts movement ended in 1915, the year in which Gustav Stickley's empire collapsed and, a few months later, in which Elbert and Alice Hubbard drowned aboard the torpedoed *Lusitania*.

Later, we extended the life of the Arts & Crafts movement to the year 1929, when the collapse of the stock market and the American economy pushed aside debate over styles of furniture as families struggled for survival. When, on closer examination, we realized that even as late as 1938 well-known Arts & Crafts firms, including the Roycrofters, L. & J.G. Stickley Furniture, J.M. Young Furniture, Kalo Silver, Van Briggle Pottery, Rookwood Pottery and Tiffany Studios still remained in business, we then decided that the Arts & Crafts movement was still breathing when World War II took center stage.

The post-war infatuation with new technology, from plywood and aluminum to lacquer and polyurethane, prompted the Modernism era, in which fad replaced fashion, if just for a few decades. Beanbag chairs, chrome coffee tables, walnut veneers, molded plywood and fiberglass furniture competed for the public's attention with the one style which never seemed to fade away — Colonial Revival. And while it might require what the poet William Wordsworth called "a willing suspension of disbelief," those experimental forms made of chrome, glass and plywood could trace their linage back to Gustav Stickley's call for "a new style of furniture which would be simple, durable, comfortable ... and to do away with all needless ornamentation." Their clean, crisp lines and independence from unnecessary decoration rode an invisible current which had sprung from the shores of England a century earlier in the words of William Morris and John Ruskin.

Many Americans began searching for a style that would retain those clean, simple lines while demonstrating the strength and durability of hand craftsmanship. In 1972 they had their first opportunity to view an assemblage of what for decades had been dismissed, as one prominent author labeled it, as the "chunky charm of mission oak." Entitled "The Arts & Crafts Movement in America," the first traveling exhibition of Arts & Crafts furniture, pottery, metalware, textiles and art opened at Princeton University and demonstrated once and for all that Arts & Crafts was the first truly American style of decorative arts.

Widespread acceptance of the Arts & Crafts style did not come overnight, but, each year after what became known as the Princeton Exhibition of 1972, authors, editors and publishers responded to the demand for more information on the furniture of Gustav Stickley, the metalware and books of the Roycrofters, the pottery of William Grueby, Artus Van Briggle and George Ohr, the art of Arthur Wesley Dow and the architecture of Frank Lloyd Wright. Original forms were discovered languishing in attics, antiques shops and Adirondack cabins. What began as a trickle of articles and antiques erupted into a waterfall of books, magazines and house plans, furniture, pottery and lighting, carpets, curtains and clocks, tile, metalware and artwork. Call it a revival, a reawakening or a renaissance, by 1988 the Arts & Crafts style, the Arts & Crafts movement and the Arts & Crafts philosophy had returned to prominence once again.

Bruce E. Johnson

Arts & Crafts Terminology

ALS IK KAN   "The best I can."

AMMONIA FUMING   Arts & Crafts furniture was fumed in a tent with ammonia. This reacted with the wood's tannic acid and turned the wood a medium-brown color.

CORBELS   A bracket of wood, projecting from the face of a chair leg or side of a cabinet. Generally used as a support but they became decorative elements of Arts & Crafts furniture.

CRAFTSMAN   Gustav Stickley is best known for his straight-forward furniture, sometimes called "mission" or "Craftsman furniture." Also the name of his workshops and farms.

DOWELS   Round sticks of wood used to secure a tenon into a mortise. The dowel was left exposed to serve as a decorative element and well as serving a function.

INLAY   The material or act of inserting smaller pieces of wood into grooves or cavities cut into a workpiece.

KEY   A tapered wedge of wood tapped into a hole or slot cut into a protruding tenon in order to lock the tenon in place; also referred to as a 'keyed tenon.'

MACKMURDO   Among the most successful enterprises in England was the Century Guild, a collective of designers and artisans organized in 1882 by architect A. H. Mackmurdo (1851-1942), who studied under and traveled alongside John Ruskin. The Century Guild also produced what many consider the first literary journal dedicated to the ideals of the emerging Arts & Crafts philosophy of design and decoration, *The Hobby Horse* (1884-1892).

MEDULLARY RAYS   In quartersawn material, where the wood is cut into boards with the growth rings roughly perpendicular to the face of the board, the medullary rays often produce beautiful figure such as silver grain, medullary spots, pith flecks, etc.

MISSION   The monks of the California Missions made their own furniture because they had to. Having the right idea of the simple life, and the belief that beauty and durability were best displayed in the plain, straight-lined effect, they origi-nated the now so-called Mission design.

MORTISE AND TENON   The end of one of the members is inserted into a hole cut in the other member. The end of the first member is called the tenon, and it is usually narrowed with respect to the rest of the piece. The hole in the second member is called the mortise. The joint may be glued, pinned or wedged to lock it in place.

Mortise and Tenon joint

PINNED (JOINT)   Critical mortise-and-tenon joints were generally pinned with wooden pegs sanded flush with the surface of the wood.

Pinned Mortise and Tenon joint

PRAIRIE SCHOOL   The works of the Prairie School architects are usually marked by horizontal lines, flat or hipped roofs with broad overhanging eaves, windows grouped in horizontal bands, integration with the landscape, solid construction, craftsmanship and discipline in the use of ornament. Horizontal lines were thought to evoke and relate to the native prairie landscape.

QUARTERSAWN   Boards that are created by first cutting a log into quarters and then creating a series of parallel cuts perpendicular to the tree's rings.

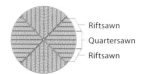

Riftsawn
Quartersawn
Riftsawn

TABORET   A small table made by Arts & Crafts furniture makers.

WHITE OAK   Wood of choice for Arts & Crafts furniture makers. When quartersawn, it reveals distinctive grain patterns including medullary rays, flake and close, straight grain.

Bibliography

Bamberger, Bill and Davidson, Cathy N.. *Closing: The Life and Death of an American Factory*, W.W. Norton & Co., NY, 1998.

Bartinique, A. Patricia, editor. *Kindred Styles: The Arts & Crafts Furniture of Charles P. Limbert*, Published by Gallery 532, New York, 1995.

Brady, Linda Hubbard, editor. *The Book of the Roycrofters*, catalogs 1919, 1926, House of Hubbard, East Aurora, NY, 1995.

Brady, Nancy Hubbard, introduction. *Roycroft Hand Made Furniture Catalog*, 1906, reprinted by the House of Hubbard, East Aurora, NY, 1973.

Brunk, Robert S., editor. *May We All Remember Well*, Vol. 1, Brunk Auction Services, Publisher, Asheville, NC, 1997.

Cathers, David. *Furniture of the American Arts & Crafts Movement*, Turn of the Century Editions, Philmont, NY, 1996.

Cathers, David. *Gustav Stickley*, Phaidon Press: London, 2003.

Catalog of Roycroft Furniture And Other Things, 1906, reprinted by Turn of the Century Editions, New York, NY, 1981.

Champney, Freeman. *Art & Glory: The Story of Elbert Hubbard*, Kent State University Press, Kent, Ohio, 1968.

Clark, Dr. Michael and Thomas-Clark, Jill. "The Quaint Art Furniture Company of Syracuse, New York", *Style 1900*, vol. 9, no. 3, August 1996.

"Elbert Hubbard Talks of The Professions," *Atlanta Constitution*, March 3, 1909.

Elder, Paul. *An Arts & Crafts Book Shop in Greater San Francisco*, San Francisco, 1906.

Gray, Steven. *The Early Work of Gustav Stickley*, Turn of the Century Editions, Philmont, NY, 1996.

Grove Park Inn brochure, ca. 1919, private collection.

Hamilton, Charles F. *Roycroft Collectibles*, A.S. Barnes & Company, San Diego and New York, 1980.

Holmes, Margaret. "White Furniture Completes Its First Century", *The Enterprise Newspaper*, Mebane, NC, January 28, 1981.

Hubbard, Elbert. "The Inn Superbus Maximus," *The Fra*, March, 1913.

Hubbard, Elbert. *The Roycroft Shop: A History*, The Roycroft Print Shop, East Aurora, NY, 1908,.

Hubbard, Elbert. *White Hyacinths*, The Roycroft shops, East Aurora, NY, 1907.

Johnson, Bruce. *Built for the Ages: A History of the Grove Park Inn*, The Grove Park Inn Resort and Spa, Asheville, NC, 2003.

Johnson, Bruce. "Eleanor Vance, Charlotte Yale and the Origins of Biltmore Estate Industries," Brunk, Robert S., editor. *May We All Remember Well*, Vol. 2, Brunk Auction Services, Asheville, NC, 2001.

Kylloe, Ralph. *Rustic Artistry for the Home*, Gibbs-Smith, Publisher, Salt Lake City, 2000.

Kylloe, Ralph, editor. *The Collected Works of Indiana Hickory Furniture Makers*, Rustic Publications, Nashua, NH, 1989.

Lamoureau, Dorothy. *The Arts & Crafts Studio of Dirk Van Erp*, San Francisco Craft & Folk Art Museum, San Francisco, 1989.

Lifetime Furniture: Grand Rapids Bookcase & Chair Company, ca. 1911, reprinted by Turn of the Century Editions, New York, 1981.

Limbert Furniture Catalog No. 119, reprinted by Turn of the Century Editions, New York, 1981.

Lydell, Boice, editor. *Karl Kipp and His Work at the Tookay Shop*, 1912 catalog, The Roycroft Arts Museum, East Aurora, NY, 1992.

Lydell, Boice, editor. *Tookay Catalog*, ca.1914, Roycroft Arts Museum, East Aurora, NY, 1992.

MacMillan, E. J.. *Syracuse China News*, Syracuse China Corporation, Syracuse, NY, 1931.

McConnell, Kevin. *Roycroft Art Metal*, Schiffer Publishing, West Chester, PA, 1990.

Marek, Don. *Arts & Crafts Furniture Design: The Grand Rapids Contribution*, 1895-1915, Grand Rapids Art Museum, Grand Rapids, MI, 1987.

Rago, David and Johnson, Bruce. *The Official Price Guide to American Arts & Crafts*, 3rd ed., House of Collectibles, New York, 2003.

Roycroft Hand Made Furniture, 1912, House of Hubbard reprint, East Aurora, NY, 1973.

Rust, Robert and Turgeon, Kitty. *The Roycroft Campus*, Arcadia Publishing, Charleston, SC, 1999.

"Secretary Bryan Is Guest Of Honor At Great Banquet That Dedicates Grove Park Inn," *The Sunday Asheville Citizen*, Asheville, NC, July 13, 1913.

Seely, Fred L.. *Grove Park Inn* brochure, Asheville, NC, ca. 1919.

The White Furniture Company Catalog, Mebane, NC, 1927.

"The White Line" catalog, The White Furniture Company, Mebane, N.C., 1912.

Via, Marie and Searl, Marjorie. *Head, Heart and Hand: Elbert Hubbard and The Roycrofters*, University of Rochester Press, Rochester, NY, 1994.

Index

More great titles from Popular Woodworking

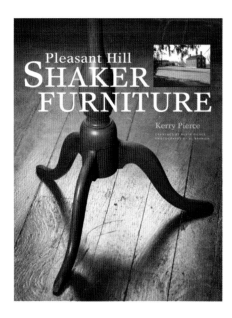

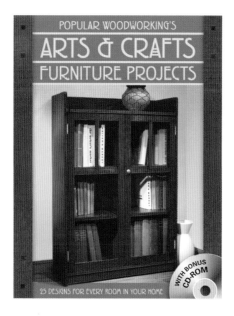

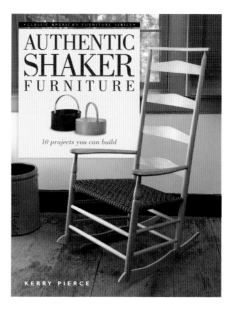

PLEASANT HILL SHAKER FURNITURE

By Kerry Pierce

Take a virtual tour through one of the remaining shaker communities. study the history, the lifestyle and delve deeply into the furniture created by these gifted craftsmen. includes painstakingly detailed measured drawings of the original furniture pieces and hundreds of beautiful photos. learn the secrets of shaker construction while learning about the shaker's themselves.

ISBN 13: 978-1-55870-795-5
ISBN 10: 1-55870-795-6
hardcover, 176 p., #Z0564

POPULAR WOODWORKING'S ARTS & CRAFTS FURNITURE PROJECTS

This book offers a collection of twenty-five Arts & Crafts furniture projects for every room in your home. Some projects are accurate reproductions while others are loving adaptations of the style.

A bonus CD-ROM contains ten projects and ten technique articles to provide even more information on construction and finishing.

ISBN 13: 978-1-55870-846-4
ISBN 10: 1-55870-846-4
paperback w/CD-ROM, 208 p., #Z2115

AUTHENTIC SHAKER FURNITURE

by Kerry Pierce

The classic grace of the Shaker style is captured in twenty timeless furniture projects built using a combination of hand and power tools. With step-by-step photos and Pierce's clear instruction, you will discover how to build each unique creation, including:

• An armed rocker and a straight-back chair
• A drop-leaf table and a sewing desk
• Hanging boxes, bentwood boxes, clothes hangers and more!

ISBN-13: 978-1-55870-657-6
ISBN-10: 1-55870-657-7
paperback, 128p, #70607

These and other great woodworking books are available at your local bookstore, woodworking stores, or from online suppliers.

www.popularwoodworking.com